Exploitation

Exploitation

Perspectives from Philosophy, Politics, and Economics

Edited by
BENJAMIN FERGUSON AND MATT ZWOLINSKI

OXFORD
UNIVERSITY PRESS

Oxford University Press is a department of the University of Oxford. It furthers
the University's objective of excellence in research, scholarship, and education
by publishing worldwide. Oxford is a registered trade mark of Oxford University
Press in the UK and certain other countries.

Published in the United States of America by Oxford University Press
198 Madison Avenue, New York, NY 10016, United States of America.

© Oxford University Press 2024

All rights reserved. No part of this publication may be reproduced, stored in
a retrieval system, or transmitted, in any form or by any means, without the
prior permission in writing of Oxford University Press, or as expressly permitted
by law, by license, or under terms agreed with the appropriate reproduction
rights organization. Inquiries concerning reproduction outside the scope of the
above should be sent to the Rights Department, Oxford University Press, at the
address above.

You must not circulate this work in any other form
and you must impose this same condition on any acquirer.

Library of Congress Cataloging-in-Publication Data
Names: Ferguson, Benjamin, editor. | Zwolinski, Matt, editor.
Title: Exploitation : perspectives from philosophy, politics, and economics /
edited by Benjamin Ferguson and Matt Zwolinski.
Other titles: Exploitation (Oxford University Press)
Description: New York, NY : Oxford University Press, [2024] |
Includes bibliographical references and index. |
Identifiers: LCCN 2023040879 (print) | LCCN 2023040880 (ebook) |
ISBN 9780190256951 (hardback) | ISBN 9780190256968 (paperback) |
ISBN 9780190256982 (epub)
Subjects: LCSH: Exploitation.
Classification: LCC BJ1474.5 .E975 2024 (print) | LCC BJ1474.5 (ebook) |
DDC 179—dc23/eng/20231129
LC record available at https://lccn.loc.gov/2023040879
LC ebook record available at https://lccn.loc.gov/2023040880

DOI: 10.1093/oso/9780190256951.001.0001

Contents

1. Introduction — 1
   Benjamin Ferguson and Matt Zwolinski

PART I WHAT EXPLOITATION IS

2. Sacrificing and Forgoing: A Deontic View of Exploitation — 13
   Gijs van Donselaar

3. Exploitative Transactions and Corrective Justice — 31
   Christopher Mills

4. "But Where Does It Stop?": Exploitative Structures and Exploitative Actions — 57
   Mirjam Müller

5. Fair Trade, Bargaining, and Respect for Persons — 79
   Hillel Steiner

PART II WHAT MAKES EXPLOITATION WRONG

6. Who Is Wronged by Wrongful Exploitation? — 93
   Brian Berkey

7. Two Faces of Exploitation: Moral Injury, Harm, and the Paradox of Exploitation — 113
   Ruth Sample

8. Exploitation Across Time: Climate Change, Public Debt, and Resource Depletion — 139
   Nicola Mulkeen

PART III APPLIED ISSUES IN EXPLOITATION THEORY

9. Unequal Exchange and International Justice — 161
   Roberto Veneziani and Naoki Yoshihara

10. Exploitation, Children and Childhood, and Parental
    Responsibilities   187
    Samantha Brennan

11. Labor Exploitation: A Left-Libertarian Analysis   203
    Roderick T. Long

12. Decommodification as Exploitation   229
    Vida Panitch

13. Exploitation Does Not Justify Prohibiting
    Canadian Paid Plasma   253
    Mark Wells and Peter Jaworski

Index   275

1
Introduction

Benjamin Ferguson and Matt Zwolinski

1. Three Questions

Most research on exploitation tends to address the following questions: What is exploitation? Why is it wrong? What should we do about it? These are, of course, interrelated. Whether and why exploitation is wrong will depend in part on what kind of behavior we take the concept to pick out, and the kind of responses that exploitation calls for will be shaped by the nature of its wrongs. Answers to the last question, about how we should respond to exploitation, also inform discussions of topics such as sweatshop labor and plasma donation. Furthermore, different disciplines approach the concept of exploitation in different ways. For some Marxists, exploitation is a pervasive and inextricable part of capitalist economies; some neoclassical economists argue we cannot make sense of the idea of exploitation within competitive markets. Between these two extremes exist a wide range of theories, methods, and approaches to exploitation. This volume brings together a broad group of scholars in philosophy, political science, economics, and law who approach exploitation from a variety of perspectives. Though they are informed by disciplinary approaches, the essays in this volume individually and collectively offer a novel and interdisciplinary perspective on the concept. The authors' contributions build upon, but also challenge, received answers and theories of exploitation. In what follows we introduce and contextualize each of the authors' contributions while summarizing the debates surrounding common responses to the above three questions.

Benjamin Ferguson is at the Department of Philosophy, University of Warwick, benjamin.ferguson@warwick.ac.uk, http://benjaminferguson.org/. Matt Zwolinski is at the Department of Philosophy, University of San Diego, mzwolinski@sandiego.edu, http://mzwolinski.com.

2. What Is Exploitation?

Although accounts of exploitation and fair exchange can be traced from Aristotle (1984) through Aquinas (1945) to the Scottish Enlightenment (Hodgskin 1832), Marx's technical definition of exploitation (Marx 1867; Elster 1985) is as good a place as any to mark the origins of contemporary approaches to the concept. His definition of exploitation as the unequal exchange of labor is as simple as it is contentious.

Commentators have found much to disagree about, including what kinds of labor should be equalized (Nozick 1974, 258–259), whether Marx thought such exploitation was morally problematic (Wolff 1999; Wood 1981), and even whether labor is really what's behind Marx's concerns (Cohen 1979). Contemporary accounts of exploitation often begin with a working definition of exploitation as "taking unfair advantage" that is broader than Marx's, yet perhaps even more contentious. In the most general sense, the contemporary debate about what exploitation is focuses on two dimensions. The first concerns whether exploitation is best understood as a structural feature of systems and institutions or as a feature of discrete transactions between agents. The second concerns whether exploitation is, at its core, a distributive phenomenon that concerns how benefits are distributed or an attitudinal phenomenon that involves expressions or dispositions of disrespect and domination.

2.1. Agents or Structures?

Defenders of structural accounts of exploitation argue that if we focus only on the interactions between individual agents, we will exclude many paradigmatically exploitative situations because in many cases it is the system as a whole, rather than the discrete actions of individuals, that is exploitative. Advocates of structural approaches to exploitation understand this general claim in a variety of ways. Some argue that in many cases victims of exploitation are in a position to be exploited because of background structural injustices (Zwolinski 2012; Sample 2003); others claim that social systems structure and limit the options of disadvantaged groups in a way that advantages more powerful groups (McKeowan 2016); some claim that sometimes victims of exploitation "cannot point to or name any particular individual as [the] exploiter" (Wollner 2019, 147).

The challenge for structural accounts is to show that cases of structural exploitation are not reducible to agential accounts and to do this "*without* assuming the existence of any strange or mysterious entities" (Wollner 2019, 148, emphasis added). Here it is important to distinguish exploitation from vulnerabilities that leave one liable to be exploited. Agential accounts of exploitation are compatible with non-agential (or institutional) sources of vulnerability. In his contribution to this volume Hillel Steiner defends an account of exploitation on which A exploits B when A gains more and B less than either would have gained in the transaction if it were not for unjust background circumstances. Steiner's account is agential, but also compatible with historic and systemic injustice. Social structures may be such that they unjustly disadvantage B vis-à-vis A without any member of society (A included) intending that the structures make B vulnerable. Yet, we can still identify A as the party who gains unfairly at B's expense. That is, it is A who exploits B, even if social structures are responsible for B's initial disadvantage.

What about the claim that victims of exploitation cannot point to any individual as the exploiter? Can we make sense of this idea without invoking mysterious entities? One reason to think that such exploitation exists is to consider cases of exploitation in global supply chains like those that operate in the garment industry and utilize sweatshops. These supply chains include many links: minimally, the workers in the sweatshops, the factory that employs them, retailers, and ultimately consumers. Now, if we adopt an agential account of exploitation, on which exploitation is a property of discrete transactions, if workers are exploited, then they must be exploited by the factory. Why? Because the only agent workers exchange with is their employer, the factory. For the same reason, if consumers exploit, they must exploit the retailer. Yet, these descriptions seem to miss something. There is a sense in which the claim that it's the factory that exploits workers is odd, especially when what they pay workers is dictated by the price retailers offer for the product. If factories gain unfairly from workers only to pass all this illegitimate gain on to retailers, the claim that factories exploit—which is entailed by agential theories—rings false. Unlike strict agential accounts, structural accounts can make sense of the far more natural claim that retailers (or consumers) exploit workers. Note that this departure from strict agential accounts does not, however, entail that workers are exploited without being able to identify their exploiter (except in the narrow sense of being epistemically unable to identify the *particular* consumer agent who exploits). Mirjam Müller's contribution to this volume attempts to make sense of these structural cases while preserving room for individual actions, in particular the ways that individuals can be responsible for reproducing the structural relations that create structural exploitation. Roderick Long takes the opposite approach in his article, pointing out that even individualist, libertarian accounts can make sense of both private exploitation, particularly in labor markets, and exploitation by the state, a form of exploitation that bears much in common with structural exploitation.

Accounts of exploitation that depart most strongly from agential accounts are non-transactional. On these accounts—discussed in Roemer (1982, 1985), taxonomized by Yoshihara and Veneziani (2018), and employed in Veneziani and Yoshihara's contribution to this volume—exploitation is not a relation between two agents in the economy but rather "refers to the relationship between a person and society as a whole" (Roemer 1985, 31). To be exploited, then, is not to find oneself the victim of another's bad behavior but rather to find oneself occupying a particular and unfavorable economic position in the economy as a whole.

Although it is tempting to understand the differences between structural and agential accounts as a deep disagreement about what exploitation is, we think this characterization would be a mistake. Rather, these different approaches pick out different phenomena. Regardless of how we use the label "exploitation," it seems true that the general structure of economic systems can place some individuals in unfair and subaltern social and economic positions compared to others. It seems equally true that being in such a position can also be the result of the distinctive behavior of particular agents. And the existence of either of these forms of disadvantage is, at least *pro tanto*, morally undesirable. Of course, the differences between the approaches remain important, not least because the eradication of exploitation requires different kinds of intervention depending on whether the exploitation in question is agential or structural.

2.2. Distribution or More?

The second main debate about what exploitation is centers on whether it should be understood as a purely distributive phenomenon, where A exploits B just in the case where the social surplus is maldistributed between the two, or whether exploitation involves certain kinds of dominating behavior or holding disrespectful attitudes toward another, or, perhaps, whether it involves both. Many of the best-known analyses of exploitation (Arneson 2013; Goodin 1987; Wertheimer 1996; Zwolinski 2012) assume it is purely distributive. Yet, characterizing exploitation as mere unfair gain seems to miss out characteristics of the behavior (Wolff 1999) and contemporary accounts (Vrousalis 2013; Ferguson 2021) increasingly focus their attention on properties beyond distribution. Hillel Steiner's many articles on exploitation (Steiner 1984, 1987, 2013, 2018) fit squarely within the purely distributive camp. However, in his contribution to this volume he shows how respect can be incorporated in—and, indeed, used to ground—these distributive approaches, thus bridging the two approaches.

Exploitation theorists also disagree about how the maldistribution that—at least partly—characterizes exploitation should be understood. Many theorists advocate substantive accounts of fair distribution, arguing, as Marx did, that the goods exchanged should in some sense be equal, or, as more recent authors have argued (Sample 2003; Snyder 2008), that the benefits of exchange should at least meet the basic needs of the parties involved. Others defend procedural accounts, which argue that fairness is characterized not by a particular distribution but rather by a lack of procedural flaws in the generation of a given distribution. Gijs van Donselaar's contribution questions whether this distinction makes sense—or at least whether it is as sharp as it might first appear. Christopher Mills also discusses this distinction in his contribution, which considers whether contract law should be concerned with exploitation. The orthodox position is that it should not. Since contract law is not concerned with distributive injustice and exploitation *is* a distributive injustice, exploitation does not fall under contract law. However, Mills argues for a more pluralistic law of contracts that provides room to address at least some of the wrongs associated with exploitation.

3. Is Exploitation Wrong?

This brings us to the second main question of exploitation theory—why, if at all, is exploitation wrong? On one hand, the answer seems clear. Exploiters use the disadvantage of others to enrich themselves, offering the disadvantaged a raw deal when they could easily give them more. The wrong of such behavior has been variously characterized as disrespectful, unfair, a failure to treat others as ends in themselves, and so on. Regardless of which of these concepts ultimately grounds exploitation, it seems that exploiting is clearly wrong and wrong for one of these (in the end, fairly similar) reasons. On the other hand, there exist powerful theoretical arguments that significantly complicate this intuitive and straightforward verdict.

In many transactions labeled exploitation, it seems that there is no general moral obligation to transact. Although the parties have an apparent conditional obligation to transact fairly if they choose to transact, they may also permissibly refrain from transacting. Further, when these transactions are mutually beneficial, transacting makes both parties better off. There is good reason to think that if a situation increases all parties' welfare, then it is also morally superior to the status quo. But this means that so long as transacting is mutually beneficial, it is morally superior to not transacting, even if the benefits that the transaction brings are maldistributed. And if not transacting is morally permissible, then it seems that any mutually beneficial transaction must be too, since acts better than permissible acts are permissible too (Ferguson 2016, 2020). If this line of reasoning is correct, then it seems exploitation—at least when mutually beneficial—cannot be wrong.

Ruth Sample, Brian Berkey, and Nicola Mulkeen all address exploitation's wrong(s) in their contributions. Sample's article focuses directly on this paradox. She argues that the conclusion that exploitation is not wrong depends on a too-narrow appeal to its unfairness. Sample argues that some exploitations involve more than just the wrong of unfairness; they also involve moral injury (Hampton 1999). Thus, even if we conclude that exploitation cannot be impermissible because it is unfair, it may nevertheless be so when it involves moral injury. Brian Berkey also challenges the above argument, and like Sample, he thinks it relies on an overly restrictive account of exploitation's wrongs. However, Berkey does not argue for an expansion of the ways in which exploitation wrongs the exploited; rather, he argues that the scope of those whom exploitation wrongs is wider than we might first think. In particular, Berkey claims that part of the wrong of exploitation is external to the transaction itself because we can expand the scope of wronged parties to those who could have but did not participate in the exchange. Finally, Nicola Mulkeen also expands the scope of exploitation and the parties it affects by drawing attention to the possibility of exploiting future people, in particular, via public debt and resource depletion. Mulkeen's account has direct and obvious implications for how we structure and distribute the costs and benefits of social policy over time.

4. What Should Be Done About Exploitation?

This leads us naturally to the third main question covered by exploitation theorists: what, if anything, should we do about it? Many authors have concluded that even if exploitation's unfairness, moral injury, or other wrong-making features make it morally wrong, in cases of mutually beneficial exploitation, state or other third-party intervention aimed at stopping exploitation should not be allowed since mutually beneficial exploitation confers welfare benefits on the exploited. Yet, in some cases—situations in which exploitation stems from structural injustice or where public policies directly cause exploitation—intervention may be appropriate or even morally required. Whether exploitation should be prohibited or tolerated depends on the context of the cases involved. Four of the papers in this volume provide analyses of exploitation in the context of particular cases. Samantha Brennan assesses whether and when children are exploited by their parents. Brennan points out that although childhood experiences are developmentally important, they are also intrinsically valuable. Parents, she argues, have obligations to nurture both kinds of experience in their children. When they make the mistake of only instrumentally valuing the goods of childhood, they exploit their children. Vida Panitch considers whether prohibiting the commodification of goods such as sex and organs might *cause*, rather than prevent, exploitation. She concludes that by reframing these exchanges as gift exchanges, anti-commodification advocates deceive the disadvantaged parties in these exchanges and engender unfair and exploitative interactions. Roberto Veneziani and Naoki Yoshihara explore the relationship between exploitation, international justice, and migration. They show that international inequalities, class relations, and various forms of exploitation arise from differences in per capita endowments of productive assets across countries. Finally, Mark Wells and Peter Jaworski consider whether the practice of paying people for blood plasma should be prohibited in Canada on grounds of exploitation. They apply a broad range of accounts of exploitation to the question and conclude that the practice is not, generally, wrongfully exploitative. Although these articles are primarily applied, the authors also make novel and interesting theoretical contributions along the way.

5. Conclusion

The picture that emerges from the articles in this volume is one of a nuanced and complex topic. Exploitation triggers some of our most fundamental moral intuitions and arises in a wide variety of scenarios. Yet, despite its prevalence and the rawness of the responses it provokes, pinning down just what it is, why it is wrong, and how we should respond to it is surprisingly difficult. The authors included here do a fantastic job of advancing the philosophical discourse on exploitation, offering inventive and careful discussions that shine a new light on a perennial and fascinating topic.

References

Aquinas, Thomas. 1945. *Summa Theologica*. In *Reflections on Commercial Life*, edited by P. Murray, 91–115. New York: Routledge.
Aristotle. 1984. *Nichomachean Ethics*. In *The Complete Works of Aristotle*, edited by J. Barnes, 1729–1867. Princeton, NJ: Princeton University Press.
Arneson, R. 2013. "Exploitation and Outcome." *Politics, Philosophy, and Economics* 12: 392–412.
Cohen, G. 1979. "The Labour Theory of Value and the Concept of Exploitation." *Philosophy and Public Affairs* 8, no. 4: 338–360.
Elster, J. 1985. *Making Sense of Marx*. Cambridge: Cambridge University Press.
Ferguson, B. 2016. "The Paradox of Exploitation." *Erkenntnis* 81, no. 5: 951–972.
Ferguson, B. 2021. "Are We All Exploiters?" *Philosophy and Phenomenological Research* 103, no. 3: 535–546.
Ferguson, B., and S. Köhler. 2020. "Betterness of Permissibility." *Philosophical Studies* 177, no. 9: 2451–2469.
Goodin, R. 1987. "Exploiting a Situation and Exploiting a Person." In *Modern Theories of Exploitation*, edited by A. Reeve, 166–197. London: Sage.
Hampton, J. 1999. "Defining Wrong and Defining Rape." In *A Most Detestable Crime: New Philosophical Essays on Rape*, edited by K. Burgess-Jackson, 118–156. New York: Oxford University Press.
Hodgskin, T. 1832. *The Natural and Artificial Right of Property Contrasted*. London: B. Steil.
Marx, K. 1867. *Capital: A Critique of Political Economy*. Chicago: C. H. Kerr.
McKeowan, M. 2016. "Global Structural Exploitation: Towards an Intersectional Definition." *Global Justice: Theory, Practice, Rhetoric* 9, no. 2: 155–177.
Nozick, R. 1974. *Anarchy, State, and Utopia*. Oxford: Blackwell.
Roemer, J. 1982. *A General Theory of Exploitation and Class*. Cambridge, MA: Harvard University Press.
Roemer, J. 1985. "Should Marxists Be Interested in Exploitation?" *Philosophy and Public Affairs* 14, no. 1: 30–65.
Sample, R. 2003. *Exploitation: What It Is and Why It's Wrong*. Lanham, MD: Rowman and Littlefield.
Snyder, J. 2008. "Needs Exploitation." *Ethical Theory and Moral Practice* 11: 389–405.
Steiner, H. 1984. "A Liberal Theory of Exploitation." *Ethics* 92: 225–241.
Steiner, H. 1987. "Exploitation: A Liberal Theory Amended, Defended and Extended." In *Modern Theories of Exploitation*, edited by A. Reeve, 132–148. London: Sage.
Steiner, H. 2013. "Directed Duties and Inalienable Rights." *Ethics* 123, no. 2: 230–244.
Steiner, H. 2018. "Exploitation, Intentionality, and Injustice." *Economics and Philosophy* 34: 369–379.
Vrousalis, N. 2013. "Exploitation, Vulnerability, and Social Domination." *Philosophy and Public Affairs* 41: 131–157.
Wertheimer, A. 1996. *Exploitation*. Princeton: Princeton University Press.

Wolff, J. 1999. "Marx and Exploitation." *Journal of Ethics* 3, no. 2: 105–120.

Wollner, G. 2019. "Anonymous Exploitation: Non-Individual, Non-Agential and Structural." *Review of Social Economy* 77, no. 2: 143–162.

Wood, A. 1981. "Marx and Equality." In *Issues in Marxist Philosophy*, edited by J. Mepham and D. Hillel-Ruben, 4:195–221. Sussex: Harvester Press.

Yoshihara, N., and R. Veneziani. 2018. "The Theory of Exploitation as the Unequal Exchange of Labour." *Economics and Philosophy* 34, no. 3: 381–409.

Zwolinski, M. 2012. "Structural Exploitation." *Social Philosophy and Policy* 29, no. 1: 154–179.

Zwolinski, M., B. Ferguson, and A. Wertheimer. 2022. "Exploitation." In *The Stanford Encyclopedia of Philosophy* (Winter 2022 edition), edited by E. Zalta and U. Nodelman. https://plato.stanford.edu/archives/win2022/entries/exploitation/.

PART I
WHAT EXPLOITATION IS

2
Sacrificing and Forgoing
A Deontic View of Exploitation

Gijs van Donselaar

1. A Horn of Plenty

Shipwrecks and the wide range of human responses to them, from horror to hallelujah, are a fertile field for exploring our moral intuitions. I will do so to some extent, in the hope of being able to establish a position from which we may look at what has been called the "paradox of exploitation" (Fergusson 2016): the idea that transactions that are mutually beneficial, such as between international apparel producers and local sweatshop workers, can still be exploitative. I will argue that the wrongness of "treating others as a means," as formulated by Kant, is central to our concern with exploitation.[1]

Here is one example of a hallelujah about a wreck, from the historical novel *Sil de Strandjutter* by Dutch author Cor Bruijn (1940):

> How lucky . . . that the wind blows so often from the northeast. God sends that wind over the world especially for the Oosterenders. What a ship! Nothing so odd you can think of, and the waves are washing it ashore, boxes and barrels and drums, all sorts of small stuff. Barrels with beer, boxes with bottles of beer, candles in boxes, candles in slices, brushes, coffee grinders, bales of paper, boxes with percussion caps, thousands, thousands of barrels with oil, bottles of cognac, tins with some sort of fish. A horn of plenty is emptied over the beaches of Terschelling. (My translation from the Dutch)

---

[1] While writing this contribution I realized that in earlier work, notably Van Donselaar 2009, I did not sufficiently stress this element of instrumentalization, which I now think is central to our understanding of exploitation. This omission may have invited Karl Widerquist's (2006) critique of my book, repeated in Matt Zwolinski's (2010) review of it and in Zwolinski and Wertheimer's survey article on exploitation (2016).

The Oosterenders are the inhabitants of the settlement of Oosterend, which is situated on the far east end of the island of Terschelling. On one side it has a long coast facing the North Sea. In the old days, depending on the winds, the sea would be dangerous for passing merchant ships, and frequently they would wreck in a gale, after which their valuable cargo would be washed up the shores of Terschelling to the profit of the beachcombers, especially those of Oosterend.

Many of us would probably feel a pang of moral discomfort about having one's windfalls being dependent on the misfortune of others, as the benefit of the washed-ashore cargo is dependent on the drowning of sailors and the losses for merchants. We may prefer to live in a world without shipwrecks and without the consequent horn of plenty. We would hesitate, I assume, to actually celebrate (as the passage above seems to do) the wreck of ships, even though these wrecks would be to our advantage. On the other hand, what good would there be in letting a horn of plenty spoil on the beaches? Indeed, wouldn't it be a waste and a shame not to drink the cognac?

This is not to deny that the pang of moral discomfort can be real enough, and motivationally effective. Author Bella Bathurst, in her wonderful study of the various practices of beachcombing, salvaging, and looting of wrecked ships around the British Isles in past centuries, reports that some inhabitants of the Scottish island of Swona (whom we will meet in a different capacity below) refused to take home tins of peaches from a particularly disastrous wreckage in 1937, even though the tinned peaches "would have been the most incredible, delicious thing they'd ever tasted." Their reason: "women and bairns had died on that wreck" (Bathurst 2006, 95).[2]

Nonetheless, while allowing for the possibility of such moral hypersensitivity, I think that at worst the Oosterenders who took the cognac can be thought of as a kind of scavenger, not as predators—vultures, perhaps, but not harpies. They may have an interest in wrecks, but they are bystanders who could not have altered the course of events. And their enjoyment of the spoils cannot be rejected as "exploitative."

Daphne du Maurier's grim novel *Jamaica Inn* (2015, originally published in 1936) also features a historical community of inhabitants of a treacherous

---

[2] Bathurst suggests that the premature death of women and bairns (children) was considered extraordinary, while for adult males going to sea, early death was a risk that was taken for granted. I commend this book to all moral philosophers. It makes us aware of how unruly the waters are that *we* are trying to navigate.

coastal area, this time in Cornwall. Here, however, the heroine discovers a gang of "wreckers" (headed by her own uncle) that lures passing merchant ships to their ruin by setting up decoys on the rocky shore, false lights suggesting safe harbor, so that the wreckers will then be able to reap the spoils of disaster.

Bathurst (2006, 220–222) observes that Du Maurier's Gothic tale is based on "rumors" that are vehemently contradicted by the modern Cornish. But, fact or fiction, our moral judgment will not likely waver in a case like this. The wreckers are involved in what we may call the core case of exploitation. They intentionally cause shipwrecks, drownings, and merchant losses in order to reap the benefits of their misery. The wreckers cannot regard their benefits as "God sent," as the Oosterenders did, because it is not God but themselves who send the benefits. The wrecker strategy is close to downright piracy.

The distinction seems clear. Reaping the benefit of another's misery may be uncomfortable, but it is not exploitative in itself, as in the case of the Oosterenders of Terschelling. It is only if the misery of others is intentionally caused by the reapers of the benefits that their benefits are exploitative, as with the wreckers of Cornwall.

Yet, I want to argue there is a problem with the neatness of this distinction. I have not been able to trace a novel for illustration, but I did find a novelist to serve my purposes, or rather Bella Bathurst did. Her book begins with a long quote from Robert Louis Stevenson's *Records of a Family of Engineers*. Stevenson recounts his father's chilling experience on board the *Regent*. Early at dawn the ship is drifting on a windless swell toward the dangerous coast of Swona in Scotland (again). At the head of the beach the sailors discern a small hamlet; the inhabitants are all still asleep. And since they hope to escape being wrecked if a boat is launched from the shore to tow the *Regent* to safety, they fire a gun to alarm the Swonans. Awakened, the inhabitants appear on the beach, one by one. They observe the ship in trouble but stay perfectly inert: "not a hand was raised; but all callously awaited the harvest of the sea." Fortunately, the ship's sail then catches a timely breeze, and the *Regent* is saved (Bathurst 2006, xiii–xiv). Evidently, this time the Swonans suffered no pang of moral discomfort at the prospect of benefiting from the misery of others.

How should we judge the moral attitude of *these* Swonans and their like? They were not the active predators the Cornish were rumored to be—they did nothing. But neither were they, as the Oosterenders were, innocent bystanders who merely profited from an accident they could not have prevented—they did nothing. Bathurst concludes:

> There were also a few instances which fell between active and passive wrecking. As Robert Louis Stevenson pointed out, there were parts of the country where coastliners sinned by omission, having done so little to prevent wrecks that they were, in effect, encouraging them. (Bathurst 2006, xvii)[3]

2. Exploitation by Omission

Whether or not exploitation is a sin (in the biblical sense) is something to be determined by others, but I will argue that the Swonans who refused to save the *Regent* were guilty of exploitation by omission.

However, my argument proceeds on an important assumption—namely, that moral agents, if they are to be of good will and if they are to treat others as ends in themselves, will answer to at least a minimal duty of benevolence— what Kant calls "duties of love." They are prepared to make sacrifices on behalf of others in distress. Such duties may be discretionary and raise no corresponding claim rights. And, as I shall take them, there may also be legitimate restrictions to such sacrifices, such as if an attempted rescue operation would be life-threatening or if an agent's special duties to their near and dear would have priority. I will not consider how and at what level these reasonable limits on sacrifices should be set, but I take it for granted that moral agents can be criticized for being too inconsiderate about the ill fate of others, for failing to suffer a pang of moral discomfort in the face of disaster for others.

Let me therefore address the behavior of the Swonans as follows. Their refusal to rescue the *Regent* is determined *only* by their desire for the "harvest of the sea," implying that in the absence of such an anticipated harvest they would have been ready to take on the small cost of launching a boat and tow the *Regent* to safety—as the sailors were hoping. So, the Swonans recognize a reason to save lives (or prevent misery) compelling them to make a certain

---

[3] In an earlier version of this paper, written some time ago, in trying to make my point, I cooked up imaginary examples of precisely this nature. Dissatisfied with that, I searched the internet for real-life examples, and that brought me—via a vital reference (Rufus and Lawson 2009, 66)—to Bathurst's book. I was happy not only that she presented to me the Swonans but also that she, like me, identified them as a special category of "sinners."

sacrifice to do so, but now that they would have to do without the value of the spoils on top of that sacrifice, they refrain from the rescue. Let us put it thus: the cost of a rescue operation can be thought of as consisting of two elements—that which the Swonans would have to *sacrifice* (S), which is the launching of the boat, and that what they would have to *forgo* (F), which are the spoils, the harvest of the sea.

The Swonans regard (S) as acceptable but (S + F) as prohibitive. For simplicity, think of $10 as the monetary equivalent of (S), $90 as the equivalent of (F), and so $100 as the equivalent of (S + F). Their omission to rescue the *Regent* is therefore strategic. It will obtain them $90 they would otherwise not have had. In the way they deliberate they are instrumentalizing the drowning of the sailors and the losses of the merchants.

In order to bring this out more clearly, consider a parallel community that faces a similar choice to rescue a ship in trouble but without anticipating any spoils because it happens to be a mere passenger ship without any worthwhile cargo to harvest, let alone a horn of plenty. For the counterparts, however, the rescue operation would require them to sacrifice $100, which is equivalent to what (S + F) is for the Swonans. And the counterparts regard that figure as prohibitive (for reasons that we may or may not find convincing—as I said, on this I will not speculate). Schematically:

	Swonans	Counterparts
Sacrificing (S)	$10	$100
Forgoing (F)	$90	$0
Aggregate (S + F)	$100	$100

Yet, the counterparts, in omitting the rescue, cannot be accused of instrumentalizing the foreseeable shipwreck and the misery it causes because the wreck is not required for the parallel community to have access to the value of (F). They already have (F), and they might well have a great sense of relief if the ship was saved in the end by a timely breeze, as happened to the *Regent*. For the actual Swonans, such a sense of relief is inconceivable. They cannot but have regretted that breeze because it robbed them of (F).

For both the Swonans and their counterparts the following holds:

If we do not rescue, there will be a wreck. (i)
If there is a wreck, we will have (obtain/keep) the value of (F). (ii)

If we do not rescue, we will have (obtain/keep) the value of (F). (iii)
Because we want to have (obtain/keep) the value of (F), we do not rescue. (iv)

For the Swonans only, something stronger holds, namely:

If we do not rescue, there will be a wreck. (i)
If *and only if* there is a wreck, we will have (obtain/keep) the value of (F). (ii′)
If we do not rescue, we will have (obtain/keep) the value of (F). (iii)
Because we want to have (obtain/keep) the value of (F), we do not rescue. (iv)

3. Consequentialism

From a straightforwardly consequentialist point of view the reasonings, or attitudes, of the Swonans and their counterparts are morally equivalent, since their conclusions (and subsequent decisions and outcomes thereof) are the same, and therefore equally morally justified or equally morally unjustified, depending on the balance of bad and good consequences for the islanders on the one hand and the sailors and merchants on the other.[4] Consequentialists will not recognize a relevant moral distinction between sacrificing and forgoing. For the consequentialist, therefore, the following equivalence holds:

It is morally right not to forgo (F) on top of the sacrifice of (S) if and only if it is also morally right not to sacrifice the equivalent value of (S + F).

But then the consequentialist likewise would justify the predatory actions of the wreckers from *Jamaica Inn* if overall consequences were better on balance compared to their not interfering with the ships.[5] And this demonstrates that consequentialists cannot attribute any moral significance to exploitation at all, whether by the action of the wreckers or by the omission of the Swonans.

We are not unfamiliar with this consequentialist incapacity. The Swonans desire to obtain the spoils of the shipwreck (F) and therefore they intend the

---

[4] "Straightforward" consequentialism, such as classical utilitarianism, attaches no relevance to the distribution of the consequences over those involved. What is to be maximized is the *aggregate* or *average* value of the consequences (which of the two it is does not concern us here).

[5] This is the way that Shelly Kagan (1989) argues in favor of consequentialism.

shipwreck. Their counterparts desire to keep the equivalent of (F) but they do not therefore intend the shipwreck, even if it is foreseeable. As said, the counterparts would have been perfectly happy if there were no shipwreck at all. The counterparts can be said to regard the shipwreck as *collateral damage* from their desire to keep (F). This is not true for the actual Swonans: without the foreseeable shipwreck they would have no access to (F) and they cannot regard it as collateral damage. It is intended damage. The damage is no side effect.

Of course, the distinction I use here between the foreseeable but not intended collateral consequences of omissions and the intended consequences of omissions is familiar. It should remind us of a distinction that we know from just war theory, that between the foreseeable but not intended (collateral) consequences of actions and the intended consequences of actions. The idea is that a government that wants to deliver a decisive blow to its enemy by bombing a crucial arms factory and accepts as collateral damage the deaths of a number of innocent civilians in the plant's neighborhood should be judged differently than a government that deliberately bombs a civilian neighborhood, with a comparable number of victims, with the purpose of demoralizing the enemy and pressing it to surrender. In the latter case the victims are intended and required to achieve victory. In the former case, the victims are not intended and not required to reach victory. Were no innocent victims consequent upon bombing the enemy arms plant, it would be a great relief for the bombing government. Just as the timely breeze that rescued the *Regent* would be a relief for the Swonans' counterparts. Such a government might even consider spreading flyers with a warning just before the bombing of the plant, in order to minimize the damage. This is not among the latter government's considerations. The latter government is what we call a terrorist; the former government faces a dilemma, or even a tragic choice. The former has an incentive to minimize the damage; the latter doesn't.

4. Sacrifice and Reservation Price

After this rather lengthy stage-setting, we should now return to the original question: how can mutually beneficial transactions still be exploitative? Matt Zwolinski, who turns out to be a fellow impending-wreck analyst, discusses an example from Wertheimer (1996) of a vessel in trouble that was rescued by a tugboat, but only after a payment of £1,000 to the tugmaster was agreed upon.

> In the current case ... the result of the transaction was not to set back the interests of the vessel's owner, but to advance them. The owner of the vessel was much better off being rescued, even at a cost of GBP 1,000, than he would have been had the tugmaster taken no action at all. The agreement to which they came, far from being harmful, was actually mutually beneficial, at least when compared to the alternative of no transaction at all. Relative to this alternative, where the tugmaster receives no money and the vessel in distress receives no rescue, both parties experience an increase in utility. This suggests that a proper understanding of exploitation will make room for mutually advantageous, as well as harmful, exploitative transactions. (Zwolinski 2007, 705)

So, I will try to explain what that proper understanding of exploitation, making room for mutually advantageous transactions, amounts to.

But first we must remove a potential source of confusion. It is tugboats' job to keep incoming commercial vessels secure, and the tugboats cannot be kept afloat if tugmasters are not paid for their services. Tugmasters are part of a practice, like that of doctors or bakers, whose essential services to others could not continue to exist if they were not paid. The prospective willingness of potential victims of a wreck to pay tugmasters is a condition for the very possibility of the existence of tugboats and their masters. So, the parallel between tugmasters and the Swonans would be flawed, if this is the case. If they forwent the benefit of a wreck, the Swonans would not lose their capacity to sacrifice what is required to prevent the wreck; if the tugmasters were denied the benefit of preventing a wreck, they would have no tugboat with which to prevent wrecks.

To avoid this ambiguity, we should concentrate on encounters with potential rescuers who are not dependent for their existence *in their capacity as rescuers* on being paid by those who need rescue. An example is given by Chris Meyers (2004, 324–325). A man demands certain sexual services from a woman whose car broke down in the desert in return for driving her to the safety of a nearby town. I think we would not stop at calling this behavior "exploitation"; the apt word would be "extortion." Nonetheless, the transaction this brute is after is mutually beneficial (assuming the woman prefers living after being abused to the alternative of death by dehydration).

Could he claim that his position is more like that of the Swonans' counterparts than like that of the Swonans themselves? Could he argue that the sacrifice required for saving the woman is prohibitive? If he did, he should be criticized for his lack of concern for others in distress—again, for being a brute. He is already on his way to town, and he has already halted, so he merely needs to open the door and endure her company for a while. If he claims that this is too much for him, then it is more likely he is lying. The extortionist is not avoiding a prohibitive sacrifice; he is caught with the mere intention not to forgo the spoils of an exploitative deal. The core of his exploitative behavior is that he insists on an (outrageous) reward for doing what he has moral reason to do.

Nonetheless, the possibility of communication, agreement, and transaction opens an opportunity for rescues that would otherwise not happen—namely, precisely in those cases in which a sacrifice for a rescue *is* (perceived to be, correctly or not) prohibitive, as in the case of the Swonans' counterparts. In such cases, potential rescuers evidently need an incentive to do the rescuing, and if they have an incentive, it means that their position will be improved once they act upon it. And such an incentive can be established through a deal with those who need to be rescued.

But if we uphold the objection to exploitative behavior, it follows that potential rescuers should insist on no more than their "reservation price" for the rescue—that is, the price that would minimally move them to perform. Pressing for more than that would be pressing for an exploitative benefit. It means that potential rescuers should not exercise the full force of their bargaining power, on pain of being exploiters.[6] So, what is that reservation price? It is a full compensation for the sacrifice plus the smallest possible increment in benefits, say $1. And then we have it, a Pareto improvement without exploitation: the rescuer benefits ($1), the one who is rescued benefits and is not exploited.[7]

---

[6] Normally a reservation price is contrasted with the market price: if the market price for X is below my reservation price, I will purchase X; if the market price is higher than my reservation price, I will not purchase. Here, however, since there is no market, we must contrast the reservation price with the maximal attainable bargaining result.

[7] If we regard instrumentalization as characteristic of exploitation, it is obvious that we need to turn to Immanuel Kant to look for groundwork. But some exegesis is required if we want to capture the deontic objection to exploitation by omission. A person of good will, Kant says, will answer to the categorical imperative. The categorical imperative knows various formulations; the one that is of most interest here is "Act so that you use humanity, as much as in your own person as in the person of every other, always at the same time as an end and never merely as a means" (Kant 2002, 42). The German original of this passage reads as follows: "Handle so, dass du die Menschheit, sowohl in deiner Person, als in der Person eines jeden andern . . . niemals bloß als Mittel brauchest" (Kant

5. Libertarianism

The despair of sweatshop workers is so obvious that it needs no long rehearsal here. They earn less, often much less, than what would bring them up to the international poverty line, which is about $2 per day. They work for long hours under unhealthy, sometimes dangerous conditions and have no affordable access to healthcare or other essential facilities. Basically, their lives consist of working, eating, and sleeping, without the enjoyments so many others are accustomed to. They work to continue their biological existence but cannot hope to achieve any fulfillment beyond that. Finally, the manual labor they perform is drudgery—routine and mechanical. With or without an inquiry after their rights, these are not the dismal lives one would wish human beings to endure, and it is only natural that many in the West feel a pang of moral discomfort once they realize that their own extensive access to all kinds of goods, indeed luxury goods, is dependent on sweatshop work, even if they realize that most sweatshop workers would be worse off, perhaps starving, without their employment by sweatshops.

The question that concerns us is whether sweatshop workers are exploited by their employers. According to Matt Zwolinski, "since . . . providing *no* monetary benefit does not violate anyone's rights, and since a contract whereby sweatshops agree to provide *some* benefit does not in itself violate anyone's rights, it follows that such contracts are not exploitative" (2007, 711). I will call this the "libertarian" position. There are several complications with it. If contracts that do not violate rights are by definition non-exploitative—assuming we take rights as "side constraints" as Robert Nozick (1974) does,

---

1968, 429). As in the translation by Allen W. Wood, quoted above, *brauchen* is usually translated in English as "using," as if *brauchen* were the same as *gebrauchen*. Now, the word "using" suggests that the user indeed *acts*—interferes with, or manipulates what is used. To use something we must drink it, or hammer with it, or drive in it, etc. And in that sense the Swonans cannot be said to be using the *Regent*'s sailors or the owners of its cargo. They did nothing except wait. And to say that you are waiting for something to happen (for the train, for the rain to stop, for Godot, or for the harvest of the sea) means that you are doing nothing. But at least in modern German, *brauchen* means not "using" but "needing." There is a subtle but significant difference between the imperative not to act in such a way that you will *use* others as a means and the imperative not to act in such a way that you will *need* others as a means. The latter formulation will rule out the strategic omission of the Swonans as a violation of the imperative, even if the former might not. Meanwhile, I think the best word for an English translation of *brauchen* would be "treating," because it avoids the difficulty of identifying its opposites, whether it would be "using"/*gebrauchen* as a means or "needing"/*brauchen* as a means. If you let others drift toward their ruin in order to get access to their goods, you are certainly not treating them as ends in themselves. And you are certainly not of good will. It also avoids the grammatical clumsiness of saying that we could be "using [or needing] others as an end in themselves." Kant (2017, 24) indeed has "treating" as the translation.

so that the rights of others circumscribe the space in which we are morally free to act at our discretion—then we bounce upon the problem of coerced contracts. Two neighbors hold property rights over their parcels. Neighbor A has no particular interest in building a high structure on her land, but neighbor B has no right that such a structure is not built. He has no right to the beautiful view he enjoys over A's land. Yet, A builds a high and ugly wall on her land after all, just to spoil B's view, and she offers to demolish the wall, but only in return for a substantial payment from B. If B consents and contracts to make the payment, then under the libertarian definition the contract is not exploitative, since by stipulation there is no rights violation involved in it; B has no right to the view. But can we maintain that B is not instrumentalized by A, not exploited? If we maintain that such contracts are not exploitative, then it should be concluded that we have no right not to be *coerced*, because A might as well have threatened to build the wall unless B makes a payment for not building it.[8] This is bad news for Friedrich Hayek (2006), who argued that to be free in the libertarian sense essentially means to be free of coercion. As it turns out, then, even some core cases of non-mutually-beneficial exploitation will not be viewed as exploitative by libertarians as long as no rights are violated.[9]

But Zwolinski could have avoided these complications, had he wanted to, by stipulating that the rights of sweatshop workers are not violated and that their contracts are not coerced.[10] I will continue to discuss the argument as such. But as such, there remains a difficulty with libertarianism, which is acute for the present analysis: it is unable to make a morally relevant distinction between collateral damage and intended damage, whether from actions or from omissions. In this regard, *bien étonnés de se trouver ensemble*, libertarians are in the same league with consequentialists. Consider again the terrorist government that deliberately bombs a civilian neighborhood. It intends the loss of innocent lives in order to press the enemy to surrender. So, according to libertarian standards, this constitutes a rights violation, and a

---

[8] I address such cases, including some historical legal cases, in Van Donselaar 2009. I argue that the law of torts can (and should) be structured in such a way as to avoid exploitation by coercion.

[9] A crucial subtlety here: the transaction may still seem mutually beneficial, but the *possibility* of the transaction is not, because it invites the behavior of the exploiting party. See Nozick (1974, 85) on "unproductive exchanges."

[10] Those who are acquainted with the work of Thomas Pogge (2002, 2005) will agree that these stipulations are not at all innocent. The long history of European colonialism has affected the conditions of many contemporary Asians, Africans, Latin Americans, and South Americans, and it may be that these conditions now leave them no alternative but to accept sweatshop labor.

serious one. Now compare this with a government that accepts the loss of innocent lives as collateral damage, as a foreseeable but morally regrettable side effect of bombing an arms factory. Then, according to libertarian standards, this also constitutes a rights violation, and an equally serious one. Actions violate rights or they don't, and libertarians cannot appreciate a morally relevant distinction between exploitative and non-exploitative rights-violating actions. For both consequentialism and libertarianism only the outcomes of actions, characterized in a certain way (respectively, as maximizing good consequences or as not violating rights), are relevant in judging their legitimacy. Unlike Kant, they fail to look at the *actor* (or the omissor) and the actor's good will: the actor's intentions or motivations.

But then it is equally obvious that when *no* rights violations are involved, libertarians can also not appreciate a morally relevant distinction between exploitative and non-exploitative omissions. Even if they were to admit that strategic omissions are exploitative, they would not object to them for that reason, because they violate no rights (and are not coerced). They will see no moral difference between the Swonans and their counterparts for the same reason that they see no difference between a terrorist bomber and a tragic bomber. So, instead of arguing that sweatshop workers are not exploited since their rights are not violated, they should be arguing that *it does not matter* whether they are exploited, as long as their rights are not violated. Again, libertarians will review an intuitively morally problematic interaction, and they will ask if any rights violations are involved. If not, there is no further question to be asked. But if there is a rights violation involved, there is also no further question to be asked. Characterizing actions or omissions as "exploitative" does not determine their legitimacy. Libertarians have other criteria for that. Whether or not people's lives are instrumentalized, whether or not they are treated as means to an end, is of no libertarian concern.

6. Swona Incorporated?

In what sense, then, can sweatshop workers be regarded as being exploited by their employers, even though their (uncoerced) contracts do not violate their rights? Of course, international producers of apparel are not charities; they are profit-seeking and competitive firms under market pressure. But are they driven by market forces to set their sweatshop wages as miserably low as they do? In that case we should ask what, exactly, "market forces" are.

Royal Philips in Eindhoven, the Netherlands, a producer of consumer electronics and lightbulbs, was not a charity but, from its early years up to the 1960s, offered packages of benefits to its workers that were way above what the market would enforce. It built comfortable and affordable housing for the workers; it built schools and playgrounds for their children. Philips created public parks. It built a football stadium, a concert hall, and a museum exhibiting technological developments. On top of all that, Eindhoven did not witness a single layoff for decades in a row: workers who became redundant in one position were not sacked but instead were scrupulously prepared for a transfer to another position. When it came to social security, it was said, Philips was as good as the government. Nonetheless, Philips continued to be an immensely profitable firm.

All kinds of cynical responses to Philips's "corporate social responsibility," as it would nowadays be called, may imply that in the end such behavior was to Philips's own advantage, because it created a sense of loyalty among the workers (which it did) and avoided labor unrest. But then the question becomes why, if it would be to their advantage in the end, international producers of apparel are not doing the same for their sweatshop workers.

A relevant factor may be that Philips was always far ahead as a technological innovator and that its innovations were mostly patented. In that sense Philips could be considered as a near monopolist that would not lose any significant market share by accepting the higher production costs that were required to maintain its social responsibility. It could afford its generosity.

So, we need to ask in what sense *competitive* international corporations can afford or not afford to raise the wages of their sweatshop workers. Basically, there are two scenarios: one is "benign" and the other is "vicious," and these scenarios have radically distinct moral implications. I discuss the benign scenario first, with a highly stylized example.

Consider a corporate producer of apparel that employs 100 sweatshop workers who together sew 100 shirts each day, for a daily wage of $1 each. And each day the producer sells 100 shirts in the West for $30 each. The producer, however, reads about the World Bank's poverty line of about $2 per day and realizes with a pang of moral discomfort that his employees earn much less than that. So he starts calculating. If he raises the daily wage of his workers to $2 while other production costs remain equal, and therefore raises the price for the shirts by $1 dollar to $31, he will sell 10 fewer shirts each day. Presently, corporate profit is $3,000 from sales minus $100 in wages: $2,900 each day. If wages are raised, *ceteris paribus*, corporate profit would be $2,790 from sales minus $200 in wages: $2,590. The difference of $310 consists of a sacrifice of $100, which is the advantage for the sweatshop workers, plus a remainder of $210, which is what the producer would forgo due to a loss of market share. It means that the corporation, if it raises wages, will lose ~11 percent in revenues, consisting of a sacrifice of ~3.5 percent and an exploitative benefit forgone of ~7.5 percent. In this case, the loss is no trifle, but it is the price that is paid for not being an exploiter. And it is difficult to see why, if (and only if) business results are sufficiently comparable, it would be a price a corporation could not afford to pay.

Do not mistake this as an attempt at "realism"; apart from the simplified figures that are used, there is a host of relevant considerations that are not addressed (and which I will address in discussing the vicious scenario later). It just suggests a method for separating a sacrifice from what is forgone in the books of the corporation: the sacrifice is equal to the advantage of the sweatshop workers. If the sacrifice is acceptable to the producer but the further costs from losing market share, whatever they are, turn out to be prohibitive, then the latter are equal to the corporation's exploitative advantage if wages are not raised.

So, if an international corporation that produces apparel or whatever argues that it cannot afford to raise the wages of its sweatshop workers or improve their labor conditions because of the vulnerability of its market share, it implies that it *would* have raised wages or improved their conditions if no market share were at stake—that is, if the corporation were a monopolist. In that case it should admit that the part of its market share it would lose because of the raises or improvements is an exploitative benefit of its strategic omission to raise workers' wages or to improve workers' labor conditions. It should admit that its strategy is Swonan. If the corporation is unwilling to admit as much, because it is disagreeable to admit it, then it implies that the corporation would have neither raised wages nor improved labor conditions if it had been a monopolist. But then the appeal to its market vulnerability is redundant, or rather a fig leaf that hides from perception that the corporation is not willing to sacrifice anything at all to give its workers better lives. In that case it should admit that it fits the classical Marxist image of the capitalist who, market pressure or not, seeks to squeeze all possible surplus value of their labor out of his workers, and instrumentalizes them as nothing more than beasts of burden that must be kept alive and sufficiently fit to carry the burden, but who have no right to complain because otherwise they would starve. And that too is a disagreeable thing to admit, because, again, it indicates that the corporation fails to treat its own employees with a minimal concern for the quality of their lives, that it fails to be of good will. Disagreeability prevails, one way or the other.

7. Oosterend Incorporated?

Let us turn to what I call the vicious scenario. The repercussions of raising wages or improving conditions of sweatshop workers can be more serious than just losing an affordable share of sales in the West; or, rather, losing such a market share itself may have further repercussions. Thus, Robert Mayer (2007, 617), referring to Nike and Reebok, observes:

> Both the manufacturing and retail sectors of the apparel industry are intensely competitive and businesses in both sectors do go bankrupt with some frequency. Profit margins in the manufacturing sector do not seem excessive and in the retail sector they are notoriously tight....
>
> In this type of environment, the minimum profit necessary to survive is in fact the profit that can be made. With declining profits a business loses shareholder confidence, cannot raise capital or borrow on favorable terms.

And then we should say that the corporation, indeed, cannot afford the raises or improvements; it would cease to exist.

But still, this is not the end to relevant questions. What is so bad about the bankruptcy of a corporation that cannot survive except by paying its workers subsistence wages? Some business ethicists, such as Elaine Sternberg (2000), have tried to model firms and corporations after the Aristotelian view of natural organisms—that is, with a telos of their own. So if a firm went bankrupt, it would be like an animal dying, and that is bad for the animal. But corporations are not natural organisms. They may be legal creatures, and may even be called legal persons, but legal creatures are creatures of the state, not of God or of nature.[11] So, if we ask what is bad about the disintegration of an international corporation headquartered in the West, we must ask what

---

[11] Gangs of mercenary assassins—*illegal* non-natural persons—also fall apart if they do not accept the next assignment for a murder. Of course, it cannot be maintained in general that it is all right to do mischief because if one did not do the mischief, then others would do it. A mercenary assassin, operating on a market for murder, is not excused for accepting the next assignment for a hit by pointing out the fact that if he did not take it, one of his competitors would.

is bad for its natural composites, the natural persons who are its so-called stakeholders. Who are they? There are the investors, who, predictably, will redirect their investments. There are the well-trained CEOs and administrative staff, who will lose their well-paid jobs. A part of them may be absorbed by the competitors whose business opportunities will now increase, but if not, the consequences would remain limited for them. And that is because their *citizenship* rights in Western countries preclude that they will be reduced to misery, perhaps comparable to that of sweatshop workers elsewhere. The same would be true for others who lose business because of the bankruptcy, such as some apparel retailers.

But even if we accept that the repercussions of the bankruptcy of an international apparel corporation for its natural composites in the West are greatly ameliorated by the more or less robust social security systems (more so in Europe and less so in the United States), it cannot be denied that some will suffer a setback to their interest. So, there is some bad in a bankruptcy, even if we do not think of firms as animals. Would there be any good in it? We must now turn to the last category of the corporation's stakeholders, those whose interests we were concerned with to begin with, and these are the sweatshop workers themselves. As observed by Mayer (2007), they may gain for a while from their raised wages and improved conditions, but shortly afterward they will lose their jobs as their employer goes bankrupt and then they will end up in a worse condition, perhaps starve, than they were in when still on sweatshop wages, or they end up anew in the employment of one of the other apparel corporations that can now usurp the market share of the one that went bankrupt.[12]

If, and only if, what Mayer says is correct, that "the minimum profit necessary to survive is in fact the profit that can be made," and if a bankruptcy would not improve the sweatshop workers' situation, then, in terms of the distinction I used earlier, it follows that each corporation's reservation price for labor is equal to its market price, which is the price at the level of sweatshop wages as they are. As it turns out for a dismal conclusion, an individual international corporation cannot improve the position of its sweatshop workers. It lacks the power to do so. The international labor market would then appear

---

[12] In Van Donselaar 2013 I argue against the editors of *The Economist* (2004) that improvements of labor conditions in the developing world may seriously affect consumers in the West. Even if their budget remains the same, the *range* of products they can purchase will no longer include what is now produced by sweatshops. The new budget line will merely intersect with the present one and not fully include it. It implies that those with presently vested interests in sweatshop labor have a reason to regret progress in the Third World. This is a caveat to the argument above.

to be an untamable beast, as is the sea that washes ashore the losses of sailors and merchants, while these losses cannot be prevented by refusing the spoils. The difference, then, between the benign scenario and the vicious scenario is that in the former there is room between the non-exploitative reservation price for labor and its exploitable market price, whereas in the latter case there is no such room to be exploited. Which scenario is actually the case is something to be decided by economic, not moral, analysis. But I hope to have indicated what the economist should be looking for.

If the vicious scenario turns out to be the actual one, one might still hope that good-willed international corporations, competitors for labor, would make an effort to bind each other by covenant in setting sweatshop wages at an acceptable level, leaving a level playing field on which to continue competing with each other. Such a covenant would turn the competitors into a quasi-cartel, not for setting prices but for setting wages. Alternatively, one might hope that critical consumers in the West show themselves en masse prepared to pay higher prices for the sweatshop manufactures they routinely purchase.

But as long as such hopes remain unfulfilled, and given that the vicious scenario is the actual one, international apparel corporations have an opportunity to join the Oosterenders of Terschelling in their hallelujah:

> How lucky ... that destitution visits so many parts of the world. God sends that destitution especially for the Westerners. What a trade! Nothing so odd you can think of, and the ships are bringing it in, containers full of it. Containers with apparel and sneakers, containers with sugar, coffee, tea, and chocolate. And consumer electronics in containers: smartphones, tablets, TV sets. Hand-stitched footballs, furniture, carpets, thousands, thousands of barrels with palm oil, tins with some sort of fruit. A horn of plenty is emptied over the beaches of the West.

If they find there is something distasteful in rejoicing like this, it must be because of their still remaining pang of moral discomfort.

References

Bathurst, B. 2006. *The Wreckers: A Story of Killing Seas, False Lights and Plundered Ships*. London: Harper Perennial.
Bruijn, C. 1940. *Sil de strantjutter*. Nijkerk: Callenbach.

du Maurier, D. 2015. *Jamaica Inn*. London: Virago Press.
The Economist. 2004. "Poverty and Inequality: A Question of Justice?" (editorial). March 11, 2004. http://www.economist.com/node/2499118.
Ferguson, B. 2016. "The Paradox of Exploitation." Erkenntnis 81, no. 5: 951–972.
Hayek, F. 2006. "Freedom and Coercion." In *The Liberty Reader*, edited by D. Miller, 80–99. Edinburgh: Edinburgh University Press.
Kagan, S. 1989. *The Limits of Morality*. Oxford: Clarendon Press.
Kant, I. 1968. *Grundlegung zur Metaphysik der Sitten*. Akademie-Ausgabe Kant Werke IV. Berlin: Walter de Gruyter.
Kant, I. 2002. *Groundwork for the Metaphysics of Morals*. Edited and translated by A. W. Wood. With essays by J. B. Schneewind, M. Baron, S. Kagan, and A. Wood. New Haven, CT: Yale University Press.
Kant, I. 2007. *Groundwork for the Metaphysics of Morals* Translated by H. Nottas. https://www.academia.edu/38519368/Groundwork_for_the_Metaphysic_of_Morals.
Mayer, R. 2007. "Sweatshops, Exploitation, and Moral Responsibility." *Journal of Social Philosophy* 38: 605–619.
Meyers, C. 2004. "Wrongful Beneficence: Exploitation and Third World Sweatshops." *Journal of Social Philosophy* 35: 319–333.
Nozick, R. 1974. *Anarchy, State, and Utopia*. Oxford: Blackwell.
Pogge, T. 2002. *World Poverty and Human Rights: Cosmopolitan Responsibilities and Reforms*. Cambridge: Polity Press.
Pogge, T. 2005. "Real World Justice." *Journal of Ethics* 9: 29–53.
Rufus, A., and K. Lawson. 2009. *The Scavengers Manifesto*. New York: Tarcher/Penguin.
Sternberg, E. 2000. *Just Business: Business Ethics in Action*. New York: Oxford University Press.
Van Donselaar, G. 2009. *The Right to Exploit: Parasitism, Scarcity, Basic Income*. New York: Oxford University Press.
Van Donselaar, G. 2013. "Not on Venus: Global Poverty and Causal Innocence." *Krisis: Journal for Contemporary Philosophy* 1: 42–46.
Wertheimer, A. 1996. *Exploitation*. Princeton, NJ: Princeton University Press.
Widerquist, K. 2006. "Who Exploits Who?" *Political Studies* 54: 444–464.
Zwolinski, M. 2007. "Sweatshops, Choice, and Exploitation." *Business Ethics Quarterly* 17, no. 4: 689–727.
Zwolinski, M. 2010. Review of G. Van Donselaar, *The Right to Exploit*. *Ethics* 121, no. 1: 228–232.
Zwolinski, M., and A. Wertheimer. 2016. "Exploitation." In *Stanford Encyclopedia of Philosophy* (Fall 2016 edition), edited by E. N. Zalta. https://plato.stanford.edu/entries/exploitation/.

3
Exploitative Transactions and Corrective Justice

Christopher Mills

1. Introduction

Exploitative transactions are transactions where one party wrongfully benefits by taking unfair advantage of another party's bargaining position.[1] These transactions raise important questions of distributive and corrective justice. These domains of justice differ from each other by conforming to distinctive internal logics and conferring different types of reasons to agents. Conceiving of exploitation in either distributive or corrective terms shapes our priorities when responding to exploitation. Distributive responses to exploitation seek to understand how public policies can reduce the background inequalities that give rise to exploitation.[2] Corrective responses to exploitation seek to understand how legal institutions can prevent or negate the actions of those exploiting the vulnerabilities of their fellow citizens.[3] How we seek to conceive of and respond to the problem of exploitative transacting should thus lead us to think more deeply about the relationship between distributive and corrective justice.[4]

This relationship between domains of justice is especially important to the law of contracts. These laws govern legally enforceable transactions and appear well suited to respond to moral concerns about exploitative transactions.

Thanks to Christian Twigg-Flesner for discussion of the doctrinal elements of this chapter and to Adam Slavny, Ben Ferguson, and Matt Zwolinski for comments on a draft of this chapter. An early version of this work was presented at Warwick's Centre for Ethics, Law, and Public Affairs. Many thanks, as always, to colleagues and participants for their critical and constructive feedback.

[1] Arneson 1992; Ferguson and Steiner 2018.
[2] For example, Wertheimer 1996, 8–10; Sample 2003, 169–170.
[3] For example, Bigwood 2005.
[4] Exploitation is not unique in this regard. Historical injustices raise similar questions about how corrective and distributive principles should relate to each other. For example, see Blomfield 2021.

However, contract law is often thought to be a legal means of enforcing corrective justice within bipolar correlative contracting relationships rather than a political tool for pursuing distributively just outcomes between all citizens.[5] Contract law determines when legally enforceable agreements form, what legal duties parties to an agreement owe one another, and how disputes between parties should be resolved. Courts will respond to correctively unjust features of exploitation within this correlative relation while leaving general distributive worries about exploitation to other institutions.

Our understanding of the wrong-making features of exploitative transactions and their relationship to distributive and corrective justice has important consequences for contract law. In this chapter I explore some of these consequences. In section 2 I identify a somewhat orthodox legal position that exploitation is a *normatively redundant* category within contract law.[6] This redundancy stems from the combination of two claims: first, that the law may *exclude* distributive concerns over exploitative transactions (as background considerations of distributive injustice) when pursuing corrective justice, and second, that any correctively unjust features of exploitation that the law responds to merely *replicate* already present corrective features of the law (such as concerns about enforcing involuntary agreements). The orthodoxy that results from these two claims suggests that debates concerning exploitation's normative features promise to add little to contract law. The law should pursue corrective justice and, in doing so, will likely have neither the appetite nor the ability to prohibit or compensate for exploitative transactions.

I then offer arguments against both claims and the plausibility of this orthodoxy. In sections 3 and 4 I argue that the exclusion claim requires us to employ a distinction between distributive and corrective injustice that is more challenging than the orthodoxy assumes. This makes it difficult to exclude exploitation from contract law *even if* you believe that exploitation is primarily a distributive problem. In section 5 I argue that the replication claim is most plausible if we adopt a narrow and monistic view about the purpose of contract law. Against this monistic tendency, I argue in favor of pluralism about the purposes of contract law. This pluralistic approach ensures that the law is more inclusive and better able to respond to exploitation than the orthodoxy suggests.

---

[5] For example, Weinrib 2012, 136–140, 210–214.
[6] For a negligence-based argument toward a similar conclusion, see Bigwood 2005.

2. Identifying an Orthodoxy

Exploitation is a common and morally significant complaint in market-based economies marred by substantial inequalities. Yet it plays a relatively minor role in the law of contracts. To see why, consider the relationship between philosophical and legal debates concerning exploitation.

The primary philosophical question raised by exploitation concerns its wrong-making features. There is broad conceptual agreement that exploitation involves taking unfair advantage of others, but as disagreement about fairness is widespread, disagreement about what constitutes unfair advantage-taking and which real-world phenomena should be considered wrongfully exploitative proliferates.[7] For simplicity's sake, we can identify three rough categories of philosophical theory within this landscape.

First, we can distinguish between theories that favor a broad *structural* understanding of exploitation and theories that favor a narrower *transactional* understanding. Groups of people can plausibly claim to suffer exploitation even if some individual members of the group are sometimes free to participate in some non-exploitative transactions. Furthermore, not all forms of exploitation primarily take the form of discrete transactions. This chapter focuses on the narrower category of exploitative transactions because legally enforceable transactions are the domain of contract law.

A wide range of possible explanations of wrongfulness remain within this narrowed category of exploitative transactions. These explanations contrast in how they respond to questions of *voluntariness* and *mutual benefit*.[8] What we can call *broad transactional* theories draw on a wide range of explanatory concepts, including duress or harm, to explain why exploitative transactions are wrong. In contrast, *narrow transactional* theories seek to explain why consensual and Pareto-superior transactions may be considered wrongful. This narrower range of transactions cannot result from force (as they are consensual) and must benefit one party while leaving the other party no worse off (as they are Pareto-superior), and so we cannot explain their wrongfulness according to duress or harm. Other explanations must provide this answer, such as the unfair distribution of benefits between parties, the presence of historical injustice, or the disrespectful treatment of one party by another.[9]

---

[7] Richard Arneson (1992, 350) suggests that there are as many accounts of exploitation as there are of fair treatment.
[8] Ferguson and Steiner 2018.
[9] Wertheimer 1996, ch. 7; Steiner 1984; Sample 2003, ch. 3.

These two distinctions produce three rough categories of philosophical theory: (1) structural theories, (2) broad transactional theories, and (3) narrow transactional theories. Debate rages between and within these categories. We will return to them shortly.

The primary legal question concerning exploitative transactions revolves around whether contract doctrine can be properly understood to prohibit exploitative transactions. This interpretive affair seeks to understand the motivating rationale behind different vitiating factors found in the law (such as duress, misrepresentation, undue influence, and unconscionability). Depending on how we interpret the relevant cases and statutes, we can come to different conclusions about exploitation's place within contract law as it is practiced.

Four prominent doctrinal themes guide answers to this interpretive question in English law. First, courts commonly require contracting parties to exchange value with each other through the doctrine of consideration. This requirement prevents transactions from being wholly one-sided. However, courts focus on determining the presence of value rather than judging the relative equity of the transfer of value between the parties. The consideration provided by the parties must be sufficient but need not be adequate to establish the reciprocal basis of contractual liability. As a result, parties have a wide scope of discretion to voluntarily determine how value is distributed between them.[10] Second, courts do not seek to protect parties from bad bargains that they voluntarily agree to.[11] Interference with the performance of a contract that disadvantages one party when that party has voluntarily assumed the risk of that disadvantage is often objected to as paternalistic. Third, courts favor grounding the validity of contracting in questions of procedural fairness rather than substantive fairness. As a result, substantive unfairness in the distribution of benefits between contracting parties alone is unlikely to invalidate a contract without some corresponding procedural unfairness.[12] Fourth, courts prefer that parties benefit from a baseline statutory protection of bargaining power. Judicial interventions in pursuit of inequality of bargaining power have been unpopular for at least two reasons: that sufficiency of bargaining power is favored over equality of bargaining power, and that statutory intervention by parliament is favored over courts developing

[10] Chen-Wishart 2013.
[11] Davies 2019.
[12] Cartwright 1991, 214–216.

the common law in this area.[13] Together, these doctrinal themes suggest that contract law is rarely concerned with exploitation and is poorly equipped to prevent or remedy exploitative transactions.

These philosophical and legal debates have important conceptual connections. The interpretative task within the legal debate partially depends on how we conceptualize exploitation. Whether we can identify a concern with exploitation within the doctrine depends on how we characterize the concept, and this, in turn, depends on the most plausible philosophical understanding of the wrong-making features of exploitation. These debates also have important normative connections. The question of whether contract law *should* concern itself with preventing exploitation or compensating parties who become entangled in exploitative transactions (rather than the interpretative question of whether it can be understood as doing so) depends on whether the wrong-making features of exploitation conflict with the interests that contract law should legally protect. This, in turn, is a question concerning the motivating principles of contract law.

When we consider the normative relationship between philosophical and legal debates in this way, a certain orthodoxy emerges.[14] The two ideals that are commonly thought to motivate contract law are matters of freedom, autonomy, and voluntariness, on the one hand, and matters of fairness, reciprocity, and mutual benefit, on the other.[15] These two ideals interact with narrow and broad transactional theories of exploitation in different ways.

Voluntariness and mutual benefit between parties are the same values that narrow transactional theories of exploitation seek to accommodate. Narrow transactional theories seek to discover what, if anything, is morally wrong with consensual Pareto-superior exchanges. These characteristics help ensure voluntary and beneficial transactions between parties. Thus, the motivating ideals of contract law appear *prima facie* compatible with narrow transactional exploitation. If contract law is commonly understood to protect voluntary agreements that beneficially distribute rights and obligations between parties, then contract law should not prevent or remedy narrow transactional exploitation.

The ideals of voluntariness and mutual benefit interact with broad transactional theories of exploitation differently. Broad transactional theories do

---

[13] Beale 1986; Thal 1988; Cartwright 1991, ch. 9.
[14] This orthodoxy resembles Patrick Atiyah's "traditional dogma of contract law" concerning the adequacy of consideration and the fairness of exchange (Atiyah 1986, 329).
[15] Sandel 1998, 106–109.

not focus on the narrow inquiry about the wrong-making features of consensual Pareto-superior exchanges. These theories instead appeal to a broader range of wrong-making features of exploitation, such as the absence of valid consent or the presence of harm, in seeking to understand exploitative transactions. This difference creates the possibility that contract law should concern itself with broad transactional exploitation even if it should not concern itself with narrow transactional exploitation.

This apparent possibility comes to naught, however, for the following reasons. First, contract law permits us to voluntarily expose ourselves to the risk of some loss or harm by upholding bad bargains. Second, although contract law does not permit involuntary agreements to be enforced, the reasons why such agreements are rendered voidable have nothing to do with exploitation and everything to do with more basic vitiating concerns. So, contract law should either permit broad transactional exploitation on the grounds of upholding bad bargains or constrain such transactions for more fundamental vitiating reasons. Insofar as exploitation is consensual, then it should be legally permitted; insofar as exploitation is not consensual, then it should be prohibited due to involuntariness.

This orthodox understanding of the normative relationship between the philosophical and legal exploitation debates suggests that exploitation is a normatively redundant category within contract law. Narrow transactional exploitation need not conflict with the motivating principles of contract law. Broad transactional exploitation conflicts with these principles only when it does so according to other, more rudimentary vitiating reasons. Neither narrow nor broad theories of exploitative transactions appear to offer novel independent normative guidance to the sorts of contractual exchanges the law should enforce.

From this orthodoxy, it is tempting to conclude that contract law should not concern itself with preventing or remedying exploitative transactions. This conclusion will chime with those who are alive to the often harsh realities of commercial life. If contract law is the legal basis of trade and if successful trade in modern economies sometimes requires parties to open themselves to exploitation, then the law must permit consensual exploitation. According to this line of thinking, further debate around this topic should be relegated to philosophical niceties and should not disrupt the predictability and security that contract law offers commercial parties. Insofar as we recognize exploitation as a pressing moral concern, we must turn to other institutions to combat it.

I have significant doubts about this orthodoxy and the conclusion that follows from it. The first doubt stems from the orthodoxy's ability to exclude matters of distributive justice. Let us now consider this issue in greater depth.

3. Corrective and Distributive Justice in Ideal Theory

The orthodoxy suggests that although exploitative transactions raise important moral concerns, many of these concerns are better dealt with by institutions other than contract law. Let us call this part of the orthodoxy the *exclusion claim*—the law may legitimately exclude distributive concerns about exploitative transactions from deliberation because the law ought to exclude considerations of background distributive injustice when pursuing corrective justice.

In this section and the next, I explore both principled and pragmatic defenses of the exclusion claim. The principled argument suggests that corrective and distributive justice are separate and exclusive domains of justice that ought to be pursued by different institutions. The pragmatic argument suggests that contract law is a less effective means of preventing exploitation than public policy. I offer a two-step response against these arguments and the exclusion claim. The first step concerns the distinction between corrective and distributive justice in ideal theory.

To exclude distributive justice from the pursuit of corrective justice in contract law, we must first distinguish between these domains of justice. Arguments in favor of the distinction between corrective and distributive justice often begin with a lesson from the Lyceum. In Book V of his *Nicomachean Ethics*, Aristotle outlines three distinctions between different types of justice.[16] First, he conceives of justice as an other-regarding virtue that applies to both lawfulness and fairness.[17] Lawfulness forms the basis of the complete virtue of *universal* justice, and fairness forms the basis of the partial virtue of *particular* justice. Second, the category of particular justice is divided between fairness in the *distribution* of common goods between citizens and fairness in the *rectification* of specific transactions of personal goods between two parties. Third, the category of rectificatory fairness is divided

---

[16] For the importance of Aristotle's arguments to private law thinking, see Weinrib 2012, ch. 3. For helpful commentary on Aristotle's arguments, see Polansky 2014. For critique, see Williams 1981.
[17] Aristotle 1129a 33–35.

between fairness within *voluntary* transactions (such as sales, purchases, and loans) and fairness within *involuntary* transactions (such as theft, assassination, and assault).[18]

Although Aristotle's category of universal justice raises interesting questions about the relationship between law, politics, virtue, and vice, we can set it aside for our purposes. Instead, we should focus on Aristotle's three categories of fairness—(i) fairness in the distribution of common goods, (ii) fairness in rectification within voluntary transactions, and (iii) fairness in rectification within involuntary transactions. These categories roughly map onto our modern categories of (i) distributive justice, (ii) corrective justice in contract law, and (iii) corrective justice in tort law and punitive justice in criminal law.

For Aristotle, distributive fairness concerns the distribution of common goods between citizens in proportion to some measure of merit.[19] Achieving Aristotelian distributive fairness requires us to maintain a geometric relation of different ratios between citizens. Distributive unfairness persists when we fail to distribute common goods according to this general pattern (for example, out of proportion to the relevant measure of merit). In contrast, rectificatory fairness concerns a state of equilibrium between parties in response to involuntary gains or losses in personal goods.[20] Achieving Aristotelian rectificatory fairness requires us to maintain an arithmetic relation between involuntary personal losses and gains from an interaction. Rectificatory unfairness persists when these personal losses and gains are disproportionately forced upon one party to the benefit of another (achieving disequilibrium between the parties). Whereas distributive fairness apportions out goods according to merit, rectificatory fairness sets aside questions of merit to apportion out gains and losses in response to particular injuries.

We can accept Aristotle's general claim that each domain of justice is governed by a distinctive logic without accepting his specific substantive accounts of each domain. Although modern debates over justice rarely talk

---

[18] Aristotle 1130b 30–1131a 9.
[19] Aristotle §5.3.
[20] Aristotle §5.4. Both categories of rectificatory fairness respond to the same worry—unfairness arising from involuntary gains and losses. But they do so in two different circumstances—voluntary and involuntary transactions. Involuntary transactions result in involuntary gains and losses. If I steal something from you, then my gain is your involuntary loss. Involuntary gains and losses can also result from voluntary transactions. If I make a deal with you and you gain more than you bargained for at my expense, then your gain is my involuntary loss.

in terms of geometric and arithmetic relations, we find echoes of Aristotle's distinctive logics in modern debates over the requirements of justice in ideal theory.[21] According to John Rawls, ideal theory idealizes across two important considerations—strict compliance with the principles of justice and the presence of favorable historical, social, and economic conditions.[22] Employing this level of abstraction makes the demands of distributive justice very clear. However, strict compliance obscures many of the demands of corrective justice. There is little to correct when individuals strictly comply with their rights and duties. Therefore, understanding the relationship between these domains of justice in contract law requires us to consider their relation across both ideal and non-ideal theory. We will consider ideal theory first before turning to non-ideal theory.

Ideal theory highlights two important normative relations between the domains of justice. First, distributive justice governs the background against which we make our judgments of corrective justice by providing us with the pattern of legitimate holdings and rights that form the baseline from which parties incur their corrective duties.[23] Second, corrective liabilities can alter the pattern of distribution. Losses, gains, and remedies can all have important distributive effects.[24]

These relations ensure that corrective and distributive justice have complex and dynamic effects on each other. This raises the question of the extent to which distributive factors should play a legitimate role in corrective decisions (and vice versa). The orthodoxy's exclusion claim requires a negative answer to this question in contractual matters. Distributive factors should not play a legitimate role in corrective decisions in contract law. However, philosophers disagree on this important matter, as the following contrast between two liberal egalitarian theories of justice demonstrates.

A prominent example of separating out corrective and distributive justice in ideal theory can be found in Rawls's theory of justice as fairness. Rawls famously argues in favor of basic liberties, fair equality of opportunity, and the difference principle via his original position.[25] Robert Nozick's libertarian

---

[21] Englard 2009.
[22] Rawls 2001, 12–14; Stemplowska and Swift 2012.
[23] For doubts, see Coleman 1992, 350–354; Perry 2000, 260. The claim that corrective judgements should track morally legitimate entitlements rather than distributively just entitlements is compatible with distributive considerations playing some role in our corrective decisions because one (but not the only) important consideration for moral legitimacy is distributive justice.
[24] For further discussion of the connections between private law and distributive justice, see Lucy 2007, 328.
[25] Rawls 1971.

objection to justice as fairness objects that maintaining this pattern of distribution unfairly disturbs voluntary transactions between citizens.[26] Nozick instead favors a historical account of distributive justice that requires fair rules of initial resource acquisition alongside protections for voluntary transactions.

Rawls's response to this libertarian objection separates out rules that govern the basic structure of society from rules that govern decisions made by individual citizens. Voluntary exchanges can be morally compromised if the background circumstances are not themselves morally just.[27] Justice as fairness is aimed at governing the basic structure—the major social, political, and economic institutions in a society. A just basic structure secures background justice against which citizens cooperate and pursue their differing conceptions of the good. This produces two types of social rules—rules that individual citizens can be reasonably expected to follow and rules that are constitutive of legal institutions.[28] These different types of rule allow corrective justice to play a local role in contractual disputes against a distributively just basic structure.[29]

Rawls's rule-based distinction faces two important objections. First, it is unclear whether Rawls can plausibly restrict the site of distributive justice to the basic structure. As G. A. Cohen argues, Rawls ambiguously construes the basic structure as the background social framework and first subject of justice.[30] There is a sense in which the basic structure is constituted by institutions that are coercive, and there is a sense in which the basic structure is constituted by norms that have profound effects on our lives.[31] This ambiguity puts pressure on Rawls's claim that the basic structure is an institutional concept and that justice as fairness applies to institutions rather than individual decisions. If our principles of distributive justice should apply to the basic structure and the basic structure is constituted by coercive institutions, then the effects of our principles of distributive justice may be less profound than they otherwise could be. Alternatively, if we understand the basic structure in the broader sense to include norms that have profound effects on our lives, then the principles of distributive justice should also apply to our

---

[26] Nozick 1974, ch. 7.
[27] Rawls 2005, 262–269.
[28] Rawls 2005, 268.
[29] Bigwood 2003, 73–79.
[30] Cohen 2008, 132–138.
[31] Rawls 1971, 7–11; 2005, 257–288; 2001, 10–12. For discussion of the roughness of this distinction, see Rawls 2001, §4.3.

everyday choices that reflexively interact with these norms. The institutional focus of the basic structure is secured at the risk of losing its profound effects on our lives. The profound effects of the basic structure are secured at the risk of losing its institutional focus. From this tension, Cohen concludes that Rawls cannot plausibly restrict justice as fairness to the basic structure.

Second, even if the basic structure is a stable site of distributive justice, Rawls may still be unable to exclude contract law from it. Rawls excludes contract law from the basic structure on the basis of epistemic demandingness.[32] However, if the basic structure is meant to provide rules that help citizens cooperate on fair terms and autonomously pursue their differing conceptions of the good, then contract law must reside within the basic structure alongside property law.[33] If justice as fairness applies to the basic structure, and contract law is part of the basic structure, then contract law becomes one legal institution through which distributive justice is legitimately pursued. Once courts start pursuing distributive justice in contract law, however, it becomes unclear how considerations of corrective justice can be pursued alongside considerations of Rawlsian distributive justice.[34] The rule-based distinction that Rawls offers in response to the libertarian challenge threatens to collapse as contract law appears to be governed by both sets of rules.

Rawls's rule-based separation faces significant objections about whether it can exclude distributive considerations from the pursuit of corrective justice in contract law. To avoid these objections, we can pursue a unified approach to justice, such as that suggested in Ronald Dworkin's theory of equality of resources.[35] According to Dworkin, governments have a duty to treat every citizen with equal care and concern. Dworkin favors making an equal share of resources available for each citizen to consume or invest as they wish across their lifetime. Like Rawls, Dworkin's approach to distributive justice has its own division of labor that seeks to avoid pitting private choice against public responsibility.[36] However, whereas Rawls divides this labor between different sorts of rules, Dworkin divides this labor between different forms of responsibility.

---

[32] Rawls 2005, 265–269.
[33] Fried 1981, 20–21.
[34] Scheffler 2015. See also Kordana and Tabachnick 2005; Freeman 2018.
[35] Dworkin 2000. Although Dworkin does not adopt Rawls's methodology, a similarly ideal mode of theorizing plays a significant role in his argument. For explanation of Dworkin's "inside-out" and "outside-in" approach, see Dworkin 2000, 3–4.
[36] Dworkin 1986, 295–301.

Dworkin argues that judgments of public and private responsibility should be compatible with equal concern and respect. This includes the creation and enforcement of our property scheme.[37] The property scheme governs the terms according to which citizens can own private property and transfer it between them via contractual rights. When considering ambiguous rules or attempting to resolve clashes between *prima facie* rights under this scheme, Dworkin argues that citizens should be led by considerations of equality of resources.[38] When pursuing these tasks, citizens are determining what the property scheme, properly understood, should be taken to be. This requires us to discover the relative importance of the rights at stake for us in our overall life plans, subject to important normative qualifications.

Although this discovery is epistemically demanding, Dworkin does not believe that these epistemic demands require a stark separation of corrective and distributive principles.[39] Rather, equality of resources should both provide the entitlements that corrective justice seeks to protect (by governing the background distribution of benefits and burdens against which disputes over the property scheme will arise) and help to resolve corrective disputes between property owners. Equality of resources should govern our understanding and interpretation of society's property scheme, which includes the laws of contract.[40] This is what makes Dworkin's theory unified in a manner that Rawls's theory is not.

These two prominent liberal-egalitarian theories of distributive justice demonstrate two contrasting visions of the relationship between corrective and distributive justice in ideal theory. This contrast raises important challenges for proponents of the orthodoxy. Aristotle's claim that the domains of justice have different normative structures and governing logics allows us to distinguish between the domains of justice. Once we have done so, the exclusion of distributive justice from the pursuit of corrective justice in contract law requires us to be able to and have good reason to separate out these domains of justice in practice. Rawls's rule-based separation of these domains supports exclusion but faces significant objections. It is unclear whether justice as fairness can be successfully excluded from contract law. In contrast, Dworkin's responsibility-based separation of these domains does not support exclusion. Equality of resources seeks to combine distributive

---

[37] Dworkin 1986, 301–312.
[38] Dworkin 1986, 303.
[39] Dworkin 1986, 300, 306–307.
[40] For criticism that Dworkin's account is ambiguous on this point, see Perry 2000, 263.

and corrective considerations in the creation and enforcement of our property scheme. Both domains of justice are pursued together in a unified manner, offering a very different vision of the possible relationship between corrective and distributive justice in ideal theory.

4. Exploitation and Non-Ideal Theory

Sceptics may respond that the above contrast demonstrates little. Even if Dworkin is correct to suggest that we should include distributive considerations within contract law, the law is a poorer mechanism for achieving distributive justice than public policy. Our lack of principled reasons to exclude distributive considerations from contract law does not defeat our pragmatic reasons to pursue different forms of justice via different institutions. The second step of my argument against the exclusion claim demonstrates the limits of this pragmatic response in exploitative contexts. This step requires us to move to the level of non-ideal theory. Doing so relaxes the assumptions of strict compliance and favorable circumstances. Citizens can now fail to comply with their rights and duties, and face worse historical, social, and economic conditions. Non-ideal circumstances give rise to exploitation as a pervasive issue because individuals can differ greatly in their relative bargaining strengths and can be motivated to take unfair advantage of another's bargaining weakness for their own benefit.

The move to non-ideal theory highlights further features of the complex and dynamic relationship between domains of justice. We have seen that even when we assume strict compliance and favorable circumstances, the separation of these domains need not support the exclusion of distributive justice from contract law. Relaxing our assumptions leads distributive and corrective duties to further inform each other. Our judgments of corrective justice may differ depending on whether the gains and losses between parties derive from distributively just or unjust holdings. Furthermore, those who fail to comply with their distributive duties may incur corrective duties. The non-ideal relationship between the domains of justice is more complex and more dynamic. Consequently, the challenges facing the exclusion claim become more pressing.

Non-ideal theory highlights further features of the relationship between the domains of justice because important characteristics of corrective justice are no longer obscured by ideal theory's strict compliance assumption.

The assumptions of ideal theory help us to understand the demands of distributive justice but only provide us with a general sense of the demands of corrective justice. Moving to non-ideal theory ensures that theories of corrective justice now have more detailed guidance to offer because non-compliance gives rise to more wrongs that can be understood in corrective terms. Conversely, theories of distributive justice now face a more complex philosophical challenge because the guidance they provide us must plot a route toward achieving distributively just outcomes from our current non-ideal circumstances.

The move to non-ideal theory helps us better understand the place of exploitative transactions within the domains of justice. Consider the distinctive logics and normative structures identified by Aristotle. Corrective justice concerns agent-relative reasons, pre-institutional moral reparative duties, and bipolar relations between parties.[41] Distributive justice concerns agent-general reasons, institutional political distributive duties, and patterned relations between citizens. When contrasted in this manner, we can see how distributive and corrective solutions to exploitation differ. Distributive solutions prioritize the responsibilities of political institutions to prevent exploitable circumstances from arising. These solutions will likely require the provision of a particular pattern of resources or rights to citizens to prevent the background circumstances that give rise to exploitative transactions. In contrast, corrective solutions prioritize the responsibilities of contracting parties not to take unfair advantage of bargaining weaknesses. These solutions will likely rely on courts to enforce pre-institutional duties that transacting parties owe to each other to avoid or repair private wrongs.

A pragmatic defense of the exclusion claim requires distributive solutions to exploitative transactions to somehow crowd out corrective solutions. If this is the case, then even in the absence of principled reasons for excluding distributive considerations from contract law, we still have pragmatic reasons for excluding these considerations. There are three sorts of skeptical argument that could defend the exclusion claim on pragmatic grounds. Let us consider each in turn.

The first skeptical argument concerns *aptness*. If it can be shown that the wrong-making features of exploitative transactions are most plausibly understood as forms of distributive injustice, then distributive solutions will be a more apt response to this form of injustice. Remembering that we set aside

---

[41] Coleman 1995, 66.

structural theories of exploitation in section 2, let us consider the prospects of transactional theories of exploitation.[42] The transactional nature of these theories ensures that we can plausibly understand them in corrective terms: Exploitative transactions occur within bipolar relations between contracting parties. These transactions conflict with pre-institutional moral reasons to not unfairly exploit our bargaining position or to compensate those who are wronged when we do so. These reasons attach to exploiters in an agent-relative manner (e.g., rather than to wealthier bystanders). Indeed, David Miller argues that the "particular moral force" of exploitation reflects the fact that exploitation is not merely a distributive injustice resulting from a transaction but rather the reprehensible action of an agent who benefits themselves when they had less reprehensible alternatives available to them.[43] If Miller is right, then the distinctive agential wrong-making features of exploitative transactions are most plausibly understood as correctively unjust.[44] This undermines the skeptic's claim that distributive solutions are a more apt response than corrective solutions. While distributive solutions seek to prevent exploitable circumstances from becoming pervasive, corrective solutions speak directly to the distinctive wrongs of exploitative transactions.

The second skeptical argument concerns *efficacy*. Distributive solutions to exploitation preempt corrective solutions. Distributive solutions reduce the pervasiveness of exploitable circumstances, and so fewer wrongs will occur that need correcting. This means that even if distributive solutions are less apt, their wide pursuit as a matter of public policy will leave contract law with little corrective work to do. There are two ways of interpreting this efficacy argument—one that supports the exclusion claim and is critical to the unified project and another that does not support the exclusion claim and is friendly to the unified project.

The critical interpretation of the efficacy argument that supports the exclusion claim suggests that unified approaches to justice will ultimately exclude distributive considerations from contract law in practice because these considerations will have been preempted by public policy. This critical interpretation relies on a slip between ideal and non-ideal theorizing.[45] Ideal

---

[42] One possibility open to the skeptic is to recast the orthodoxy as arguing that structural theories of exploitation are more plausible than transactional theories of exploitation, and that (structural) exploitation is normatively redundant in contract law. This argument will attract objections from transactional theorists, and its plausibility will depend on the role that contract law plays in upholding the exploitative structure.

[43] Miller 1987, 161. On the importance of alternatives, see Horton 2019.

[44] Wertheimer 1996, 298–299; Malmqvist and Szigeti 2021.

[45] Thanks to Andrew Williams and Victor Tadros for helping me develop this claim.

theory demonstrates how the idealized application of principles of distributive justice may prevent pervasive exploitable circumstances. As we move into non-ideal theory, exploitation becomes a pressing normative concern due to the non-ideal circumstances we face. Non-ideal circumstances include exploitable circumstances where the demands of distributive justice are not being met. Thus, skeptics who claim that the idealized application of principles of distributive justice will preempt corrective solutions to exploitation that arises in (non-ideal) exploitable circumstances miss the point. These solutions respond to exploitation in non-ideal circumstances by demanding we move toward the assumptions of ideal theory. As we have seen, the assumptions of ideal theory are strict compliance and favorable circumstances. Under these conditions, exploitation is (of course) less likely. But that abstract fact does not help us much in the non-ideal circumstances we face. After all, it is the pervasiveness of (non-ideal) exploitable circumstances that makes exploitation a pressing normative concern in the first place.

This critical efficacy argument denies the premise of the problem under investigation rather than offering a defensible solution to it. Whether skeptics are ultimately correct that contract law is a poorer instrument of distributive justice than public policy under ideal conditions means less in our non-ideal world, where public policy fails to uphold distributive justice. In a distributively unjust world, we often face the decision between correcting particular exploitative transactions or letting them stand. The skeptics' response to victims of exploitation that some other political institution would ideally be better placed to more effectively prevent the circumstances that gave rise to their exploitation, even when the failure of that institution has contributed to their exploitation, offers victims scarce justice.

A more plausible interpretation of the efficacy argument is friendlier to the unified project and does not support the exclusion claim. Rather than moving between ideal and non-ideal theory, the friendly interpretation functions solely at the non-ideal level and avoids the false binary of the critical interpretation. The friendly interpretation suggests that when pursuing both distributive and corrective solutions to exploitation in tandem and allowing distributive considerations to play a role in shaping corrective solutions (as the unified approach suggests), whatever preemption does occur in our distributively unjust world will reduce the risk of disruption to the function of contract law that proponents of the orthodoxy fear could be caused by allowing distributive considerations to inform our corrective solutions to exploitative transactions. The exploitative circumstances that cause these considerations to play this role will be less pervasive when the state pursues distributive and corrective justice in a unified manner. Some exploitative circumstances that would otherwise give rise to exploitative transactions requiring corrective solutions will in effect be preempted by distributive policies. Corrective solutions to exploitative transactions will only be required when distributive policies fail to preempt exploitative circumstances in this manner. But this does not mean that corrective solutions should not be sensitive to distributive matters, as the exclusion claim suggests. The mere fact of preemption does not necessarily support exclusion. Rather, preemption is one factor within the complex and dynamic relationship between domains of justice that a unified approach to justice must respond to when spreading the task of pursuing different forms of justice across different institutions.

The third skeptical argument develops the *disruption* concern by looking for a principle internal to contract law to explain why making contract law sensitive to distributive considerations will disrupt the pursuit of corrective justice. If exclusion is less disruptive than inclusion, then the disruption avoided provides a pragmatic reason to exclude. We will explore internal principles of contract law in greater detail in the next section. For now, considering a possible principle of voluntariness will allow us to see the concerns facing this skeptical argument.

The skeptic might agree with Aristotle that contract law is a distinctive sphere of corrective justice due to the voluntary nature of the transacting that contract law governs. Corrective justice in contract law should be sensitive to the value of voluntariness. Under ideal circumstances, voluntariness can help to explain the value of freedom of contract, which in turn provides us with reasons for non-interference.[46] The skeptic might then object that distributive considerations are insensitive to the voluntary features of transacting. Imposing distributive considerations into contractual disputes threatens to interfere with parties' voluntarily agreed terms. A unified approach to justice that admits distributive considerations into contract law will therefore pollute the law's corrective aims in a manner that clashes with contract law's distinctive voluntary character.

This argument ignores another important consequence of the move from ideal to non-ideal theory. Non-ideal circumstances make voluntariness a

[46] Flanigan 2017.

double-edged sword by opening up the possibility of exploiters voluntarily taking unfair advantage of the presence of background injustice for their own benefit. The voluntary nature of the exploiter's behavior is an important part of its wrongful character, especially when the behavior is done knowingly.[47] Consequently, the move to non-ideal circumstances weakens the "protective shield" of voluntariness because, under these circumstances, exploiters may be voluntarily choosing to act against a distributively unjust background. The moral qualities of the background against which we strike our bargains inform our assessment of the bargain itself. Under ideal circumstances, this allows us to derive reasons of non-interference from the value of voluntariness. Non-ideal circumstances make it more difficult to derive the same reasons of non-interference. As Aditi Bagchi argues, there is no inherent unfairness in allowing background injustice to play a role in determining liability in this manner.[48] Those who "choose to operate under the direct shadow of distributive injustice" voluntarily assume the risk that those injustices might work against their attempts to benefit from such injustices.[49] Skeptical appeals to the value of voluntariness to defend the exclusion claim face serious concerns. Voluntariness makes contract law a distinctive sphere of corrective justice, but it need not give us reasons to exclude distributive considerations from contract law under non-ideal circumstances.

5. The Purposes of Contract Law

In the previous two sections I have argued against both principled and pragmatic defenses of the exclusion claim. We must now consider the second part of the orthodoxy identified in section 2—the *replication claim*. This claim suggests that if we do grant exploitative transactions a place within contract law, the correctively unjust features of exploitation that the law responds to will merely replicate features already legally catered to (such as concerns about enforcing involuntary agreements). This is a second potential source of normative redundancy for exploitation in contract law.

I suggest that the replication claim is most plausible if we accept a *monistic* view of contract law. Monists reduce the nature of corrective justice

---

[47] Ferguson 2021.
[48] See Bagchi 2008, 116–136; 2014, 201–202.
[49] Bagchi 2008, 126.

in contract law to a single core theme or family of themes.⁵⁰ According to this view, contract law has a narrow remit and little reason to cater to considerations beyond that remit. However, we should reject monistic views of contract law in favor of a *pluralistic* view instead. Pluralists accept that corrective justice in contract law must be sensitive to a broad range of normative factors that should be balanced against each other in cases and statute.⁵¹ Contract law should admit a broader range of considerations into the justification of the law. This opens up greater conceptual space for contract law to respond to exploitative transactions and, in turn, avoids replication by not reducing complex normative issues to single-value considerations.

The monistic argument for the replication claim might proceed as follows. Contract law primarily concerns the legal enforcement of particular promissory obligations. This enforcement relies upon the normativity of performance and breach that, in turn, derives from the voluntariness of the acts of will that bind parties together through their exchange of promises. Corrective justice requires us to prohibit or compensate involuntary losses resulting from this exchange of promises. If the law understood thusly is to concern itself with exploitative transactions, then we must understand transactional exploitation in terms of an involuntary loss.

The argument for understanding transactional exploitation in terms of an involuntary loss might then rely on the fact that exploitable circumstances are often materially unequal circumstances. Significant material inequality can cause significant inequality of bargaining power within individual transactions and impose volitional pressure upon parties to accept unfair terms. This pressure may threaten the voluntariness of parties' decision-making. One party might believe that they had "no choice" but to accept the exploitative offer on the table, and the other party might exploit this belief to their benefit. The monist may conclude from this apparent absence of choice that exploitation is a vitiating concern, but not a novel vitiating concern independent from preexisting doctrines. Involuntary losses are already vitiated in the law (for example, via the doctrine of duress). Consequently, exploitation ends up adding nothing of independent normative weight to contract law's to-do list.

---

⁵⁰ On monism in contract law, see Fried 1981.
⁵¹ On pluralism in contract law, see Saprai 2019a.

This monistic understanding of the purpose of contract law can explain why broad transactional exploitation should be either legally permitted if voluntary or prohibited if involuntary, according to more fundamental vitiating reasons. This understanding makes the rights and wrongs of enforcing exploitative transactions revolve around the concept of voluntariness. There are significant philosophical and legal doubts about the plausibility of this monistic view.

Philosophically, whether material inequality can generate the type of pressure on our decision-making to render the resulting decision involuntary is contested. Some philosophers argue that we cannot make sense of involuntariness without reference to background distributive considerations and that these considerations can undermine the voluntariness of our decisions even in the absence of intentional coercion.[52] Others demur, arguing that inequality of bargaining power can bring about unjust outcomes but need not bring about involuntary outcomes.[53] Some of the complexities being navigated here concern how the concept of voluntariness is employed in the process of vitiation, the relevant standard of voluntariness, and how this standard interacts with volitional pressure. These complexities trace back to foundational normative disagreements concerning the relationship between law, morality, compatibilism, and freedom of the will. Monism must provide satisfactory answers to these challenging complexities and disagreements to make the theory philosophically workable.

Legally, this monistic approach also faces significant doctrinal issues to contend with. Using the doctrine of duress as an illustrative example, we can see two key doctrinal features that this theory struggles to explain. First, it struggles to explain why the doctrine has developed away from coercion of the will and toward illegitimate pressure as the *grounds* of duress.[54] There are many ways in which pressure can be illegitimate in the eyes of the law and explaining this broad doctrinal development in narrow monistic terms is challenging. Second, even if a monistic account of the grounds of duress were sound, it would struggle to plausibly explain the *process* of vitiation. What should follow from the monistic argument is that exploitative transactions are rendered void because an involuntary agreement is no agreement at all. But this would not be the legal result of vitiation in this context. Vitiation

---

[52] Kronman 1980, 495–497; Olsaretti 2004, ch. 6.
[53] Wertheimer 1996, 264–271; Bigwood 2003, 105–111; Zwolinski 2007, 701–702.
[54] Atiyah 1982.

would likely render a contract voidable rather than void. Monistic theories cannot explain why victims of exploitation would incur *pro tanto* promissory obligations that they can then choose to either set aside or enforce. If the exploitation is involuntary, then no valid enforceable promises were exchanged between parties. The *pro tanto* obligation seems to mysteriously appear out of thin air.[55]

These philosophical and legal doubts should lead us to reject a monistic understanding of the purpose of contract law in favor of a pluralistic understanding of the purposes of contract law. Pluralism has two significant benefits in this regard. First, it provides a more convincing rationale for contract law's bipartite nature. As we saw in section 2, contract law is commonly thought to be motivated by two sets of values—matters of freedom, autonomy, and voluntariness on the one hand and matters of fairness, reciprocity, and mutual benefit on the other hand.[56] This bipartite nature is reflected throughout contract law. For example, it can be found in the debates between autonomy-based and utility-based justifications, between promissory-based and reliance-based theories of obligations, between procedural and substantive accounts of fairness, and between market-individualist and consumer-welfarist ideologies.[57] Monism can explain why we should favor one side of these debates. However, it struggles to explain why we find these bipartite distinctions throughout contract law. Pluralism suggests that this pattern is not a repeating conceptual mistake. Rather, it is evidence of the constant need to consider and balance various competing values within the law. Monism resists the complexity of this balancing, favoring instead to reduce normative issues to single-value considerations. We have seen the philosophical challenges that this reductive tendency creates.

The second benefit that pluralism provides is a better explanation of the purpose and function of vitiation within contract law. Monism favors what Mindy Chen-Wishart calls a one-step "consent-in, lack-of-consent-out" picture of vitiating factors. Chen-Wishart contends that such a view "is normatively skewed, lacks fit with the law, lacks transparency, and takes an

---

[55] For discussion of undue influence, see Saprai 2019a, 27–30, 108–113. For discussion of duress, see Saprai 2019b.
[56] Sandel 1998, 106–109.
[57] Wertheimer 1996, 38–41; Fried 1981; Atiyah 1986, chs. 2, 11; Adams and Brownsword 1987.

unrealistic and disrespectful view of the complainant's rationality."[58] She favors an alternative two-step "defeasibility approach" where the conditions of liability are established by satisfying the requirements of formation *before* it is determined whether the complainant can defeat this claim via vitiating factors. Such an approach balances multiple factors, including those beyond the complainant's state of mind. Chen-Wishart emphasizes five relevant factors; two general legal factors (public policy and administrability) and three specific contractual factors (responsibility in contract formation, refusal to assist wrongdoers or exploiters, and protection of vulnerable parties from harsh outcomes).[59] The pluralistic nature of this account of vitiation allows it to provide a more plausible explanation of both the grounds and process of various vitiating factors than the monistic account outlined above.[60]

The philosophical and legal challenges that monism in contract law faces should raise further doubts about the orthodoxy. Rejecting monism and adopting a more pluralistic understanding of the purposes of contract law opens up more conceptual space within both the grounds and function of the law. This greater conceptual space, in turn, admits more ability and appetite to respond to exploitation than the orthodoxy assumes. The risk of replication diminishes significantly once we resist the temptation to reduce the philosophical and legal complexities raised by exploitative contracting to narrow questions of voluntariness.

6. Conclusion

There is much more left to be said about the status of exploitative transactions within contract law. There is further detail to provide about the nature of exploitation within contractual contexts and further objections to contend with once this detail is in hand. I do not pretend to have offered a comprehensive explanation of exploitation within contract law in this chapter. Rather, I have raised a series of objections against an orthodox view within

---

[58] Chen-Wishart 2014, 295.
[59] Chen-Wishart 2014, 298–305.
[60] Chen-Wishart's response to concerns over apparent conflicts between these values relies upon Dworkin's account of interpretive concepts. Chen-Wishart 2014, 315. For further analysis, see Dworkin 1985, ch. 7; 1986, ch. 2; 2011, ch. 8.

the law that relies upon the exclusion and replication claims. Some may still believe that they have reasons to doubt exploitation's role within contract law. I have argued that the exclusion and replication claims should not be among them.

References

Adams, J., and R. Brownsword. 1987. "The Ideologies of Contract." *Legal Studies* 7: 205–223.
Aristotle. 2009. *The Nichomachean Ethics*. Translated by D. Ross. Oxford: Oxford World Classics.
Arneson, R. 1992. "Exploitation." In *Encyclopedia of Ethics*, edited by L. Becker, 350–352. New York: Garland.
Atiyah, P. S. 1982. "Economic Duress and the 'Overborne Will.'" *The Law Quarterly Review* 98: 197–202.
Atiyah, P. S. 1986. *Essays on Contract*. Oxford: Clarendon Press.
Bagchi, A. 2008. "Distributive Injustice and Private Law." *Hastings Law Journal* 60: 105–149.
Bagchi, A. 2014. "Distributive Justice and Contract." In *Philosophical Foundations of Contract Law*, edited by G. Klass, G. Letsas, and P. Saprai, 193–211. Oxford: Oxford University Press.
Beale, H. 1986. "Inequality of Bargaining Power." *Oxford Journal of Legal Studies* 6: 123–136.
Bigwood, R. 2003. *Exploitative Contracts*. New York: Oxford University Press.
Bigwood, R. 2004. "Contracts by Unfair Advantage: From Exploitation to Transactional Neglect." *Oxford Journal of Legal Studies* 25: 65–96.
Blomfield, M. 2021. "Reparations and Egalitarianism." *Ethical Theory and Moral Practice* 24: 1177–1195.
Cartwright, J. 1991. *Unequal Bargaining: A Study of Vitiating Factors in the Formation of Contracts*. Oxford: Clarendon Press.
Chen-Wishert, M. 2013. "In Defence of Consideration." *Oxford University Commonwealth Law Journal* 13: 209–238.
Chen-Wishert, M. 2014. "The Nature of Vitiating Factors in Contract Law." In *Philosophical Foundations of Contract Law*, edited by G. Klass, G. Letsas, and P. Saprai, 294–318. Oxford: Oxford University Press.
Cohen, G. A. 2008. *Rescuing Justice and Equality*. Cambridge, MA: Harvard University Press.
Coleman, J. 1992. *Risks and Wrongs*. Cambridge: Cambridge University Press.
Coleman, J. 1995. "The Practice of Corrective Justice." In *Philosophical Foundations of Tort Law*, edited by D. Owen, 53–72. Oxford: Oxford University Press, 1995.
Davies, P. S. 2019. "Bad Bargains." *Current Legal Problems* 72: 253–286.
Dworkin, R. 1985. *A Matter of Principle*. Cambridge, MA: Harvard University Press.
Dworkin, R. 1986. *Law's Empire*. Oxford: Hart.
Dworkin, R. 2000. *Sovereign Virtue: The Theory and Practice of Equality*. Cambridge, MA: Harvard University Press.

Dworkin, R. 2011. *Justice for Hedgehogs*. Cambridge, MA: Harvard University Press.

England, I. 2009. *Corrective and Distributive Justice: From Aristotle to Modern Times*. New York: Oxford University Press.

Ferguson, B. 2021. "Are We All Exploiters?" *Philosophy and Phenomenological Research* 103: 535–546.

Ferguson, B., and H. Steiner. 2018. "Exploitation." In *The Oxford Handbook of Distributive Justice*, edited by S. Olsaretti, 533–555. Oxford: Oxford University Press.

Flanigan, J. 2017. "Rethinking Freedom of Contract." *Philosophical Studies* 174: 443–463.

Freeman, S. 2018. "Private Law and Rawls' Principles of Justice." In *Liberalism and Distributive Justice*, 167–194. Oxford: Oxford University Press.

Fried, C. 1981. *Contract as Promise: A Theory of Contractual Obligation*. Cambridge, MA: Harvard University Press.

Horton, J. 2019. "The Exploitation Problem." *Journal of Political Philosophy* 27: 469–479.

Kordana, K., and D. Tabachnick. 2005. "Rawls and Contract Law." *George Washington Law Review* 73: 598–632.

Kronman, A. 1980. "Contract Law and Distributive Justice." *Yale Law Journal* 89: 472–511.

Lucy, W. 2007. *Philosophy of Private Law*. Oxford: Clarendon Press.

Malmqvist, E., and A. Szigeti. 2021. "Exploitation and Remedial Duties." *Journal of Applied Philosophy* 38: 55–72.

Miller, D. 1987. "Exploitation in the Market." In *Modern Theories of Exploitation*, edited by A. Reeve, 149–165. London: Sage.

Nozick, R. 1974. *Anarchy, State and Utopia*. Oxford: Basil Blackwell.

Olsaretti, S. 2004. *Liberty, Desert and the Market*. Cambridge: Cambridge University Press.

Perry, S. 2000. "On the Relationship Between Corrective and Distributive Justice." In *Oxford Essays in Jurisprudence: Fourth Series*, edited by J. Horder, 237–263. Oxford: Oxford University Press.

Polansky, R. 2014. "Giving Justice Its Due." In *The Cambridge Companion to Aristotle's Nicomachean Ethics*, edited by R. Polansky, 151–179. Cambridge: Cambridge University Press.

Rawls, J. 1971. *A Theory of Justice*. Cambridge, MA: Belknap Press of Harvard University Press.

Rawls, J. 2001. *Justice as Fairness: A Restatement*. Cambridge, MA: Belknap Press of Harvard University Press.

Rawls, J. 2005. *Political Liberalism: Extended Edition*. New York: Columbia University Press.

Sample, R. 2003. *Exploitation: What It Is and Why It's Wrong*. Lanham, MD: Rowman & Littlefield.

Sandel, M. 1998. *Liberalism and the Limits of Justice*, 2nd edition. Cambridge: Cambridge University Press.

Saprai, P. 2019a. *Contract Law Without Foundations: Toward a Republican Theory of Contract Law*. Oxford: Oxford University Press.

Saprai, P. 2019b. "Promising Under Duress." *Law and Philosophy* 38: 465–480.

Scheffler, S. 2015. "Distributive Justice, the Basic Structure, and the Place of Private Law." *Oxford Journal of Legal Studies* 35: 213–235.

Stemplowska, Z., and A. Swift. 2012. "Ideal and Nonideal Theory." In *The Oxford Handbook of Political Philosophy*, edited by D. Estlund, 373–390. Oxford: Oxford University Press.

Steiner, H. 1984. "A Liberal Theory of Exploitation." *Ethics* 94: 225–241.
Thal, S. N. 1988. "The Inequality of Bargaining Power Doctrine: The Problem of Defining Contractual Unfairness." *Oxford Journal of Legal Studies* 8: 17–33.
Weinrib, E. J. 2012. *The Idea of Private Law*. Oxford: Oxford University Press.
Wertheimer, A. 1996. *Exploitation*. Princeton, NJ: Princeton University Press.
Williams, B. 1981. "Justice as a Virtue." In *Moral Luck: Philosophical Papers 1973–1980*, 83–93. Cambridge: Cambridge University Press.
Zwolinski, M. 2007. "Sweatshops, Choice, and Exploitation." *Business Ethics Quarterly* 17: 689–727.

4
"But Where Does It Stop?"
Exploitative Structures and Exploitative Actions

Mirjam Müller

1. Introduction

Exploitation is messy, both in practice and in theory. To work through the messiness, (liberal) political theorists often appeal to our intuitions about different paradigmatic cases of exploitation. We are asked to consider Carole, who is stranded in the desert, and whom Jason offers to rescue in return for her entire wealth.[1] Or we are asked to imagine B being trapped in a pit, and A, who happens to have a rope, offers to get B out if B agrees to sign a sweatshop contract with A.[2] These examples are meant to invoke the reaction that Jason or A acts wrongfully because they exploit Carole or B, respectively. The examples are united in that they feature clearly identifiable agents who can be held accountable for their actions and who could have chosen not to exploit. Jason, for instance, could have given Carole a ride back to town, merely asking for a share of the gasoline costs. Instead, he turns Carole's misfortune into a possibility for profit. His act of exploitation can be explained by pointing to a specific feature about him: his intention to enrich himself. These forms of exploitation have been variously called interactional, transactional, or discretionary exploitation.[3]

Theories necessarily abstract from some aspects of reality and bring others into focus.[4] Still, we should ask what is assumed and what is left out in these examples, and whether what is assumed and left out can help to illuminate and resist exploitation's most pernicious and persistent forms under

---

[1] Meyers 2004, 325.
[2] Vrousalis 2013, 148.
[3] See, for instance, McKeown 2017; Mayer 2007; Zwolinski 2007. I will henceforth use the term "transactional exploitation."
[4] For different forms of abstraction and their role in normative theory, see O'Neill 1987; Mills 2005, 168.

contemporary capitalism. Think about sweatshop labor relations, often taken to be paradigmatic cases of global capitalist exploitation.[5] Sweatshop workers work long hours under dangerous and unhealthy working conditions and receive minimal wages. Yet, the agents who are involved in the exploitation of sweatshop workers generally operate within the confines of specific constraints: overseers in the factories who push workers to meet quotas are themselves subject to surveillance, and their job may be on the line if they fail to deliver on targets. Factory owners who employ workers on insecure contracts and push down wages tend to be subcontracted by multinational or transnational enterprises and answer to them. Those global enterprises, in turn, act under the pressure of competitive markets.

There is thus a worry that transactional accounts offer little illumination of the complex nature of contemporary capitalist labor relations. The assumption that exploitation can be explained primarily by features of the individual misses the fact that the exploiters in these situations act within historically specific social structures and often do not have much discretion about whether or not to exploit.[6] If we are looking for a few bad apples who exploit and thereby deviate from what is normally a non-exploitative relationship, we are looking in the wrong place.

The insight that exploitation is fundamentally a structural relation is not new and has figured prominently in Marxist accounts of exploitation under capitalism. Recent work on exploitation has built on this insight and put structures back at the center of exploitation theory.[7] Drawing on this work, my aim in this chapter is to develop an account of exploitation that focuses on the structural conditions of exploitation, while also highlighting the role of individual actions in reproducing structural exploitation. I propose that structural exploitation involves jointly taking advantage of a structurally embedded vulnerability to bring about a transfer of resources. Thus this account aims to strike a middle ground between transactional accounts of exploitation, on the one hand, and structural accounts, on the other.

---

[5] See, for instance, McKeown 2017 or Snyder 2010. For defenses of sweatshop labor, see Powell 2014 or Zwolinski 2007.

[6] Robert Mayer distinguishes discretionary exploitation from structural exploitation. In the former case the agent is free to decide whether or not they play for advantage. In the latter case the agent acts within a competitive market and is a price taker, hence lacks the discretion of the former. Mayer 2007, 610.

[7] See in particular McKeown 2016; Shelby 2002; Wollner 2019; Young 1990. This work also adds an explicitly normative account of exploitation to Marx's (arguably) technical notion of exploitation.

The chapter proceeds in four steps. First, I show in more detail how structural accounts depart from transactional accounts and discuss relevant recent work on structural exploitation. Second, I clarify the notion of social structures that provides the grounds for developing my account of structural exploitation. Third, I propose an account of structural exploitation that illuminates how structural exploitation is reproduced through the actions of individuals.

2. Exploitative Structures

2.1. Impersonal and Anonymous Exploitation

How can we understand the claim that a structure, as opposed to an individual, is exploitative?[8] Start with the following conversation, which John Steinbeck describes in *The Grapes of Wrath*:[9]

> "And that reminds me," the driver said, "you better get out soon. I'm going through the dooryard after dinner." . . .
> "It's mine. I built it. You bump it down—I'll be in the window with a rifle." . . .
> "It's not me. There's nothing I can do. I'll lose my job if I don't do it. And look—suppose you kill me? They'll just hang you, but long before you're hung there'll be another guy on the tractor, and he'll bump the house down. You're not killing the right guy."
> "That's so," the tenant said. "Who gave you orders? I'll go after him. He's the one to kill."
> "You're wrong. He got his orders from the bank. The bank told him, 'Clear those people out or it's your job.'"
> "Well, there's a president of the bank. There's a board of directors. I'll fill up the magazine of the rifle and go into the bank."

---

[8] Matt Zwolinski provides a helpful distinction between different forms of structural exploitation (2007, 160). One key difference is between accounts that see structures as instrumental to or enabling exploitation, and accounts that theorize structures as exploitative in and of themselves. One example of the former is Ruth Sample's account of exploitation (2003, 97–98). In this chapter I am interested mainly in the latter.

[9] Steinbeck 2000. The use of this literary example was inspired by a talk by John Filling on structural domination.

> The driver said, "Fellow was telling me the bank gets orders from the East. The orders were, 'Make the land show profit or we'll close you up.'"
>
> "But where does it stop? Who can we shoot?" . . .
>
> "I don't know. Maybe there's nobody to shoot. Maybe the thing isn't men at all. Maybe like you said, the property's doing it. Anyway I told you my orders."
>
> "I got to figure," the tenant said. "We all got to figure. There's some way to stop this. It's not like lightning or earthquakes. We've got a bad thing made by men, and by God that's something we can change."

Here is a situation where something bad is about to happen to the protagonist of the story—their house is going to be demolished—and yet they can point to no one to hold accountable. The tractor driver's response that "maybe there is nobody to shoot" expresses the sense that the protagonist is confronted by something beyond their control, alike to a natural catastrophe. As a result, the protagonist's complaint goes out into the void. And yet the protagonist knows that what is happening to them is not "like lightning or earthquakes"; it is human-made. *Someone* is doing it, even though they can point to no one *in particular*.

In a similar way, saying that a structure is exploitative relies on the idea that the exploitation is in some sense anonymous. Gabriel Wollner describes the anonymity of structural exploitation in the following way: "The victim of exploitation cannot point to or name any particular individual as her exploiter. There is exploitation even though nobody in particular is exploiting anyone in particular."[10] This echoes Marx's insight that capitalist exploitation is anonymous and impersonal.[11] Yet, while the individual, on Wollner's account, cannot point to any *particular* individual as their exploiter, it is possible to identify *exploitative positions* within a structure. According to Wollner, "an individual enjoys the status of an exploiter if her role or position within the structure is such that in order to optimize or maximize economic revenue she has to take unfair advantage of others."[12] In a similar way Nicholas Vrousalis argues that capitalism is a structure that requires, for its reproduction, a certain disposition on the part of the capitalist. In virtue of being a capitalist, the capitalist has the disposition to use their power

---

[10] Wollner 2019, 147. Anonymity can, according to Wollner, refer to both sides, exploiter and exploited. My main focus in this chapter is on the anonymity of the exploiter.
[11] Marx 1978, 205. See also Cohen 1983, 12.
[12] Wollner 2019, 157.

over the worker to extract maximum surplus value.[13] The underlying idea in both proposals is that an exploitative structure is one that features social positions where some optimize by exploiting others.[14] It is, however, somewhat random which particular individual occupies which particular position. Instead, the emphasis lies on the kind of dispositions or behaviors a social position incentivizes.

Maeve McKeown proposes a different account of structural exploitation, one that focuses more specifically on the centrality of structural force to exploitation and thus takes a closer look at the social structural processes that determine individuals' option set. According to McKeown, structural exploitation consists in "the forced transfer of the productive power of groups positioned as socially inferior to the advantage of groups positioned as socially superior."[15] McKeown develops the notion of structural force following Jeffrey Reiman. Structural force, according to Reiman is a type of force that is built into the structure of society.[16] Structural force means that individuals, in virtue of their social position within a structure (e.g., as a worker within a capitalist economy) face a limited set of options, and options outside of that set are either prohibitively costly or unacceptable. While this set of options is forced upon them, there are no particular agents who intentionally set up a structure in such a way that it leaves some agents with a limited set of options. Instead, the origin of the force is structural, in that a large number of different people uphold a structure by playing "their roles more or less unthinkingly."[17] When McKeown speaks about a forced transfer of productive power from groups who are positioned as socially inferior to the advantage of groups positioned as socially superior, she refers to this type of structural force.[18]

Similar to Wollner and Vrousalis, McKeown thus shifts the focus from the specific features of individuals to their structural positions. Consequently, the picture that emerges when we think about exploitation in structural terms is one where particular individuals are neither necessary nor sufficient

---

[13] Vrousalis 2021, 15.

[14] In a similar way, Robert Mayer argues that structural exploitation occurs when agents have no discretion to set prices, because they are locked in competition. They face a dilemma between no-transaction and exploitation. See Mayer 2007, 610.

[15] McKeown 2016, 174. See also McKeown 2017.

[16] Reiman 1987, 12.

[17] Reiman 1987, 12. Note that Reiman draws attention to the structural nature of force both in its effect and in its origin. Since my interest here lies with the structural origin of force, I will set aside its structural effect.

[18] In this, McKeown draws on Iris Young's account of structural exploitation. See Young 1990, 49.

for exploitation to take place. Structural exploitation is not about a few bad individuals who break the rules by exploiting. They exploit by acting in accordance with the rules.

The claim that particular individuals are neither necessary nor sufficient for exploitation might invite some confusion. Consider again John Steinbeck's tractor driver who concludes that "maybe there's nobody to shoot" and "maybe the thing isn't men at all." Does a commitment to the impersonality and anonymity of exploitation lead to the conclusion that the "thing isn't men at all"? In other words, do structural accounts of exploitation entail a reference to some non-human entity that exploits? Wollner has argued that a convincing account of structural exploitation needs to meet what he calls a non-mysteriousness constraint. According to him, to make sense of structural forms of exploitation we should not assume or refer to any mysterious entities.[19] The good news is that saying that exploitation is impersonal or anonymous does not require a commitment to some non-human entity, and theorists who hold structural accounts do not generally deny that exploitation is human-made.[20] To say that *no one in particular* exploits is not necessarily to say that *no human* exploits. It is, in the first place, to point out that particular features about individuals, like their *specific* motivations or intentions, do not play a central role in explaining the exploitation.

While structural accounts are right to insist that some forms of exploitation require a focus on the structural conditions under which they occur, they have paid insufficient attention to the relation between individual action and structural exploitation. They thereby fail to provide a compelling account of the mechanisms by which structural exploitation gets continuously reproduced. To explain why structural exploitation persists, structural accounts need to say more about the relation between individual action and structural exploitation and the type of actions that reproduce structural exploitation. In the following I show that the accounts of structural exploitation outlined above either fail to theorize the relation between individual action and structural exploitation or theorize it in a way that gives up much of their structural bite.

---

[19] Wollner 2019, 148.
[20] E.g., Reiman 1987, 14.

2.2. Structural Exploitation as Something Passive?

On McKeown's view, someone is exploited when they are positioned such that they are (structurally) forced to transfer their productive powers to more powerful groups, who benefit from this transfer. Members of powerful groups are not, however, themselves forcing those positioned as socially inferior to transfer their productive powers; the force is structural and emerges from many different agents going about their daily lives.[21] All they do is occupy a powerful position and accept the benefit that is transferred to them; no active advantage-taking is required of them. To the extent that this account allows for the identification of exploiters, likely those who occupy powerful positions and who benefit from the forced transfer, this identification is not based in their exploitative *actions*. On this account, exploitative relations almost turn into something passive that happens to both the exploited and the exploiters in virtue of their social positions.

While this account is helpful in bringing into the foreground the often mundane and everyday actions of individuals involved in the production of injustice, more can and needs to be said about the type of actions that reproduce exploitative structures. Exploitative structures do not reproduce themselves automatically, and while it looks like structures sometimes take on a life of their own, they are made by individuals.[22] An understanding of why they persist requires an analysis of what individuals do to keep them in place. We thus need to know more about the specific relations and the particular type of actions of individuals involved in situations where some are forced to transfer their productive powers to others. This also requires the tools to distinguish between actions that do reproduce exploitation and actions that do not.

2.3. Structural Exploitation as a Specific Structurally Embedded Act?

In their accounts of structural exploitation, both Wollner and Vrousalis offer a different understanding of the relation between individual action and structural exploitation. For Wollner, structural exploitation consists

---

[21] This assumption builds on Iris Marion Young's work on structural injustice (Young 2011, 52).

[22] This is a key insight of theories of structuration. See in particular Sewell 1992, 13.

in the act of advantage-taking to maximize economic revenues, which is incentivized by the agent's position within an economic structure. Vrousalis spells out the act of advantage-taking in terms of domination: the exploiter uses their power over a vulnerable other to extract a benefit, thereby subordinating them. Exploitation, on his account, is the "dividend of servitude."[23] Both Wollner and Vrousalis provide a clear account of the role of individual actions in the process of exploitation. Structural exploitation is, accordingly, not something passive. It is actively carried out and upheld by individuals.

Wollner's and Vrousalis's accounts are structural insofar as they focus on the social positions of the exploiters rather than on the particular attributes of those who exploit. Yet, when it comes to the acts constituting exploitation this structural nature is lost. Exploitation becomes a discrete action that can be attributed to a particular agent. Like transactional accounts, their accounts thereby miss the complex and interdependent ways in which different actions by various actors make up structural exploitation. The example of sweatshop labor shows that it is difficult to attribute the whole act of advantage-taking to one specific agent. The low wages of sweatshop workers do not typically result solely from negotiations between an individual worker and the hiring manager. Instead, they are the outcome of complex industry-wide struggles between workers and employers and reflect the power relations between different groups. Furthermore, while there are particular overseers who are responsible for monitoring the workers' pace and output, the overseers' particular actions (e.g., the threat of sanctions in case of failure to comply with requirements) do not fully explain the exploitation of the workers. For one thing, these particular individuals are unlikely to reap the whole benefit of their action. At the end of the day the profits made possible by sweatshop workers will be distributed among different actors along global supply chains. For another, their action is possible only because others do their part: push the workers to meet their quotas, threaten to fire them should they join a union, move production to places where labor is cheaper, and so on. This suggests that the actions that make up structural exploitation are not adequately analyzed in terms of independent individual actions.

Wollner is aware of the difficulties involved in assigning exploitative actions to particular individuals in situations of structural exploitation. He accounts for them by offering an account of a division of labor between different agents involved in structural exploitation.[24] On this account, different

---

[23] Vrousalis 2021, 1.
[24] Wollner 2019, 154–155.

individuals coordinate their actions in a way that amounts to exploitation, even though no *individual* actor is taking unfair advantage and benefits at somebody else's expense. For instance, in a constellation of three actors, A, B, and C, A might take advantage of B, but C is the one to benefit from A's advantage-taking. Thus, neither A nor C individually fits the bill when it comes to exploiting B. But jointly they do.[25]

Understanding different actions involved in structural exploitation in terms of a division of labor is helpful to get a first grip on the involvement of multiple agents in exploitative structures. Yet, to understand this relation in terms of a cooperative division of labor is too strong. It presupposes a form of decision-making process that is not generally present in structural relations of exploitation. Social structures, as I argue in the next section, enable and incentivize joint action in much more informal and less explicit ways. This claim is consistent with there being some cooperative divisions of labor in structural relations of exploitation, such as between the factory supervisor and the shift manager. Yet, focusing on them alone is insufficient to explain the various forms of joint actions that make up structural exploitation.

In sum, while McKeown's account captures the structural nature of exploitation, she does not provide a compelling account of the relation between individual actions and structural exploitation and thus of the way in which structural exploitation is reproduced. Wollner and Vrousalis, on the other hand, provide a clear account of the actions that make up structural exploitation. Yet, by attributing these actions to particular individuals and by explaining their relation in terms of a cooperative division of labor, their accounts lose much of their structural bite. In the following, I outline an account of structural exploitation that both retains the focus on structures and provides an understanding of the relation between individual action and exploitative structures. I start with my account of social structures.

3. Social Structures

3.1. Constraints and Opportunities

For an initial understanding of social structures, start with the assumption that our actions, our relations to others, and our relations to the world are,

---

[25] This is a shortened version of Wollner's own example.

at least to some degree, constrained and enabled by structural processes.[26] These structural processes are often thought of primarily in terms of laws and explicit rules.[27] For instance, laws regulating traffic have a clear impact on the way individuals can move through the world. But structural processes constrain and enable in less formal and less explicit ways too. To understand the effects and persistence of social structural processes, Sally Haslanger stresses the importance of cultural schemas: "culturally shared mental states and processes, including concepts, attitudes, dispositions, norms etc. that enable us to interpret and organize information and coordinate action, thought and affect."[28] Cultural schemas are best understood as tools to navigate the social world. Agents integrate schemas into their practical knowledge about the world and mobilize those schemas to guide their action. Schemas enable and constrain action by organizing us in relation to resources—things that have positive or negative value.[29] This organization takes place in social practices.

Consider the following example by Haslanger. Cooking is a social practice that organizes us in relation to food. Because we are embodied beings with physical needs, food is an essential resource and organizing access to it is a vital interest. This is where schemas come in. They tell us what counts as food in our specific context and what does not; for example, some herbs are part of one country's cuisine but not of another's. They tell us how to use and prepare the food, such as whether to cook it or to eat it raw. They also tell us what kind of actions are appropriate for the practice of cooking; for example, if I throw rice into the air, I am not engaging in the practice of cooking (I may instead be celebrating a just-married couple in some contexts). And they regulate access to food; for example, to get food I need to go to the supermarket to buy it. Consequently, cultural schemas enable and constrain action "by providing templates of interaction that favour (or discourage) certain forms of coordination with respect to a resource . . . ; and by canalizing our attitudes accordingly."[30]

Beyond rules and cultural schemas, a further set of constraints is engendered by the physical world as well as the congealed outcomes of past practices. While schemas play an important role in organizing us in relation to resources, they never fully determine the meaning of them. As Haslanger

---

[26] Haslanger 2015, 20; Young 2011, 53.
[27] See, for instance, John Rawls's understanding of the basic structure. Rawls 1971, 7.
[28] Haslanger 2015, 21. In her understanding of social structures, Haslanger draws on theories of structuration, in particular on William H. Sewell's work (e.g. Sewell 1992).
[29] Haslanger 2015, 21.
[30] Haslanger 2016, 128.

notes, "the world pushes back."³¹ The meaning of resources depends among other things on their physical characteristics, their relation to other resources, and not least their availability in a given context. For instance, the availability of a particular type of stone in an area affects the architectural style. Similarly, a society's access to natural resources, such as oil, affects its energy politics, the country's wealth, and so on. Beyond the physical world, the outcomes of past social practices also play an important role. Iris Young argues that "the accumulated effects of past actions and decisions have left their mark on the physical world, opening some possibilities for present and future action and foreclosing others."³² Consider as an example the housing market. The decision to invest in social housing affects the availability of affordable living space long after these decisions were taken. In that sense, decisions about how specific resources, such as housing, should be allocated and organized determine their availability long after these decisions have been made. In short, social structural processes that involve formal rules, schemas, resources, the physical world, and the outcomes of past practices constrain and enable action.

3.2. Social Positions and Structural Vulnerability

These constraints and opportunities define different social positions that are characterized by different possibilities for action.³³ For instance, in sweatshop labor the set of options available to the agents in these relations is shaped fundamentally by their access to capital (financial resources, land, information technologies, and so forth). Sweatshops recruit their workforce from a pool of workers who generally lack access to and control over resources that would allow them to sustain themselves without working in a sweatshop. In a capitalist economy, access to resources that allow people to satisfy their needs, the most basic being hunger, the need for shelter, and the need for clothing, is generally mediated through wage labor for those who do

---

³¹ Haslanger 2017, 157.
³² Young 2011, 53. While Young, similarly to Haslanger, draws on theories of structuration (in particular William Sewell or Anthony Giddens), her notion of structure is different from Haslanger's. Young's understanding of structure, however, nicely complements Haslanger's account and illustrates different ways in which structures constrain and enable.
³³ Which positions individuals occupy within a structure depends on different factors, including race, gender, sexuality, ability, and age. Different authors have spelled this out with reference to membership in a social group. See, for instance, Haslanger 2004; Young 1990, 42–48.

not own or control capital. This restates the basic Marxist insight that those who do not own capital need to sell their labor power to get a crack at living. Sweatshop workers are in a position where the options available to them to meet their needs are severely limited. Within that option set, sweatshop labor is one of the better options, compared to alternative employment or unemployment. The lack of alternative options brings sweatshop workers in a position of structural vulnerability vis-à-vis sweatshop employers. The fact that they cannot easily walk away from an offer gives sweatshop employers greater bargaining power and means that sweatshop workers are bound to accept bad working conditions and low wages.

In that sense, the constraints and opportunities define positions of vulnerability and power, loosely understood in terms of the set of options or room to maneuver, available to different agents and how this structures the relations between them.[34] It is important to note that vulnerability and power must not be understood in a binary sense: the shift supervisor who threatens to report the workers should they not meet quotas has power over the workers and the workers are vulnerable to them. But they themselves respond to the factory managers, who in turn have power over the shift supervisor, and the shift supervisors are vulnerable to them. Vulnerability and power are thus best understood in relative terms.

In short, social structures entail different social positions that are associated with different constraints and opportunities. An understanding of the way in which these constraints and opportunities work to bring some in positions of vulnerability and others in positions of power, is central to understanding structural exploitation.

4. Structural Exploitation

4.1. Taking Advantage of Structural Vulnerability

The existence of a structurally embedded relation marked by vulnerability and power does not by itself constitute structural exploitation. I follow Nicholas Vrousalis in assuming that exploiters occupy positions of (relative) power and that this is a necessary condition for exploitation.[35] It is

---

[34] In my understanding of power and vulnerability I roughly follow Vrousalis 2013.
[35] For further defenses of power as a necessary condition for exploitation, see Vrousalis 2013; Shelby 2002.

not, however, a sufficient one. Not everyone who is in a position of power therefore occupies the position of an exploiter. I propose that someone occupies the position of an exploiter when they are incentivized to participate in taking advantage of another's vulnerability to bring about a transfer of resources. For instance, sweatshop supervisors are incentivized to push workers to meet quotas, sweatshop managers are incentivized to keep wages low, and multinational enterprises are incentivized to move production to low-wage places, like Bangladesh or Cambodia. Before I say more about what it means to participate in taking advantage of someone else's vulnerability, I want to clarify in which sense this proposal differs from McKeown's and how it addresses the concern about the role of individuals in relations of structural exploitation.

To say that structural exploitation involves taking advantage of someone's vulnerability to bring about a transfer of resources means that exploitation involves more than simply occupying a powerful position and benefitting from a forced transfer. It involves carrying out specific actions to that end—namely, actions that form part of taking advantage of others. These actions are incentivized by the social position an agent occupies. Yet, a social position does not entirely determine the course of action. Instead, social positions allow for and incentivize several different actions to be carried out. They structure *possibilities* for action, rather than determining these actions. Social positions do not provide a full template of how that position needs to be filled. Thus there is some leeway in occupying a social position, and some potential to push its boundaries.[36]

One implication of this is that those who are in a position where they are exploitable have different options available to them and hence there is some (limited) space for resistance. In sweatshop labor relations, contracts are the outcomes of struggles between workers and employers. These outcomes depend on the distribution of power between different groups—for example, the existence of unions or the availability of alternative options for workers to sustain themselves. Workers form unions, they go on strike, they mobilize consumer boycotts, and so forth to push for better working conditions and higher wages. Their exploitation does not come about by itself. The exploited

---

[36] This proposal builds on Robin Zheng's discussion of the nature of social roles. According to Zheng, a social role entails a set of expectations that apply to an individual in virtue of occupying this role and which are enforced through a variety of sanctions. However, these expectations never fully specify how an occupier of a particular role is supposed to perform that role. Roles are, on Zheng's view, undefinable. There is hence some space in deciding on how to perform a social role. Following Zheng, I assume that this holds equally for social positions. Zheng 2018, 873.

have an interest in not being exploited, even when the latter is their best available option. Exploiters need to use their power and overcome resistance. Differently put, in order to bring about a transfer of resources, the vulnerability of the workers needs to be taken advantage of. Structural exploitation thus involves specific actions. It is not just the fact that exploiters benefit from occupying a powerful position through the transfer of resources; they are actively involved in processes that bring about this transfer, and thus they participate in taking advantage of vulnerable others.

4.2. Joint Advantage-Taking

In which sense do agents participate in taking advantage of vulnerable others? I argued above that the actions involved in bringing about a transfer of resources are not independent individual actions that can be attributed to particular agents. To say that someone participates in taking advantage of vulnerable others is to say that their actions contribute to the advantage-taking and that their contribution is dependent on others doing their part. This interdependence is not, however, best understood in terms of a cooperative division of labor, in the sense Wollner has suggested. I argued above that understanding these acts as a cooperative division of labor is too strong. It does not sufficiently account for the informal and less explicit ways in which structural processes hold different actions together.

The question then is how the actions of different individuals hang together such that they all form part of exploitation—taking advantage of another's vulnerability to bring about a transfer of resources. I propose that the connection between different actions of advantage-taking is best understood in terms of a shared economic practice. I understand practices, following Haslanger, as "collective solutions to coordination or access problems with respect to a resource." Practices organize access to and distribution of resources by referring to schemas. Wage labor can, in this sense, be understood in terms of a solution to the organization of the production and distribution of economic goods under capitalism. It is organized according to particular schemas, such as contractual freedom, the logic of competition and profit maximization. On this view, the actions of agents within wage labor relations are interdependent not in virtue of a joint decision to divide up labor. Instead, they hang together in virtue of forming part of a collective solution to a particular problem. The specific actions of individuals in turn depend on their particular social positions.

In sum, I propose to understand structural exploitation as individuals jointly taking advantage of the structural vulnerability of workers to bring about a transfer of resources. This account departs from transactional accounts by focusing on the structural conditions that enable and constrain the action of both exploited and exploiters. Exploitation, on this account, is not the result of someone being an asshole. It is the result of someone occupying a social position that incentivizes them to exploit. At the same time, this account does not lose sight of the actions of individuals. The joint acts of individuals, which are held together by the social practice of wage labor, are necessary for the reproduction of structural exploitation. In the remainder of this chapter, I will outline in more detail how structural exploitation is reproduced and highlight the role of individual action in this reproduction.

5. Reproducing Exploitation

I argued above that occupying a social position structures the space of action for individuals and provides incentives to act in accordance with the constraints and opportunities. To say that a social position incentivizes a specific action is to say that it gives agents reasons to carry out this action. A social position gives agents reason to carry out a particular action when the constraints and opportunities that apply to this social position single it out as one of the best options. For example, in a choice between unemployment and wage labor in a sweatshop, it is reasonable for workers to sign the contract. Social structures, however, do not just confront agents as external entities. Structures are produced and reproduced through the actions of individuals within them.[37]

The use of schemas has an impact on resources—that is, on what counts as a resource, or how it should be used (rice boiled in a pot is food, rice thrown into the air celebrates a newly wedded couple). This is not a one-way street. As William Sewell puts it, "Resources, we might say, are read like texts, to recover the cultural schemas they instantiate."[38] They teach and

---

[37] For a detailed account of how individual action reproduces social structures, see Sewell 1992, 13. See also Young 2011, 59–62.
[38] Sewell 1992, 13.

justify schemas. Consider the following example. The resource of care work is organized through gendered schemas. Gendered schemas, including that women are naturally disposed to care, play a role in women disproportionately occupying the position of caregivers. If care work is largely organized along the lines of gender, this in turn reinforces gendered schemas about care work. Thus the practice of caregiving reproduces itself in its gendered form. The fact that individuals act by employing schemas to access and distribute resources has the effect of reproducing structural constraints and possibilities. Structural exploitation is reproduced in this way, as I will now show in more detail.

5.1. How Joint Advantage-Taking Reproduces Structural Exploitation

Structural exploitation involves jointly taking advantage of a structurally embedded vulnerability. Using their power to take advantage of the vulnerability of others does not merely allow exploiters to benefit from a transfer of resources; it also, in the process, sustains (and sometimes increases) the power advantage. When exploiters exploit, they bring about an unequal transfer of resources. Resources are closely connected to power, insofar as individuals can mobilize them to influence the action of others and to further their own ends.[39] An unequal transfer of resources from the vulnerable to the powerful stabilizes the power of the latter and maintains the vulnerability of the former. For instance, a worker who barely makes a living and who has no savings to fall back on will find it difficult to join a union if that means risking losing their job. While some workers might eventually own sufficient capital to become independent of wage labor, this is not a route that is open for all.[40] At the same time, capitalist accumulation increases the power of sweatshop employers, including by providing them with greater market shares or greater lobbying power.[41]

---

[39] This understanding of the role of resources builds on Iris Young's discussion of social structures. See Young 2011, 61.

[40] Cohen (1983) discusses the possibility of exiting the proletariat and gives a detailed analysis of why workers are collectively unfree, even when they are free as individuals to leave.

[41] Here, my understanding of how the power advantage is reproduced through the unequal flow of resources draws on Tommie Shelby's account of reproductive exploitation. See Shelby 2002, 408.

Exploitation does not, however, merely reproduce a specific resource distribution. Above I argued, following Haslanger, that schemas play an important role in making sense of the world, interacting with others, and coordinating action. Schemas tell us how particular resources should be distributed, what counts as a resource in the first place, and who should provide it. Hence they play a central role in organizing resources. When it comes to the unequal transfer of resources involved in exploitation, we need to take a closer look at the schemas that govern this distribution. These schemas involve assumptions about the value of the resources that are exchanged. For instance, assumptions about the value of the activities typically involved in sweatshop labor, such as sewing or assembling, play an important role in the remuneration of this work. Gendered and racialized schemas furthermore determine who carries out which kind of activities. For instance, during her fieldwork in garment factories in Indonesia, Teri Caraway found that tasks that were assumed to involve more physical strength were normally carried out by male workers.[42] In addition, racial schemas affect who is considered to be an exploitable worker in the first place. This is highlighted in Gargi Bhattacharyya's discussion of racial capitalism and the ways in which racial differentiation excludes racialized workers from forming part of the formal workforce altogether.[43] Schemas thus have an impact on the way in which resources are distributed. The resulting distribution in turn affirms the schemas: sweatshop workers generally take home very low wages. This in turn confirms and sustains the schema that the activities involved in sweatshop labor do not command a high exchange value.

As a result, the power of the exploiters is continuously reproduced through the act of exploitation. In volume 1 of *Capital* Marx states:[44]

> It is no longer a mere accident that capitalist and worker confront each other in the market as buyer and seller. It is the alternating rhythm of the process itself which throws the worker back onto the market again and again as a seller of his labour power and continually transforms his own product into a means by which another man can purchase him. In reality, the worker belongs to capital before he has sold himself to the capitalist.

---

[42] Caraway 2005, 414.
[43] Bhattacharyya 2018, 42.
[44] Marx 1992, 723.

It is, indeed, no accident that exploiter and exploited confront each other *as* exploiter and exploited. Exploitation continuously reproduces its own conditions of possibility.

5.2. How Do Individuals Relate to Structural Exploitation?

The above has important implications for the way individuals within a structure relate to exploitation. Human action is constrained and enabled by the schemas and resources available. Social structures are reproduced if individuals act in accordance with these constraints and opportunities and thus with the incentives provided by their social position. So if someone occupies the position of an exploiter, they are incentivized to exploit. This, however, does not mean that their action is entirely determined by their social position. While human action is constrained and enabled by the schemas and resources available to them, individuals have some leeway in how they occupy a social position. Schemas often do not have definitive content and may be transposable; for instance, marriage once was only between people of two opposite genders, while today (at least in some contexts) people of the same gender can get married too, and the meaning of the term "marriage" has changed accordingly. Resources may change as well; for example, the availability of digital means of communication has radically transformed possibilities for organization. Furthermore, as I argued above, social positions within structures do not necessarily incentivize only one particular action and spell it out in full detail. They structure the space of possibilities, but they do not determine one specific course of action. This means that individuals who occupy exploitative positions have the possibility of not exploiting. Acting in defiance of the constraints and opportunities of one's social position usually entails costs, and for some exploiters these will be prohibitive. There may be hard choices between staying competitive and raising wages. In some instances, a non-exploitative deal may not be available and hence exploiters face the option between no transaction and exploitation. In others, however, there is more room for maneuver and those who occupy an exploitative position do not need to exploit. It is also important to note that the space for deciding which actions to take will depend significantly on how much power different agents hold.

This again raises the issue of an exploiter who does not exploit, albeit in a slightly different way. In response to McKeown I asked whether it is helpful (or plausible) to conceptualize exploitation in a way that understands it merely in passive terms; I was thus interested in the contents of the concept. I am here interested in the actualization of that content. Under the assumption that structural exploitation involves participating in taking advantage of someone's vulnerability in order to bring about a transfer of resources, can individuals occupy the position of an exploiter when they never exploit?

In response to this, recall that structures and social positions do not exist independently of those who occupy them. They are produced and reproduced through the action of individuals. Individuals have some leeway with regard to how they fill their social position, and they have the option to push the boundaries and sometimes even to act against the incentives of the social position. This means that it is in principle possible that an agent who occupies an exploitative social position does not exploit. If, however, enough individuals stop exploiting, this will influence how constraints and opportunities related to social positions are reproduced. An exploitative social structure, like any other social structure, requires individual action to exist. This does not suggest that individuals can change structures by themselves. But enough individuals need to reproduce their social positions for the structure to continue to persist. Consequently, while particular agents do not have to exploit, there needs to be a sufficient number of agents who exploit for an exploitative structure to be reproduced.[45]

6. Conclusion

The account of structural exploitation I proposed departs from existing accounts of exploitation in two ways. In moving the focus away from specific individuals and their intentions toward the structural conditions that constrain and enable their actions, it follows other structural accounts of exploitation. Unlike them, however, it highlights the importance of accounting for the relation between individual action and the structural conditions under which these actions occur and which they, in turn, reproduce. In doing so, it strikes a middle ground between accounts that focus too much on particular individuals and accounts that risk losing sight of individuals

---

[45] This raises difficult question about the number of individuals that need to uphold a social structure and the type of actions they need to carry out for the social structure to persist over time. I take these to be empirical questions that go beyond the scope of this chapter.

altogether. I want to close this chapter by highlighting two implications for the possibilities of resisting structural exploitation.

First, the charge of exploitation does not go out into the void, even when the exploitation is structural. While there are no particular exploiters, there are exploitative social positions that are occupied by agents who exploit. A closer look at how these social positions are reproduced reveals that they are produced in action: their reproduction requires the employment of schemas governing a particular resource distribution that secures the power of the exploiter. This is done by agents. Yet, the claim that exploitation should be understood as jointly taking advantage of vulnerability does not imply that individual agents can or should be blamed. Instead, it aims to shift the focus to the underlying power mechanisms that allow and incentivize exploiters to exploit. The specific ways in which schemas and resources interact to define an exploiter's social position are historically and contextually specific. Understanding them requires a detailed and historically embedded empirical analysis. While this goes beyond the scope of this chapter, I hope that my work here provides some theoretical vantage points for such an analysis.

A second and related implication is that any form of resistance to exploitation will require bringing about a shift in the specific power advantages. This can take place at different levels and at different points simultaneously. For instance, a power shift might come about through the redefinition of schemas. Jobs that previously were understood as low skilled or less valuable came during COVID-19 to be understood as essential. Whether or not this will actually lead to a change in the material conditions—for example, bringing about higher wages—will depend to some extent on how this shift in understanding affects a shift in resources. A shift in resources can also bring about a shift in power, as when new technologies make possible new ways of organizing and resistance. There is no doubt, however, that bringing about a shift in the power advantage will be a collective task.[46]

In sum, the protagonist of *The Grapes of Wrath* is right: exploitation is not like lightning or earthquakes. There are exploiters who exploit. Yet, transactional accounts will only get us so far. Instead of focusing on the bad character or specific intentions of particular individuals, an analysis of structural exploitation requires an understanding of the structural processes by which exploitative structures are reproduced.

---

[46] For a detailed analysis of the type of responsibility and action required to resist structural injustice, see Young 2011.

References

Bhattacharyya, G. 2018. *Rethinking Racial Capitalism: Questions of Reproduction and Survival*. London: Rowman & Littlefield International.

Caraway, T. L. 2005. "The Political Economy of Feminization: From 'Cheap Labor' to Gendered Discourses of Work." *Politics and Gender* 1, no. 3: 399–429.

Cohen, G. A. 1983. "The Structure of Proletarian Unfreedom." *Philosophy and Public Affairs* 12, no. 1: 3–33.

Haslanger, S. 2004. "Oppressions: Racial and Other." In *Racism in Mind*, edited by M. Levine and T. Pataki, 97–123. Ithaca, NY: Cornell University Press.

Haslanger, S. 2015. *Critical Theory and Practice*. Assen: Koninklijke Van Gorcum.

Haslanger, S. 2016. "What Is a (Social) Structural Explanation?" *Philosophical Studies* 173, no. 1: 113–130.

Haslanger, S. 2017. "I—Culture and Critique." *Aristotelian Society Supplementary Volume* 91, no. 1: 149–173.

Marx, K. 1978. "Wage Labour and Capital." In *The Marx-Engels Reader*, 2nd edition, edited by R. C. Tucker. New York: W. W. Norton, 1978.

Marx, K. 1992. *Capital: Volume 1: A Critique of Political Economy*. London: Penguin Classics.

Mayer, R. 2007. "Sweatshops, Exploitation, and Moral Responsibility." *Journal of Social Philosophy* 38, no. 4: 605–619.

McKeown, M. 2016. "Global Structural Exploitation: Towards an Intersectional Definition." *Global Justice: Theory, Practice, Rhetoric* 9, no. 2: 155–177.

McKeown, M. 2017. "Sweatshop Labour as Global Structural Exploitation." In *Exploitation: From Practice to Theory*, edited by M. Deveaux and V. Panitch, 35–59. Studies in Social and Global Justice. London: Rowman & Littlefield International.

Meyers, C. 2004. "Wrongful Beneficence: Exploitation and Third World Sweatshops." *Journal of Social Philosophy* 35, no. 3: 319–333.

Mills, C. W. 2005. "'Ideal Theory' as Ideology." *Hypatia* 20, no. 3: 165–184.

O'Neill, O. 1987. "Abstraction, Idealization and Ideology in Ethics." *Royal Institute of Philosophy Lecture Series* 22: 55–69.

Powell, B. 2014. *Out of Poverty: Sweatshops in the Global Economy*. New York, NY: Cambridge University Press.

Rawls, J. 1971. *A Theory of Justice*. Cambridge, MA: Harvard University Press.

Reiman, J. 1987. "Exploitation, Force, and the Moral Assessment of Capitalism: Thoughts on Roemer and Cohen." *Philosophy and Public Affairs* 16, no. 1: 3–41.

Sample, R. J. 2003. *Exploitation: What It Is and Why It's Wrong*. New York: Rowman & Littlefield.

Sewell, W. H. 1992. "A Theory of Structure: Duality, Agency, and Transformation." *American Journal of Sociology* 98, no. 1: 1–29.

Shelby, T. 2002. "Parasites, Pimps, and Capitalists: A Naturalistic Conception of Exploitation." *Social Theory and Practice* 28, no. 3: 381–418.

Snyder, J. 2010. "Exploitation and Sweatshop Labor: Perspectives and Issues." *Business Ethics Quarterly* 20, no. 2: 187–213.

Steinbeck, John. 2000. *The Grapes of Wrath*. London: Penguin Classics.

Vrousalis, N. 2013. "Exploitation, Vulnerability, and Social Domination." *Philosophy & Public Affairs* 41, no. 2: 131–157.

Vrousalis, N. 2021. "How Exploiters Dominate." *Review of Social Economy* 79, no. 1: 103–130.

Wollner, G. 2019. "Anonymous Exploitation: Non-Individual, Non-Agential and Structural." *Review of Social Economy* 77, no. 2: 143–162.
Young, I. M. 1990. *Justice and the Politics of Difference.* Princeton, NJ: Princeton University Press.
Young, I. M. 2011. *Responsibility for Justice.* Oxford: Oxford University Press.
Zheng, R. 2018. "What Is My Role in Changing the System? A New Model of Responsibility for Structural Injustice." *Ethical Theory and Moral Practice* 21, no. 4: 869–8 85.
Zwolinski, M. 2007. "Sweatshops, Choice, and Exploitation." *Business Ethics Quarterly* 17, no. 4: 689–727.
Zwolinski, M. 2012. "Structural Exploitation." *Social Philosophy and Policy* 29, no. 1: 154–79.

5
Fair Trade, Bargaining, and Respect for Persons

Hillel Steiner

The other day I was shopping in my local supermarket and had what is these days the not uncommon experience of being confronted with a choice between a bunch of bananas labeled as "fair trade" produce and its non-fair-trade but otherwise similar counterpart. So I chose the fair trade bunch and, consequently, paid about 15 percent more for it than I would have had to pay for its counterpart. One question I want to address here is whether, in so choosing, I was acting *altruistically*. Was my behavior an act of benevolence?

My answer to this question is going to be no. To reach that conclusion, I'll begin by (i) citing the distinction between *concern* and *respect*, (ii) suggesting that it aligns closely with the difference between focusing on persons as subjects of wellbeing and persons as subjects of agency, and (iii) noting that altruism or benevolence is standardly associated with the former. Next, I'll contend that what fair trade overcomes is a respect deficit: a deficit constituted by agents' truncated scope for personal choice. Offsetting that truncation to the point of *equal* scope for choice is argued to be a requirement of justice, not altruism. Then I'll display how truncated scope for choice generates exploitation. Finally, I'll try to show how the requirement not to exploit applies to exchanges that, unlike supermarket purchases, involve bargaining.

Returning to my banana purchase, I take it that one reason to believe that my choosing the fair trade bunch wasn't altruistic is sufficiently familiar as to

---

A number of the arguments advanced here have greatly benefited from the advice of Carla Bagnoli, Chris Bertram, Colin Bird, Ian Carter, Matthew Clayton, Jerry Cohen, Stephen Darwall, Ben Ferguson, Alan Hamlin, William Lucy, Serena Olsaretti, John O'Neill, Michael Otsuka, Jonathan Quong, Ian Steedman, Zofia Stemplowska, Rebecca Stone, Peter Vallentyne, Andrew Williams, Jonathan Wolff, and Matt Zwolinski. Work on this essay was generously supported by a Leverhulme Trust Major Research Fellowship.

require only a very brief rehearsal here. It's certainly true that in shopping we standardly aim to economize: to satisfy our preferences at the least possible cost to ourselves. And this normally entails that, in a choice between any two alternatively purchasable options—each describable as possessing one and the same set of features—we choose the one with the lower price.

But, of course, the aforesaid two bunches of bananas don't quite fit this description. They don't fit it because, although both possessed one and the same set of *physical* features—that is, each was composed of six bananas of roughly the same size, shape, and shelf life—one of them possessed a *normative relational* feature the other lacked: namely, that it was produced with the aid of unexploited labor or, at least, with labor that was less exploited than that involved in the production of its lower-priced counterpart.[1]

Since the fair trade bunch possessed this additional feature, which I value,[2] I wasn't failing to be an economizing shopper in choosing it over the cheaper alternative—just as I wouldn't have been a non-economizing shopper in choosing another non-fair-trade bunch that was *more expensive* than the non-fair-trade bunch but had *seven* bananas rather than only the latter's six. So, insofar as I was simply being an archetypal *homo economicus* in making my banana choices, there's some pretty widely endorsed sense in which I wasn't acting altruistically.

But, obviously, the matter is somewhat more complicated than that. For, along with banana size, shape, and shelf life, one of the features that also figures in the formation of my preference function is banana production conditions: I *care* about the terms under which banana labor is conducted. One of the leaflets published by the Fairtrade Foundation states: "The Fairtrade Mark guarantees farmers and plantation workers the opportunity to improve their lives." Doesn't my concern for their lives being improved have some clear altruistic implication for the correct understanding of my shopping choice? If, for the same higher price that I paid for the six fair trade

---

[1] Alternative and more complex accounts of the reason why fair trade bananas might be more expensive than their counterparts are that the latter's production was subsidized (presumably, though not necessarily, by taxpayers) and that the fair trade bananas were subject to some import duty or surcharge, from which their counterparts were exempted. Both reasons, I would argue, can also be construed as involving exploitation, though not necessarily exploitation of banana producers. See Steiner 1984, 1987, 1994, 2010, 2013, 2018a, 2018b.

[2] Relevant here is the acclaimed work of mathematical economist Kelvin Lancaster, who proposes a pathbreaking revision of standard microeconomic demand theory: "The chief technical novelty lies in breaking away from the traditional approach that goods are the direct objects of utility and, instead, supposing that it is the properties or characteristics of the goods from which utility is derived" (Lancaster 1966, 133).

bananas, I could have purchased—but didn't—a non-fair-trade bunch of seven bananas, how else, other than by reference to altruism, can my actual choice be explained? And if altruism is indeed the correct explanans of my preference ordering here, wouldn't I have been doing a morally equivalent thing by instead purchasing the non-fair-trade bunch (of six) and donating the 15 percent, which I would thereby save, to a charity that supplies those banana growers with, say, decent housing?

The answer to this latter question is no, and it very much relies upon a distinction, not always clear, that is sometimes drawn between *concern* and *respect*.[3] It would be not respect but rather my *concern* for their lives being improved that would lead me to prefer the donation route. Why?

We get a tighter grip on this, I think, when we consider the significance of those two purchasing options of mine under the following imagined condition. Suppose I have good reason to believe that what those banana growers will probably do with any higher wage they receive is to spend that increment not on better housing, but rather on things like unskillful gambling, excessive drinking, and other self-harming activities. In this circumstance, my concern for them should rationally lead me to prefer the donation route over the fair trade route. Their own interests, most would agree, are uncontroversially better served by being decently housed than by contracting cirrhosis of the liver and oppressive gambling debts. So if what I want is that their lives go better, I should see to it that the benefits of my 15 percent are conferred on them in kind and not in cash. I should *resist* the urgings of the fair trade movement and, instead, give that money to Oxfam, Christian Aid, or Médecins Sans Frontières. Consigning my 15 percent to the vagaries of those workers' consumption preferences looks, at best, to be an irresponsible gamble on my part.

How, then, can the fair trade movement hope to motivate rational shoppers? What is it that it must appeal to, in order to counteract their worry that their money is in danger of being wasted? In other words, what distinctive value does it—at least implicitly—invoke in trying to persuade me not to go down the donation route with my 15 percent?

An indication of what's involved here is to be found in that same pamphlet statement I quoted previously: "The Fairtrade Mark guarantees farmers and plantation workers the *opportunity* to improve their lives" (emphasis added). As we all know, from current debates about the nature of distributive justice,

---

[3] See Dworkin 1977, xii, 182, and chs. 9 and 12; Sartorius 1984, 208–209.

to give persons the *opportunity* to do or have X is significantly different from simply giving them X. Crucially, it is to give them the *not* doing or having of X as an option rather than as an impossibility: it is to give them a *choice*. What the fair trade movement wants is that those banana growers be given the choice not to improve their lives.

Now, why on earth should I, as a rational shopper, collaborate in that kind of exercise? It's not as though I harbor some ill will against these banana growers: I don't *want* them to contract cirrhosis of the liver or oppressive gambling debts—very much the contrary. So why should I prefer to dispose of my 15 percent in such a way as to raise the probability of that happening, rather than use it to support the various effective life-improving programs of Oxfam, Christian Aid, and Médecins Sans Frontières?

One widely canvassed response, which I'm going to reject, is that while it's undeniably true that what these charities supply are various important life-improving goods and services, it's also true that being given choices is yet another important form of life improvement. So if I do indeed care about the lives of these banana growers being improved, I should be concerned not only about their housing, nutrition, and medical care but also about their being given choices. That is to say, their interests encompass having choices as well as having enhanced welfare. And that's why my 15 percent should go down the fair trade route.

This is indeed a good response, but not quite good enough. It's certainly true that acquiring choices is often a very important form of life improvement. But it's obviously not the only such form. And this implies that, in a world of limited resources, whether going down the fair trade route would supply *enough* life improvement will always be a matter of contingency. More specifically, rational shoppers who share a concern for the improvement of those lives would need to consider whether their 15 percent will bring about *more* of that life improvement by being bestowed in choice-conferring cash than in charity-conferred kind. And the answer to that question, far from being given a priori, is bound to vary from case to case.

Yet many fair trade campaigns make virtually no mention of this variability. In soliciting our custom for fair trade produce—in asking us to bestow our 15 percent in cash—they often offer us no description at all of the consumption patterns of their intended beneficiaries.[4] Nor, I think it's reasonable

---

[4] At this point, I should note that this is predominantly not true in regard to much of the fair trade movement as it currently conducts itself. For the benefits of most actual fair trade agreements

to suppose, do they consider that we should take those consumption patterns into account when we make our own shopping decisions.

Is this simply cavalier on those campaigns' part? Is it an impertinence, so to speak—asking us to make sacrifices on behalf of outcomes that, unlike the aforementioned charities, they are unwilling even to specify, let alone promise?

I think not. In urging us to increase banana growers' scope for choices rather than their welfare, what those fair traders are implicitly appealing to is *respect* and, specifically, respect for those workers as autonomous agents. The fair traders are asking me to hand over my 15 percent to these workers without regard to whether they will spend it wisely or foolishly. Now, it's pretty clear that this is *not* the sort of request with which we'd be inclined to comply if it were made on behalf, say, of our very young children. And the reason for that disinclination, obviously enough, is that—much as we love them and are deeply concerned for their welfare—we don't consider those children to be autonomous agents.

This irrelevance, of what my trading partners will do with the proceeds of our transactions, is very closely associated by Kant with the demands of justice:

> The concept [of justice] applies only to the relationship of a will to another person's will, not to his wishes or desires (or even just his needs), which are the concerns of acts of benevolence and charity. [Furthermore,] the concept of justice does not take into consideration the matter [content] of the will, that is, the end that a person intends to accomplish by means of the object that he wills; for example, we do not ask whether someone who buys wares from me for his own business will profit from that transaction. Instead, in applying the concept of justice we take into consideration only the form of the relationship between the wills insofar as they are regarded as free.[5]

today are not part of each worker's wage packet but rather go to their communities. And the range of projects they can be used to fund is typically restricted to investment in education, health care, and farming-related capital equipment. In that regard, the *moral* difference, between currently buying fair trade products and donating to those charities, is less than it would be if the 15 percent fair trade premium was paid directly to individual workers who were each vested with complete personal discretion over its expenditure. I'm very grateful to John O'Neill for drawing my attention to this fact.

[5] Kant 1965, 34.

So when Kant goes to do his shopping, what justice requires of him is that he consider only the relationship between his own scope for choice and that of those several agents whose respective goods he might alternatively purchase. What it does *not* require of him is that he consider their needs or purposes. Their needs or purposes may or may not command his respect: whether they do entirely depends on what they actually are. But what *must* command his respect—what he unconditionally owes respect to—is those persons themselves, inasmuch as they are autonomous agents. It is, if you like, their *purposiveness*, rather than their purposes, that is the proper object of the sense of respect that is clearly distinguishable from concern.

That these three ideas—justice, unconditional respect, and scope for choice—are intimately connected to one another is a view with a more than familiar ring to it. One of their more obvious points of intersection lies in the *will theory* model of rights, of which Kant was a major proponent. The will theory's central thesis is that to have a right is to have a protected choice: more specifically, it is to have the sole authority to decide whether the duty correlative to a claim right must, or need not, be performed.[6] This model of rights thereby offers considerable resistance to the view that justifications for *paternalistic* actions can be grounded in the rights of those actions' beneficiaries.[7] Hence, the association of the will theory with respect for personal autonomy is reasonably transparent, and is commonly seen as such. I would be acting paternalistically if, instead of buying the fair trade bananas, I were to purchase their non-fair-trade counterparts and donate my consequent 15 percent saving to one of those life-improving charities. That is, I'd thereby be sustaining the restriction on banana growers' scope for choice for the sake of advancing their interests, inasmuch as I'd at once be helping them to avoid the pitfalls of alcoholism and gambling indebtedness and be meeting some of their vital needs. My action would thus certainly reflect my *concern* for them. But, equally, I'd be failing to *respect* them by thereby denying them that scope for choice.

At this point, however, a serious problem evidently presents itself to us. For it's plain that I could increase their scope for choice by *far more* than this. I could choose to pay not merely 15 percent more for their bananas but

---

[6] See Steiner 1998, 239–247. By extension, one can also be said to have a will theory right if one has the sole authority to decide whether the Hohfeldian disability correlative to an immunity is or is not extinguished.

[7] It offers resistance inasmuch as a paternalistic action is one directed by an intention to override other persons' own wishes for the sake of their own interests. See Steiner 1998, 281–282, 286–288.

20 percent or 30 percent more. And on the line of reasoning pursued thus far, I'd thereby be showing those growers even more unconditional respect: I'd be enlarging their respective domains, for exercising their autonomous discretion, that much more. How can that possibly fail to be morally preferable?

Kant supplies a small part of the answer. Justice, inasmuch as what it ordains is a relationship between my own scope for choice and those of the banana growers, thereby requires us to see to it that these respective discretionary domains bear a certain *proportion* to each other. And, to make a long story very short, that required proportion is one of equality.[8] As long as any action, including any transaction, occurs within a framework where each person has an equal such domain, it cannot be unjust.

Let me hasten to add, by way of clarification, that each person having an equal such domain is not to be understood in a synchronic (what Nozick calls a "time-slice") manner. If one banana grower loses some of his time T_1 wages in unskillful gambling while another does not, the resultant inequality that obtains between them at time T_2 is *not* thereby in contravention of the equal domains requirement: it's not *that* inequality that justice requires me to remedy by paying my 15 percent more. The justice requirement is to be understood, rather, as a "starting gate" one. That is, the equality it ordains is that of a level playing field, and not what I'll call a *system of reiterative equalization*: a system that is designed to offset whatever differential personal outcomes may emerge from autonomous choices made in the course of play. For such reiterative equalization would, indeed, betoken *dis*respect for the players involved. Its particular redistributive character would be such that, in the interests of its net beneficiaries, it discounts the fact that their respective outcomes were the foreseeable results of choices made by them.

So why would justice not require me to pay 20 percent or 30 percent more for fair trade bananas? It's important, incidentally, to note that this is a question specifically about *justice*, and not about morality in general. And the answer to it is that while my paying 20 percent or 30 percent more would indeed still further enlarge those growers' discretionary domains, it would diminish mine *below* the just proportionality required to prevail between our domains. Of course, if I wish to diminish my domain and to enlarge theirs to that greater extent, my doing so would not be unjust, and it might even be morally required. But that requirement would be one enjoined not by justice but rather by some other aspect of morality—perhaps benevolence or

---

[8] Cf. Kant 1965, 37–39; Steiner 1994, 208–228.

charity. For starting-gate equality in no way prohibits me from acting altruistically toward any fellow autonomous agent, as long as it's solely at my own expense. The justice-required equality of my scope for choice with that of others is not such as to prohibit me from choosing to reduce my scope to less than theirs. What it prohibits is that reduction being done by the choice of anyone other than me.

The idea here is that paying 15 percent more for our bananas is the price of *not exploiting* banana growers: it's what we must do in order to avoid taking unjust advantage of them. Why would paying less than that be unjust? After all, injustice is standardly understood as consisting in the violation of moral *rights*. And it's certainly not obvious that paying less than that extra 15 percent would be violating any right that banana growers have. In the absence of a prior contract, no one has a *right* that I purchase their wares, let alone a right that I purchase them at a certain price.[9] I would certainly not be violating anyone's rights by simply refusing to buy any bananas at all. In what sense, then, do I commit an injustice if I buy non-fair-trade bananas at their lower price?

Let's take a step back and approach the answer to this question slightly obliquely. It's a notable fact that one thing most current theories of distributive justice tend to lack is an articulated conception of *exploitation*. That is to say, most of them fail to provide an account of how a transaction—an exchange of goods or services between two parties—can be both voluntary and one in which the things exchanged are of unequal value. At best, what we usually get are some pretty unamplified references to opaque ideas like "taking unfair advantage" or to the only slightly less opaque idea of "unequal bargaining power." Yet no one imagines that for an exchange to be just or non-exploitative, the two parties to it must literally be equally wealthy. Rather, to describe a transaction as exploitative is simply to say two things: first, that its terms of exchange would be different if, counterfactually, certain relevant background circumstances were different; and second, that the actual background circumstances differ from those counterfactual counterparts in being unjust. So what is it that can make those actual circumstances unjust?

Consider the archetypal forum for a transaction: an auction. Here we have a banana grower, Blue, trying to sell a bunch of bananas. The winning bidder

---

[9] Ben Ferguson has plausibly suggested that while it's true that no one has a right that I purchase their wares, he might be said to have a *conditional* right that I, having decided to make such a purchase, pay them a fair price for it (personal communication).

is Red, who purchases them for $1.00. Under what circumstances could Blue justifiably complain that she's been exploited, that her bananas are worth more than that and should justly have attracted a bid of at least $1.15?

There is, in fact, a wide range of such circumstances, only a couple of which I'll detail here.[10] But one circumstance that would *not* warrant that complaint is that of other persons' preferences for bananas being sufficiently strong as to prompt them to bid that higher amount. This counterfactual circumstance does not warrant a complaint of injustice, for the simple reason that justice does not require us to have stronger preferences for bananas than we do have. Justice imposes no demands whatsoever on the content of our consumption preferences per se. Its demands pertain solely to aspects of the manner and circumstances in which we go about satisfying those preferences.

Now, one background circumstance that *could* warrant that complaint is that there was another person, Green, who would have paid $1.15 but who was forcibly prevented from bidding at that auction. Whether this consideration actually *does* warrant that charge must depend upon whether Green's forcible exclusion was itself unjust: that is, a violation of Green's rights. If it was, then it is true that, in the absence of that prior injustice, the auction would have yielded a higher price for Blue's bananas than the $1.00 she received.

An alternative background circumstance that could warrant that complaint is that Blue *herself* previously suffered a rights violation—say, was robbed—and this resulted in the lowering of her *reserve price* for the auctioned bananas. Her set of indifference curves is such that, prior to that robbery, she simply would not have sold the bananas for as little as $1.00. Following the robbery, the consequent lowering of her budget line, in conjunction with that same set of indifference curves, entails that she does better to sell them at that price than not to sell them at all. Again, of course, whether this consideration actually *does* warrant the complaint of injustice must depend upon whether what Blue was robbed of was something to which she was justly entitled.

So in both of these cases and in the numerous possible variations on them, what makes that $1.00 price exploitative and unjust is the fact that those bananas would not have sold for less than $1.15 if a prior injustice—a previous rights violation—had not occurred. Red, as the winning $1.00 bidder, has (wittingly or unwittingly) benefited from the occurrence of that prior

---

[10] For more extensive lists, see Steiner 1984, 1987.

injustice, to the tune of 15 percent. That amount is what counts as the *surplus value* that Red has gained from this exchange. It's this more precise rendering of the otherwise amorphous notion of "taking unfair advantage" that conveys what is unjust about exploitation.[11] For although in that transaction Red has clearly not violated any of Blue's rights, the surplus value he has gained from it is *tainted* by the injustice of that prior rights violation, inasmuch as the terms of that transaction are a direct result of that rights violation.[12]

Now, I take it that no extended argument is needed to associate rights violations with failures to treat their victims with the kind of respect they are owed as autonomous agents. In Kantian terms, such violations curtail their victims' rightful scope for choice and thereby destroy the proportionality that justice requires to obtain between these victims' discretionary domains and those of the violations' perpetrators. So there seems to be no good reason to deny that if the injustice of rights violations is, so to speak, transmitted to the exploitations that result from them, the same transmission effect holds in regard to respect: *disrespect supervenes upon injustice*. Red, in taking unfair advantage of Blue by exploiting her, is denying her the respect he owes to her. To avoid banana growers incurring what I'll call a *respect deficit* on my account, I should not buy bananas for less than the 15 percent extra charged for fair trade bananas.

Finally, then, a brief and inadequate word about bargaining, and about how the foregoing account of respect might bear on it. Very commonly, and unlike supermarket shopping, the precise terms of a contemplated exchange are not fixed in advance and, hence, are ones over which people bargain. The terrain on which that bargaining takes place is located in whatever utility space lies between their respective reserve prices for the goods or services each wishes to exchange. Sometimes no such space exists: their respective reserve prices coincide and, consequently, they exchange at that price, with no significant bargaining involved at all.

But often there *is* some such space, and bargaining determines the division of that utility space between them: that is, how much more than their respective reserve prices they will each get if they exchange. So if I'm bargaining

---

[11] It's this rendering that also explains why exchanges between unequally wealthy parties need not be exploitative and, indeed, why it is possible—however unlikely—for a less wealthy person to exploit her more wealthy counterpart.

[12] Moreover, the fact of Blue's bananas having undersold entails that her reserve price as a bidder at subsequent auctions will be lower than it would otherwise have been, and may thus generate another underselling, which in turn may serially generate further undersellings: *exploitations compound*.

with a banana grower, my reserve price is the minimum number of bananas I'll accept in return for, say, $1.00 of my money. And, conversely, her reserve price is the minimum amount of money she'll accept in return for, say, six of her bananas. If my minimum happens to be six bananas, and hers is $1.00, then there's no bargaining to be done and we simply exchange at that price.

Suppose, however, that although her reserve price for six bananas is $1.00, I'd be willing to pay up to $1.15 for six of her bananas. This difference opens up a 15-cent space for bargaining. And the question we need to ask is whether it's okay for me to try to bargain for any of that space or, indeed, as much of it as I can get. Is it permissible for me to try to strike a deal at, say, $1.03 for her six bananas, and thereby capture 80 percent of that space?

Now what's true is that, in general, we're inclined to think that bargained terms *must* be permissible ones. For since, *ex hypothesi*, they are struck within the area of intersection between what's respectively acceptable to each transacting party, on what possible grounds could some uninvolved third party gainsay those terms and declare a particular struck bargain to be *un*acceptable? Wouldn't this be yet another instance of paternalism trying to raise its unattractive—and disrespectful—head? After all, such transactions are ones that, in Mill's phrase, occur between consenting adults. Such transactions must be presumed to be Pareto-optimal, inasmuch as both of the parties to them do as well as they can, given their respective preference orderings.

And yet, as the foregoing account of exploitation suggests, not every set of terms within that bargaining space is necessarily just. Whether some particular set of terms—some particular price—is just depends entirely on whether either of the boundaries of that space is located where it is by virtue of some prior injustice. The boundaries of the space we're considering here are, respectively, my $1.15 reserve price and that banana grower's $1.00. Suppose, however, that sometime prior to our negotiation, her reserve price for six of her bananas had been $1.10, and that what caused it to drop to only $1.00 was her then being robbed. What this entails, as we've seen, is that in the absence of that unjust robbery she would not have sold her bananas for less than $1.10, and that were she now to sell them for less than that amount, she would be thereby exploited. Accordingly, were I successfully to press her, in the course of our bargaining, to sell them to me for as little as $1.03, I would be exploiting her. That is, although the *actual* bargaining space between us is 15 cents, the *justly permissible* space is only 5 cents—the distance between $1.10 and $1.15. My pressing her *below* $1.10, my capturing *more* than 33 percent of our actual bargaining space, would amount to my showing her less than the respect to which she's entitled from me.

In short, while bargaining per se entails no disrespect, and while interference with its outcomes *can* do so, such interference is nevertheless warranted—and warranted on grounds of respect itself—when those outcomes fall outside the range of terms that might have been struck in the absence of prior injustice.

References

Dworkin, Ronald. 1977. *Taking Rights Seriously*. Cambridge, MA: Harvard University Press.

Kant, Immanuel. 1965. *The Metaphysical Elements of Justice*. Translated and edited by John Ladd. Indianapolis: Bobbs-Merrill, 1965.

Lancaster, Kelvin. 1966. "A New Approach to Consumer Theory." *Journal of Political Economy* 74: 132–157.

Sartorius, Rolf. 1984. "Dworkin on Rights and Utilitarianism." In *Ronald Dworkin and Contemporary Jurisprudence*, edited by Marshall Cohen, 208–209. London: Duckworth.

Steiner, Hillel. 1984. "A Liberal Theory of Exploitation." *Ethics* 94: 225–241.

Steiner, Hillel. 1987. "Exploitation: A Liberal Theory Amended, Defended and Extended." In *Modern Theories of Exploitation*, edited by A. Reeve, 132–148. London: Sage.

Steiner, Hillel. 1994. *An Essay on Rights*. Oxford: Blackwell.

Steiner, Hillel. 2010. "Exploitation Takes Time." In *Economic Theory and Economic Thought: Essays in Honour of Ian Steedman*, edited by J. Vint, J. S. Metcalfe, H. D. Kurz, N. Salvadori, and P. A. Samuelson, 20–29. London: Routledge.

Steiner, Hillel. 2013. "Liberalism, Neutrality and Exploitation." *Politics, Philosophy and Economics* 12: 335–344.

Steiner, Hillel. 2018a. "Exploitation, Intentionality and Injustice." *Economics and Philosophy* 34: 369–379.

Steiner, Hillel. 2018b. "Free Markets and Exploitation." In *Routledge Handbook of Libertarianism*, edited by J. Brennan, B. van der Vossen, and D. Schmidtz, 436–446. London: Routledge.

PART II
WHAT MAKES EXPLOITATION WRONG

6
Who Is Wronged by Wrongful Exploitation?

Brian Berkey

In paradigmatic cases of wrongful exploitation, the exploiting party takes advantage of the exploited party, or of a feature or set of features of the exploited party or their circumstances, in order to obtain benefits that would not have been available in the absence of the opportunity to exploit.[1] Most accounts of wrongful exploitation explain its wrongness in terms of an allegedly morally objectionable feature of the interaction between the exploiter and the exploited.[2] More precisely, these accounts tend to be aimed at explaining what is distinctively wrong with *transactions* that are exploitative despite being both voluntarily agreed to and mutually beneficial (Meyers 2004; Zwolinski 2007; Powell and Zwolinski 2012; Dänzer 2014; Ferguson 2016; Faraci 2019; Kates 2019, 28–29; Miklós 2019). This is because while interactions that are non-voluntary or harmful to the interests of at least one of the parties can also be exploitative, the most challenging ethical questions are raised by cases involving voluntary and mutually beneficial transactions that seem, intuitively, to be wrongfully exploitative.

The primary reason that voluntary and mutually beneficial transactions have been thought to raise a distinctive challenge for accounts of wrongful exploitation is that, at least in many of the central cases discussed in the literature (e.g., much sweatshop labor), the view that the transactions are wrongfully exploitative conflicts with an intuitively appealing claim, which Alan Wertheimer calls the "Nonworseness Claim" (1996, p. 289). In its most general form, the non-worseness claim states that it cannot be morally worse for a person A to engage in a voluntary and mutually beneficial transaction

---

[1] For the claim that advantage-taking in order to obtain benefits is an essential component of any account of exploitation, see Vrousalis 2018, 2.

[2] An exception is the indirect consequentialist account of the value of anti-exploitation norms offered by Richard Arneson (2013). For critical discussion of Arneson's view, see Sample 2016.

with another person B than it is for A to refrain from transacting with B altogether.³ The claim is appealing because the very same concern for the interests of those whom we tend to think are wrongfully exploited that motivates our objections to intuitively exploitative conduct seems to give us reason to reject any view on which it is better, morally speaking, to do nothing to improve their lives than it is to transact with them in ways that benefit them at least a bit (so long as they agree to the transaction).

When combined with the claim that it is permissible for an allegedly exploiting party to refrain from transacting with an allegedly exploited party, the non-worseness claim implies that the allegedly exploiting party's action is not morally worse than a permissible option. If we make the plausible assumption that options that are not morally worse than a permissible option are themselves permissible,⁴ then the conjunction of the non-worseness claim and the permissibility of refraining from transacting entails the permissibility of transacting on any terms that are both mutually beneficial and voluntarily accepted. And since it is widely assumed that at least many intuitively exploitative transactions are ones that it would be morally permissible for the allegedly exploiting party to refrain from engaging in altogether,⁵ those who aim to offer accounts of wrongful exploitation that can capture widely held intuitions both about which transactions are wrongfully exploitative and about which transactions it is permissible to refrain from engaging in generally reject the non-worseness claim (Meyers 2004; Snyder 2008, 402–403; Snyder 2013, 358; Preiss 2014; Faraci 2019; Kates 2019).

It is unsurprising that those who aim to provide an account of the wrongness of intuitively exploitative yet voluntary and mutually beneficial transactions, while holding that at least some of these transactions are ones that it would be permissible for the exploiting party to refrain from engaging in altogether, tend to claim that there are features of the transactions that explain their wrongness that would not be present if the exploiting party chose not to transact at all. After all, if such features can explain the

---

³ For roughly this formulation of the claim, though without the explicit limitation to voluntary transactions, see Wertheimer 1996, 289; Snyder 2008, 390; Bailey 2011, 238; Barnes 2013, 28. For explicit inclusion of the limitation to voluntary transactions, see Faraci 2019, 170. For formulations that include both this limitation and a requirement that no third parties are harmed, see Ferguson 2016, 956; Malmqvist 2017, 478). I discuss several variants of the claim in Berkey 2021.
⁴ For discussion of this claim, see Bailey 2011; Pummer 2016, 2019; Horton 2017; Berkey 2020a; Ferguson and Köhler 2020.
⁵ For this claim with reference to intuitively exploitative sweatshop employment transactions, see Meyers 2004; Zwolinski 2007, 699; Zwolinski 2012, 169; Barnes 2013, 38; Kates 2019, 27, 34; Preiss 2018, 885–886, 890.

wrongness of intuitively exploitative transactions, and are absent when no transaction takes place, then we will also have an explanation of how it can be possible for non-transaction to be permissible despite the fact that a wrongfully exploitative transaction would be both voluntary and beneficial to the exploited party.

The most commonly accepted view is that the feature of wrongfully exploitative transactions that explains why they are wrong is that the benefits that they produce are distributed unfairly.[6] Others have argued that the wrongness of exploitative transactions is explained by the fact that they are disrespectful or degrading (Wood 1995; Sample 2003). Because these accounts locate the wrongness of the exploiters' actions entirely in features that are claimed to be *internal* to the relevant transactions, the explanations they offer do not provide any grounds for objecting to non-transaction on the part of (potential) exploiting parties.

An additional implication of views on which the wrong-making features of wrongful exploitation are internal to exploitative transactions is that only parties to such transactions can be *directly wronged* by the exploiting parties in virtue of the fact that their conduct is wrongfully exploitative.[7] One is directly wronged by another's wrongful conduct only if one has an undefeated complaint on her own behalf against the agent for engaging in the wrongful conduct. One is directly wronged in virtue of the fact that another's conduct is wrongfully exploitative only if the features of the conduct that make it wrongfully exploitative contribute to grounding an undefeated complaint on one's own behalf against the agent for engaging in the wrongful conduct. If the features that make conduct wrongfully exploitative are necessarily internal to exploitative transactions, then only those who are parties to the transactions can have complaints on their own behalf in virtue of the fact that those wrong-making features are present.

I suspect that many proponents of views on which the wrong-making features of wrongful exploitation are internal to exploitative transactions

---

[6] Fairness-based views are accepted by Wertheimer (1996, ch. 7), Meyers (2004, 320–321), Mayer (2007a, 137–138, 141–142; 2007b, 608), Barnes (2013, 31), Dänzer (2014), Ferguson (2016, 953, 955, 966–967; 2021); Sollars and Englander (2018, 23–27), Faraci (2019), and Kates (2019, 33–34, 44–45). I suggest that these views tend to rely on an overly narrow account of the value of fairness and its relevance to the ethics of employment (Berkey 2020b).

[7] Conduct that is wrong in part because it is exploitative will sometimes be wrong for additional reasons as well. In those cases, views on which the wrong-making features of wrongful exploitation are internal to the relevant transactions can allow that individuals who are not among the parties to the transactions might be directly wronged by the exploiters, but this will have to be explained by reasons that do not play a role in making it the case that the conduct is wrongfully exploitative.

would take the fact that only parties to such transactions can be directly wronged to be an appealing feature of the general approach to explaining the wrong of wrongful exploitation that their views represent. On views of this kind, exploitation directly wrongs the exploited parties to wrongfully exploitative transactions, and *only those parties*. In the case of sweatshop employment, for example, only those employed in sweatshop labor could be directly wronged. Others might, of course, be indirectly wronged. For example, the children of an exploited sweatshop worker might be indirectly wronged by her employer's conduct, since they would be better off if their mother's wages and working conditions were not exploitative. But since failing to make those children better off is not, on the relevant views, among the features of the employer's conduct that makes it wrongfully exploitative, the children are not directly wronged.

The overall picture that follows from views on which the wrong-making features of wrongful exploitation are internal to exploitative transactions, then, is that the exploited parties to such transactions are the only directly wronged parties, and that any indirectly wronged parties must have undefeated complaints against the exploiters' conduct that are grounded in facts about how the exploitation of the directly wronged parties has affected their morally relevant interests.[8] Many will find views of this kind appealing. After all, when we are confronted with the question of who is wronged by, for example, sweatshop employment, the obvious answer is that it is those who are employed in sweatshop labor.

In the remainder of this chapter, however, I will argue that there are strong reasons to think that in some cases of wrongful exploitation, individuals who are not parties to the relevant transactions are as seriously and as directly wronged as the exploited parties to those transactions. Specifically, I claim that when we expand our focus beyond the exploitative transactions themselves, and reflect on the broader context within which many such transactions take place, we should recognize that exploitation often wrongs a much broader class of agents than those who are taken advantage of within them.[9] In particular, I argue that in at least many cases, those who would have preferred to occupy the place of the exploited party to a transaction, but were

---

[8] The range of potentially morally relevant interests that might ground claims to have been indirectly wronged can be understood quite broadly, so the claim here is compatible with any plausible moral theory and associated account of individuals' morally relevant interests.

[9] In the remainder of the chapter I will omit the qualifier "directly" when referring to direct wrongs and variants of that notion (e.g., "wronged parties"). These references should be read as referring to direct wrongs unless otherwise noted.

not selected to participate in the transaction, are wronged by the exploiting party. If this is correct, it has important implications for how we ought to understand the wrong-making features of wrongful exploitation, and for how we ought to think about the remedial duties of wrongful exploiters.

I will proceed in the remainder of the chapter as follows. In section 1, I will discuss two types of cases in which it seems plausible that those who would have preferred to become (exploited) parties to an exploitative transaction, but were not selected as transaction partners, are wronged by the exploiting parties. And I will offer an initial explanation of why this conclusion seems appealing that relies on considerations that are similar to those that motivate the non-worseness claim (but does not, strictly speaking, require that the non-worseness claim is correct). Next, in section 2, I will describe some central components of an account of the wrong-making features of wrongful exploitation that is suggested by the argument in section 1, and suggest some reasons to find an account of this type plausible. Finally, in section 3, I will note what the arguments in sections 1 and 2 seem to imply with regard to the remedial duties of wrongful exploiters. I will contrast this view with one that has recently been defended by Erik Malmqvist and András Szigeti (2021), and argue that there are important reasons to prefer the view suggested by my argument.

1. Who Is Wronged by Wrongful Exploitation?

In some cases it is clear that wrongful exploitation wrongs only the exploited party to an exploitative transaction. Consider, for example, the following case:

One Dose of Drug, One Person in Need: A has one dose of drug D, for which he paid the market price of $10. B has a medical condition that is fatal unless treated with one dose of D. There are no other sources of D to which B can gain access in time to save her life, and there is no one else in danger of dying whom A could save using his dose. A offers to give the dose to B in exchange for 90 percent of the income that she will earn for the remainder of her life. B accepts A's offer.[10]

---

[10] This is a sight variant on a case that I provide in Berkey 2021. For similar cases, see Zwolinski 2012, 156; Vrousalis 2018, 2.

In this case, it is clear that A wrongs B, and that this wrong is plausibly understood as a wrong of exploitation. A takes advantage of B's condition, and the desperate circumstances that she is in because of it, in order to obtain substantial benefits for himself. B clearly has a strong complaint on her own behalf against A's conduct. And because no one else has any similar complaint on their own behalf, it seems clear that B is the only person who is wronged by A's exploitative conduct.

It is also worth noting that in this case the fact that the transaction is mutually beneficial does not present any grounds for skepticism about the claim that A is guilty of wrongful exploitation. This is because he is obligated to provide the dose to B for at most a reasonable price (perhaps the $10 market price). Because refraining from transacting with B is not a permissible option, the non-worseness claim cannot be appealed to in order to suggest that the intuitively exploitative yet voluntary and mutually beneficial transaction must be permissible. So even defenders of the claim should accept that this is a clear and uncontroversial case of a voluntary, mutually beneficial transaction that is wrongfully exploitative and wrongs the exploited party.

If we adjust the details of the case in a particular way, however, an important reason to doubt that only those who are parties to an exploitative transaction can be wronged becomes clear. Consider the following case:

> *One Dose of Drug, Ten People in Need*: A has one dose of drug D, for which he paid the market price of $10. Ten people have a medical condition that is fatal unless treated with one dose of D. There are no other sources of D to which any of the ten can gain access in time to save their lives. None of the ten has any special entitlement to A's dose. A offers to give the dose to any one of the ten in exchange for 90 percent of the income that she will earn for the remainder of her life. All ten clearly indicate that they would like to accept this offer—indeed, each begs A to choose her. A gives the dose to B, with the result that the remaining nine all die.[11]

It seems clear that A is just as guilty of wrongful exploitation in this case as he was in the previous case. Once again, the fact that the transaction is voluntary and mutually beneficial provides no grounds for skepticism, since A is obligated to provide the dose to one of the ten and to charge no more than a reasonable price—refraining from transacting is not a permissible option.

---

[11] This is also a slight variant of a case from Berkey 2021.

In this case, however, it does not seem especially plausible to think that A wrongs B *and only B*. B is the only one of the ten people in need of the drug who was a party to the exploitative transaction, so any view on which only parties to an exploitative transaction can be wronged by wrongful exploitation will imply that only B is wronged. There are, however, several reasons to find this implication troubling. First, A did not owe it to B in particular to provide her with the dose of D for at most a reasonable price. It would have been equally permissible for him to give it to any of the other nine for a reasonable price.[12] In comparison with a range of permissible options, then, A's exploitative conduct was *much better for* B and much worse for each of the other nine than the option in which she is selected for the transaction. Because each of the ten is identically situated prior to the point at which B is selected for the transaction, and because B's selection is much better for her than it is for the others despite the fact that the transaction is clearly wrongfully exploitative, there seems to be good reason to think that if B has a complaint on her own behalf against A's conduct, then each of the others has one as well. And since B and each of the others quite reasonably prefers being selected for the exploitative transaction over not being selected, it also seems implausible to think that B's complaint is significantly stronger than those of the others. Indeed, if anything, the others' complaints would appear to be stronger.

Of course, since A has only one dose of the drug, none of the ten can have a legitimate complaint to the effect that she in particular was not given the drug for a reasonable price. Each can complain only that A failed to provide it to one of the ten for at most a reasonable price. Importantly, this complaint precisely tracks the nature of the wrong that A commits. A is obligated to provide the drug to one of the ten, and to charge at most a reasonable price. Because of this, it seems correct that each of the ten has a complaint on her own behalf when A fails to discharge his obligation. Any view that implies that only B is wronged by A's exploitative conduct in this case, then, would seem to be grounded in an inaccurate view about the nature of the wrong that A commits, since such views are incompatible with recognizing that the nine who are not selected to be parties to the transaction have complaints on their

---

[12] Perhaps in cases of this kind those in A's position are obligated to conduct a fair lottery to determine who will get the dose. My argument that giving the dose to B at an exploitative price does not wrong only B does not depend on either accepting or rejecting this requirement.

own behalf that are at least comparable in strength to B's complaint, and are therefore comparably wronged.

The central feature of the case that generates the challenge to the view that only B is wronged is that prior to its becoming the case that B is the exploited party within the relevant transaction, the exploiting party makes a choice about with whom he will transact, from among a group all of whom reasonably prefer to be selected for the transaction (despite the fact that it will be wrongfully exploitative). When this is the case, I submit, it is implausible to hold that only those who are selected for a voluntary, mutually beneficial transaction that is nonetheless wrongfully exploitative are wronged by the exploiting party. After all, in such cases the exploited party to the transaction is at least made somewhat better off in a way that she consents to, while those who are not selected for the transaction are left in the very conditions that made them vulnerable to exploitation in the first place. The fact that they are not parties to the exploitative transaction is not a reason to think that they can have no complaint on their own behalf against the conduct of the exploiting party, and so not a reason to think that they cannot be wronged by that party's wrongfully exploitative action.

It might be objected that while A does wrong all ten of the people in need of the drug, he commits the distinctive wrong of exploitation only against B.[13] Perhaps, for example, A wrongs all ten by making an exploitative proposal to them. Since the proposal was directed to all of them, all have the same complaint on their own behalf against A for making the wrongful proposal. But, the objection suggests, the other nine do not have a complaint on their own behalf against A for transacting on the proposed terms with B. Perhaps all ten would have a complaint on their own behalf if A gave the dose to no one, but so long as he gives it to one of the ten, those who do not receive it can have no complaints on their own behalf against A for transacting on the terms that he does with the one who does receive it.

There are two related reasons why we should find this objection unconvincing. The first is that it would seem to require that we think that prior to the time at which it becomes the case that B is selected for the transaction, the only duty that A has to the ten is to ensure that one of them receives the dose. This is because if he owes it to each of the ten to provide one of them with the dose for no more than a reasonable price, then all of the ten will have a complaint on their own behalf if he violates that duty—when one violates

---

[13] Thanks to Ben Ferguson and Matt Zwolinski for encouraging me to discuss this objection.

a duty that is owed to particular people, those people have grounds for complaint on their own behalf that those to whom the duty is not owed do not have.[14] It seems more natural, however, to think that A's duty to each of the ten is, from the start, to provide the dose to one of them at no more than a reasonable price, as opposed to thinking that he is first obligated to the ten to provide the dose to one of them, and then, once B has been selected to receive it, obligated to her to refrain from charging more than a reasonable price.

The second reason to find the objection unconvincing is that by transacting with B on wrongfully exploitative terms, A acts without proper regard for the interests of all ten of those in need, and indicates that he is unwilling to forgo the gains that he can obtain by insisting on exploitative terms in order to promote their interests as much as morality requires. Insofar as A's insisting on exploitative terms in his transaction with B makes it clear that he has insufficient regard or concern for the interests of all of those who are situated similarly to B, it provides all similarly situated individuals with grounds for a complaint on their own behalf against his conduct.[15]

While *One Dose of Drug, Ten People in Need* is a somewhat contrived example, in many cases that are thought to constitute paradigmatic examples of wrongful exploitation via voluntary, mutually beneficial transactions, the exploiting parties select with whom they will transact from among large groups of individuals, all of whom hope to be chosen. Consider, for example, the following quite realistic case involving sweatshop employment:

> *Sweatshop Hiring*: Firm F opens a sweatshop in a large city in a poor country. It advertises five hundred jobs in the facility that require very long hours in poor and relatively unsafe working conditions, for rather low wages that are insufficient to meet even the basic needs of a typical worker and her family. Because the wages offered by the sweatshop are nonetheless higher than

---

[14] Of course, everyone is entitled to complain on behalf of the moral community at large whenever one violates a duty.

[15] It might be suggested that A's insisting on exploitative terms in his transaction with B also suggests that he would have insufficient concern for the interests of virtually anyone, should they have been among those in need of the drug. It might then be objected that my argument therefore implies that anyone to whom A would refuse to provide the drug without extracting a wrongfully exploitative price has a complaint on their own behalf against A's conduct. This objection is unpersuasive, however, since there is a distinction between actually possessing the interests that one who engages in wrongful exploitation disregards, on the one hand, and it being the case that if one did possess those interests the wrongdoer would disregard them, on the other. There are good reasons to think that one has a complaint on one's own behalf only if one actually possesses the relevant interests (whereas anyone can object, as a matter of principle, to one's insufficient regard for the interests of others).

what typical residents of the city earn in the other forms of employment available to most people, ten thousand people apply for the positions. All of the applicants strongly prefer being chosen for one of the sweatshop jobs over continuing to work in their current occupations. F selects five hundred of the applicants and enters into voluntary and mutually beneficial yet nonetheless wrongfully exploitative employment contracts with them.

For reasons that are similar to those that made it difficult to accept that only B is wronged by A's wrongfully exploitative conduct in *One Dose of Drug, Ten People in Need*, it seems implausible that only the five hundred people hired by F are wronged by its exploitative conduct in this case. Those who are hired had no more of a claim to be hired than those who were not selected. And as a result of being hired, they are made better off, while those who were not selected remain in the worse conditions that made them vulnerable to exploitation in the first place. All of the applicants, we might think, have a complaint on their own behalf against F for its failure to provide fair or respectful or non-degrading wages and working conditions to those among the group who are hired. There is no compelling reason to think that only those who are actually hired are in a position to legitimately press this complaint on their own behalf. Prior to the firm deciding which five hundred applicants to hire, all of the applicants had the same legitimate interest in the terms of the subsequent transactions being fair/respectful/non-degrading, and none had a legitimate claim to be selected in preference to any of the others. Since those who are selected are made better off than those who are not, it seems objectionable to think that in being selected they acquire a strong complaint on their own behalf against F's conduct that those who are not as fortunate lack.

It is important to note that if my claims about who is wronged in *Sweatshop Hiring* are correct, then in many cases the group of individuals wronged by exploitative employers will be much larger than just those who applied for the positions that come to be occupied by exploited parties to the relevant transactions. To see why, consider the following extension of that case:

> *Sweatshop Siting and Hiring*: Firm F is deciding where to locate a new production site, where it will produce clothing and employ five hundred workers in sweatshop conditions. It has narrowed the options to cities X, Y, and Z. All of these cities contain large populations of impoverished citizens, and F can expect to receive at least ten thousand applications for the sweatshop jobs in whichever location it selects for the site. After

assessing the pros and cons of each location, a decision is made to locate the site in X. F advertises five hundred positions, selects five hundred of the ten thousand applicants to hire, and enters into voluntary and mutually beneficial yet nonetheless wrongfully exploitative employment contracts with them.

In this case, the same reasons that suggest that those who applied but were not hired in *Sweatshop Hiring* are wronged also suggest that those who would have applied had the site been located in their city are wronged by F's exploitative conduct. And once we recognize this, we can also see that there is no principled basis for limiting our account of who is wronged to those who would have applied and happen to live in cities that were actually considered by F as possible site locations. For example, those who live in cities that would have been suitable sites, and who would have applied had their city been considered and selected, seem to have the same relevant interests, and therefore the same basis for complaints on their own behalf, even if their city was not actually considered as a possible location for the site.

In addition to the reasons that are present in both *One Dose of Drug, Ten People in Need* and in both *Sweatshop* cases, there are further reasons that support the claim that all of those who would prefer being hired for a job in which they would be exploited over all of their other available alternatives are wronged by the exploiting parties. Most significantly, in typical labor market contexts, the presence of additional people who are both qualified and willing to accept employment of a particular type will tend to increase the bargaining power of employers and reduce the bargaining power of individual applicants, which in turn will tend to drive down wages and increase the profit margins that can be achieved by firms. Because of this, the presence of the ninety-five hundred applicants who are not hired in *Sweatshop Hiring* likely makes it possible for F to pay those who are hired less than it would have had to pay them if they were the only people willing to take the positions. There is, then, a fairly straightforward sense in which F takes advantage of the circumstances of the ninety-five hundred applicants who are not selected in order to obtain benefits that it could not have obtained in the absence of those people. It seems accurate, then, to say that F exploits these potential transaction partners in order to ensure that the terms of its exploitative transactions with those whom they do hire benefit them as much as possible, and more than those transactions would have benefited them had the additional potential transaction partners not been present.

And once we recognize that firms also take advantage of the fact that there are potential employees in one location in order to ensure that their transactions with those whom they hire in another location benefit them more than they would have had the potential employees elsewhere not been in the circumstances in which they find themselves, it seems correct to say that those potential employees are exploited as well. Firms that employ workers on wrongfully exploitative terms, then, often wrong a very large number of people in virtue of their exploitative conduct.

It is worth noting that in *One Dose of Drug, Ten People in Need*, it seems unlikely that the presence of the nine people who are not selected for the transaction would make it possible for A to benefit from his transaction with B more than he could in *One Dose of Drug, One Person in Need*. In those cases, each of the people in need would surely die without the drug, and so A is in a position to know that no matter how much he demands from B in either case, B will be willing to transact. A's bargaining power, then, cannot be expected to increase as the number of people who would prefer to be selected for the transaction increases.

This means that the case for thinking that those who would prefer to have been hired in the *Sweatshop* cases are wronged by F's exploitative conduct, despite not being parties to any transaction with F, is even stronger than the case for thinking that the nine people in need who are not selected to receive the drug in *One Dose of Drug, Ten People in Need* are wronged by A's exploitative conduct. And since the intuition that the nine who do not receive the drug are wronged by A is quite powerful, there are strong reasons to accept that the class of people wronged by the wrongfully exploitative employment practices of firms will often be very large.

I suspect that there are two main reasons why the view that wrongful exploitation can wrong people who are not parties to the relevant exploitative transactions has not previously been seriously considered in discussions of wrongful exploitation. The first is that in the cases that are typically discussed, any choices that might have been made about with whom the exploiting party will transact, from among a group of willing transaction partners not all of whom will be selected, are at best treated from the outset as irrelevant to understanding the particular wrong of exploitation, and are often ignored entirely.[16] What we should think about who is wronged in cases such as *One*

---

[16] As a representative example, consider that David Faraci opens his paper on wage exploitation (Faraci 2019) with a case involving a business owner and an employee, in which the employment relationship between the two has already been established, and the central question to be addressed

Dose of Drug, Ten People in Need, then, is not a question that has been seriously considered, since cases of this kind tend not to be explicitly discussed.

The second reason that the view that people who are not parties to exploitative transactions can be wronged by wrongful exploitation has not been seriously considered is that a central focus of many of those who hold that there is wrongful exploitation in cases such as the *Sweatshop* cases has been overcoming the challenge presented by the non-worseness claim (e.g., Meyers 2004; Barnes 2013; Faraci 2019; Kates 2019). It is typically assumed that proponents of that claim will deny that employers are guilty of wrongful exploitation in cases involving, for example, voluntary and mutually beneficial sweatshop employment, and so will deny that anyone is wronged as well.[17] In response, many have attempted to argue that, contrary to the claim, parties to a voluntary and mutually beneficial transaction can be wronged even in cases in which their transaction partners had no obligation to engage in the transaction in the first place. Because establishing this is their primary aim, the possibility that others might also be wronged in at least some cases of wrongful exploitation tends not to be considered.

If I am correct, however, this is an important oversight. If those who are not parties to wrongfully exploitative transactions can be wronged by the exploiting parties, this has implications for how we should understand the wrong-making features of wrongful exploitation, as well as for what we should think the remedial duties of those guilty of wrongful exploitation consist in. I will consider each of these issues in the following two sections.

2. The Wrong-Making Features of Wrongful Exploitation

In *One Dose of Drug, Ten People in Need*, A has an obligation to provide the dose to one of the ten for at most a reasonable price, but he is not obligated to provide it to any particular individual among the ten. By taking advantage

---

is whether the terms of employment are wrongfully exploitative despite the fact that they are voluntarily accepted and mutually beneficial, and despite the fact that the business owner had no obligation to hire or otherwise benefit the employee in the first place. I argue that Faraci's failure to consider the fact that business owners typically choose between applicants all of whom would prefer to be hired weakens his defense of a fairness-based account of the wrong of wage exploitation on which only those actually hired are wronged (Berkey 2020b).

[17] The discussions in Zwolinski (2007, 699–700) and in Powell and Zwolinski (2012) can plausibly be interpreted in this way. I argue that we should both accept a variant of the non-worseness claim and hold that much sweatshop employment is wrongfully exploitative (Berkey 2021).

of the desperate circumstances that B and the other nine find themselves in, A is able to obtain benefits that he could not have obtained had he not been in a position to exploit them. A's extracting an exploitative price for the drug from B makes it the case that he provides, on net, only a portion of the total benefit that he is obligated to provide to a member (though not any particular member) of the group of people in need.

In cases of this kind, then, the wrong of exploitation can plausibly be understood as consisting in certain ways of failing to satisfy positive duties to benefit others. When an agent has an independent obligation to benefit others to a certain extent, it is wrongfully exploitative to take advantage of the fact that others are in desperate need of a particular benefit that is among those that one is obligated to provide in order to extract benefits for oneself from the transaction in a way that makes it the case that the total amount of benefit provided to others is less than what one was morally obligated to provide.

In cases in which it is uncontroversial that an agent has a positive duty to benefit others, it is also uncontroversial that it is wrongfully exploitative to take advantage of those others and/or their circumstances in order to obtain benefits for oneself in a way that makes it the case that one fails to fully satisfy the positive duty. One important reason that this is uncontroversial is that it cannot be challenged by appeal to the non-worseness claim, since there is no permissible non-transaction baseline in comparison with which a voluntary and mutually beneficial yet intuitively wrongfully exploitative transaction is better for the exploited party. And because the positive duty in *One Dose of Drug, Ten People in Need* is not owed only to B, who happens to be the one selected for the transaction, but instead to all of the ten people in need, insofar as the wrong-making feature of A's wrongful exploitation is his failure to satisfy that positive duty, A's wrongful exploitation clearly wrongs all of them, since they are all equally owed the satisfaction of the duty.[18]

The *Sweatshop* cases are, of course, more challenging, since most people deny that firms have positive duties to benefit impoverished potential employees, either by hiring them or in some other way. I have elsewhere argued, however, that firms that benefit from global structural injustice do have obligations to benefit those who are unjustly disadvantaged, and that

---

[18] This is the case despite the fact that A's satisfaction of the duty can only in fact benefit one of the ten. The fact that they are all in need of the drug, and that A can help one of them at little or no cost to himself, makes it the case that he owes it to each of the ten to provide the drug to one of them for at most a reasonable price.

therefore the wrong of much exploitative sweatshop employment can be understood as consisting in the failure of such firms to satisfy those obligations (Berkey 2021).[19] If my argument succeeds, then at least many firms that exploit workers in sweatshops are guilty of a wrong that shares the central wrong-making features of A's conduct in *One Dose of Drug, Ten People in Need*. They might, for example, owe an obligation to all of the potential employees who would like to be selected for a job to hire a subset of them and provide wages and working conditions that meet a high enough standard to fully discharge the obligation.

While I believe that this will often be the correct explanation of the wrong that firms such as F in *Sweatshop Siting and Hiring* are guilty of, the conclusion that exploitative firms wrong all of those who would prefer to be hired for their exploitative positions, and not just those who are actually employed in those positions, does not depend on it. This is because even if firms do not have an unconditional obligation to hire or otherwise benefit badly off people who are vulnerable to exploitation, my discussion of the *Sweatshop* cases provides grounds for concluding that if a firm in fact hires people on exploitative terms, it wrongs all of those who would have preferred to be hired for the relevant positions. This can be explained in terms of a *conditional obligation* of the kind that those who reject the Nonworseness Claim typically endorse (e.g., Kates 2019, 34).

On these accounts, a firm has no obligation to hire badly off people whom it could wrongfully exploit, but conditional on actually hiring some such people, it acquires an obligation to provide them with wages and working conditions that meet certain standards (e.g., of fairness or respect). If the firm hires people on terms that do not meet these standards, it wrongfully exploits and thereby wrongs those people, and because the obligation comes to be owed to the particular people hired only once the condition of their having been hired is met, only these people are wronged by the firm's wrongful exploitation.

Once we recognize that those who are not hired but would prefer to have been have complaints on their own behalf that are at least comparable in strength to those of the people who are hired and exploited, however, we should be led to understand the structure of firms' conditional obligations in a somewhat different way. Rather than taking the condition that triggers

---

[19] For other discussions of the role that structural injustice should play in our analysis of the wrong of exploitation, see Young 2004; Zwolinski 2012; McKeown 2016; Wollner 2019; Gray 2020.

the obligations to be the hiring of particular people, we should think that the triggering condition is the decision to hire some people from among the group who would like to be hired.[20] When that condition is met, a firm owes it to all of the members of that group to hire a subset of them and to provide wages and working conditions that meet the standards for non-exploitation. When a firm fails to satisfy this conditional obligation, it wrongs not only those who are hired and therefore parties to a transaction with the firm, but also all of those who would have accepted one of the relevant positions had one been offered to them.[21]

3. The Remedial Duties of Wrongful Exploiters

Malmqvist and Szigeti (2021) note that very little has been said about the remedial duties owed by those guilty of wrongful exploitation. It should be uncontroversial that wrongful exploiters are obligated to give up at least the excess benefits that they obtained by engaging in exploitation. For example, if an exploiter gains $1,000 from an exploitative transaction, but would have gained at most $500 from the transaction had its terms been non-exploitative, then he is obligated to give up at least the $500 surplus. It also seems plausible that wrongful exploiters are obligated to direct whatever resources they are obligated to give up in order to satisfy their remedial duties to those who were wronged by their exploitative conduct.

If this is right, then views on which only parties to exploitative transactions can be wronged will imply that wrongful exploiters owe remedial duties only to their transaction partners, and ought to direct whatever resources they are obligated to give up to them. My view, on the other hand, implies that in many cases, the class of those to whom a wrongful exploiter might owe remedial duties will be much larger than the class of exploited parties to the relevant transactions.

Though they do not state this explicitly, Malmqvist and Szigeti develop their view of the remedial obligations of wrongful exploiters on the assumption that only the exploited parties to wrongfully exploitative transactions

---

[20] I make a similar suggestion in Berkey 2020b, 424–425.

[21] It is worth noting that this account of the wrong-making features of wrongful exploitation is consistent with rejecting the non-worseness claim. So while my argument in section 1 relies on certain intuitions that are similar to those that motivate that claim, my conclusion that wrongful exploitation often wrongs people who are not parties to exploitative transactions does not depend on any version of the claim being correct.

are wronged.[22] Unsurprisingly, they argue that in cases involving voluntary and mutually beneficial yet nonetheless wrongfully exploitative transactions, an exploiting party, A, owes a remedial duty to an exploited party, B, to compensate the latter by redirecting enough of the benefits that A obtained through his transaction with B to make it the case that B is as well off as she would have been had the transaction occurred on non-exploitative terms (Malmqvist and Szigeti 2021, 59).

They take their more significant contribution to consist in their argument for the claim that wrongful exploiters' remedial duties are not limited to this compensatory duty. This is because, they claim, wrongful exploitation causes what they call "relational harm" to exploited parties that must also be remedied (2021, 60–62). On their view, exploiters inflict relational harm on those whom they exploit because they view and treat their vulnerability at least primarily as an opportunity to obtain disproportionate benefits from a transaction. They claim, plausibly, that "such a stance towards other people's vulnerability is . . . incompatible with granting them a minimally acceptable (let alone equal) standing in one's relationship to them" (2021, 61). In order to remedy the relational harm that they cause, wrongful exploiters must, Malmqvist and Szigeti claim, apologize and seek forgiveness. And in the case of ongoing relationships (such as that between an employer and an employee), they must express willingness to adjust the terms of the relevant transactions so that they are made non-exploitative (2021, 63).

The first thing to note about Malmqvist and Szigeti's account of what makes it the case that wrongful exploiters inflict relational harm on those whom they exploit is that if we think about the broader context within which much exploitation occurs (as my *Sweatshop* cases require us to do), the account itself seems to imply that all of those who would like to be hired but are not suffer the same relational harm as those who are hired and thereby made parties to exploitative transactions. Firms that employ workers in sweatshop conditions, and the relevant individual decision-makers within them, will at least typically view *all* potential sweatshop employees and their vulnerable circumstances primarily as presenting opportunities to generate greater profit margins by paying low wages and requiring long hours in poor working conditions. In other words, they will be committed to a stance toward the vulnerability of all such people that is incompatible with granting them a minimally acceptable standing. Furthermore, because in the *Sweatshop* cases

---

[22] See their brief discussion of wrongful exploitation in Malmqvist and Szigeti 2021, 56–57.

the presence of additional potential employees who would be willing to accept the relevant jobs will tend to make it possible for exploiting firms to pay even lower wages to those whom they do hire than they otherwise could, the fact that they have the objectionable attitude that they do toward all of their potential employees contributes to their ability to obtain as much benefit as they do.

I argued earlier that this is a further reason, on top of those that the *Sweatshop* cases share with *One Dose of Drug, Ten People in Need*, to think that all of those who would like to be hired for the relevant positions are wronged by firms that engage in wrongful exploitation. We can now note that it also suggests that wrongful exploiters can have remedial obligations to, for example, apologize to and seek forgiveness from all of those whose vulnerabilities they viewed primarily as presenting opportunities to benefit themselves. In light of the reasons that have been noted for thinking that potential employees in the *Sweatshop* cases are not merely wronged, but are also exploited along with those who are hired, this should seem like the right conclusion. In addition, it is worth emphasizing that Malmqvist and Szigeti's own account of the relational harm caused by wrongful exploitation, properly understood, suggests that those guilty of wrongful exploitation will often have remedial duties to those who are not parties to the relevant exploitative transactions.

There are also reasons to favor a view on which compensatory duties are not owed only to the exploited parties to wrongfully exploitative transactions. In the *Sweatshop* cases, those who are hired are at least made better off than those who were initially similarly situated and would like to have been hired, but were not selected. On the view that I have suggested, firms owe it (either conditionally or unconditionally) to all of the members of the group of potential employees to hire a subset of them and provide non-exploitative terms of employment. When a firm fails to satisfy this obligation, it wrongs all of the members of that group, which suggests that all of them should be candidates for sharing in any compensation for the wrong that is later provided. Now, the fact that those who are hired perform long hours of work for the firm in poor conditions may give them a particular claim to some of the compensation that those who are not hired lack. But this claim might be thought to be counteracted, at least to some extent, by the fact that at the time that compensation might be provided, those who are not hired will tend to be, on the whole, even worse off than those who are hired. We might think that, among a group of wronged parties, those who are worst off should, all else equal, have the strongest claims to limited compensatory resources.

Recognizing that wrongful exploitation often wrongs a broader class of people than the exploited parties to the relevant transactions, then, has potentially significant implications for how we should understand both the scope and content of the remedial duties of wrongful exploiters. Because our moral concern about exploitation should be grounded primarily in a more general concern for the morally important interests of those who are vulnerable to wrongful exploitation, these implications should, I think, seem quite plausible on reflection, even if they conflict with some of our initial intuitive reactions. If I am correct, then many of those reactions are explained by the fact that our reflection on the wrong of exploitation tends to focus our attention too narrowly on factors that are internal to exploitative transactions. When our focus is appropriately broadened in ways that direct our attention to the broader contexts in which wrongfully exploitative transactions take place, we can see that a number of widely accepted claims about the wrong of exploitation should be rejected.

References

Arneson, R. 2013. "Exploitation and Outcome." *Politics, Philosophy, and Economics 12*, no. 4: 392–412.
Bailey, A. D. 2011. "The Nonworseness Claim and the Moral Permissibility of Better-than-Permissible Acts." *Philosophia 39*, no. 2: 237–250.
Barnes, M. R. 2013. "Exploitation as a Path to Development: Sweatshop Labor, Micro-Unfairness, and the Non-Worseness Claim." *Ethics and Economics 10*, no. 1: 26–43.
Berkey, B. 2020a. "Effectiveness and Demandingness." *Utilitas 32*, no. 3: 368–381.
Berkey, B. 2020b. "The Value of Fairness and the Wrong of Wage Exploitation." *Business Ethics Quarterly 30*, no. 3: 414–429.
Berkey, B. 2021. "Sweatshops, Structural Injustice, and the Wrong of Exploitation: Why Multinational Corporations Have Positive Duties to the Global Poor." *Journal of Business Ethics 169*: 43–56.
Dänzer, S. 2014. "Unfair Trade, Exploitation, and Below-Subsistence Wages." *Moral Philosophy and Politics 1*, no. 2: 269–288.
Faraci, D. 2019. "Wage Exploitation and the Nonworseness Claim: Allowing the Wrong, to Do More Good." *Business Ethics Quarterly 29*, no. 2: 169–188.
Ferguson, B. 2016. "The Paradox of Exploitation." *Erkenntnis 81*, no. 5: 951–972.
Ferguson, B. 2021. "Are We All Exploiters?" *Philosophy and Phenomenological Research* 103, no. 3: 535–546.
Ferguson, B., and S. Köhler. 2020. "Betterness of Permissibility." *Philosophical Studies 177*, no. 9: 2451–2469.

Gray, D. 2020. "Rethinking Micro-Level Exploitation." *Social Theory and Practice 46*, no. 3: 515–546.
Horton, J. 2017. "The All or Nothing Problem." *Journal of Philosophy 114*, no. 2: 94–104.
Kates, M. 2019. "Sweatshops, Exploitation, and the Case for a Fair Wage." *Journal of Political Philosophy 27*, no. 1: 26–47.
Malmqvist, E. 2017. "Better to Exploit than Neglect? International Clinical Research and the Non-Worseness Claim." *Journal of Applied Philosophy 34*, no. 4: 474–488.
Malmqvist, E, and A. Szigeti. 2021. "Exploitation and Remedial Duties." *Journal of Applied Philosophy 38*, no. 1: 55–72.
Mayer, R. 2007a. "What's Wrong with Exploitation?" *Journal of Applied Philosophy 24*, no. 2: 137–150.
Mayer, R. 2007b. "Sweatshops, Exploitation, and Moral Responsibility." *Journal of Social Philosophy 38*, no. 4: 605–619.
McKeown, M. 2016. "Global Structural Exploitation: Towards an Intersectional Definition." *Global Justice: Theory, Practice, Rhetoric 9*, no. 2: 155–177.
Meyers, C. 2004. "Wrongful Beneficence: Exploitation and Third-World Sweatshops." *Journal of Social Philosophy 35*, no. 3: 319–333.
Miklós, A. 2019. "Exploiting Injustice in Mutually Beneficial Market Exchange: The Case of Sweatshop Labor." *Journal of Business Ethics 156*, no. 1: 59–69.
Powell, B., and M. Zwolinski. 2012. "The Ethical and Economic Case Against Sweatshop Labor: A Critical Assessment." *Journal of Business Ethics 107*, no. 4: 449–472.
Preiss, J. 2014. "Global Labor Justice and the Limits of Economic Analysis." *Business Ethics Quarterly 24*, no. 1: 55–83.
Preiss, J. 2018. "Freedom, Autonomy, and Harm in Global Supply Chains." *Journal of Business Ethics 160*, no. 4: 881–891.
Pummer, T. 2016. "Whether and Where to Give." *Philosophy and Public Affairs 44*, no. 1: 77–95.
Pummer, T. 2019. "All or Nothing, but if Not All, Next Best or Nothing." *Journal of Philosophy 116*, no. 5: 278–291.
Sample, R. 2003. *Exploitation: What It Is and Why It's Wrong*. Lanham, MD: Rowman and Littlefield.
Sample, R. 2016. "Exploitation and Consequentialism." *Southern Journal of Philosophy 54*, no. S1: 66–91.
Snyder, J. 2008. "Needs Exploitation." *Ethical Theory and Moral Practice 11*, no. 4: 389–405.
Snyder, J. 2013. "Exploitation and Demeaning Choices." *Politics, Philosophy, and Economics 12*, no. 4: 345–360.
Sollars, G. G., and F. Englander. 2018. "Sweatshops: Economic Analysis and Exploitation as Unfairness." *Journal of Business Ethics 149*, no. 1: 15–29.
Vrousalis, N. 2018. "Exploitation: A Primer." *Philosophy Compass 13*, no. 2: 1–14.
Wertheimer, A. 1996. *Exploitation*. Princeton, NJ: Princeton University Press.
Wollner, G. 2019. "Anonymous Exploitation: Non-Individual, Non-Agential, and Structural." *Review of Social Economy 77*, no. 2: 143–162.
Wood, A. W. 1995. "Exploitation." *Social Philosophy and Policy 12*, no. 2: 136–158.
Young, I. M. 2004. "Responsibility and Global Labor Justice." *Journal of Political Philosophy 12*, no. 4: 365–388.
Zwolinski, M. 2007. "Sweatshops, Choice, and Exploitation." *Business Ethics Quarterly 17*, : 698–727.
Zwolinski, M. 2012. "Structural Exploitation." *Social Philosophy and Policy 29*, no. 1: 154–179.

7
Two Faces of Exploitation
Moral Injury, Harm, and the Paradox of Exploitation

Ruth Sample

1. A Paradox About Exploitation

If two persons agree to a transaction, and the transaction makes both parties better off than they were before, then how can the transaction be wrong? The commonsense answer seems to be that it cannot be wrong under these conditions, and therefore there is no prima facie good reason to interfere with the transaction. And yet many putatively exploitative interactions seem to fit this description and seem to be seriously wrong. This is at the heart of what has come to be known as "the paradox of exploitation" (Ferguson 2016). Despite the widespread appeal of the commonsense view, I shall argue that there is a way to understand the wrongness of exploitation even in such mutually beneficial transactions.

I suggest a resolution of the paradox by appealing to a distinction in tort law: the distinction between *moral injury* and *moral harm*. Jean Hampton made use of this distinction in her analysis of the wrongness of rape (Hampton 1999). She argued that in addition to the "lowering of interests" experienced by persons who are harmed by the actions of others, such persons also incur a diminishment that is distinct from, and cannot be reduced to, harm. Hampton calls this diminishment "moral injury" and argues that a moral agent diminishes another through words or actions that express a lack of respect. Tort law, she argues, makes space for actions that are wrongful but not necessarily harmful in this sense.

I have presented versions of this paper to the PPE Society, the American Society For International Law, the Carol and Lawrence Zicklin Center for Business Ethics Research at the Wharton School (University of Pennsylvania), and the University of San Diego. I would like to thank all who have graciously offered their feedback, especially Benjamin Ferguson, Subrena Smith, Katla Heðinsdóttir, and Charlotte Witt.

I rework this distinction in a way that does not rely on "expressive content" as the means by which another is diminished. In particular, I challenge Hampton's assumption that moral injury requires expressive content. However, I agree with her general point, that in cases of mutually beneficial exploitation, the exploited party may suffer moral injury even though they have not suffered a lowering of interests. Thus, although such transactions may be mutually beneficial, they may nevertheless be morally wrong by virtue of moral injury. Such wrongness, however, does not imply that those transactions ought to be prohibited. I highlight the usefulness of the distinction between moral injury and harm by examining the case of sweatshop labor. However, the paradox of exploitation is not limited to the case of sweatshops, and the resolution also generalizes to other putative cases of exploitation that involve this paradox.

2. The Case of Sweatshops

Thinking about wrongful exploitation solely in terms of harm presents a challenge to some widely shared judgments about the moral status of a number of common yet morally contested practices. The specific case that has perhaps garnered the most attention recently is that of low-wage manufacturing facilities, commonly known as sweatshops. These are factories that employ workers at very low wages in weakly regulated conditions in order to garner higher profits for owners:

> Sweatshop conditions are defined by the characteristics of a job. If workers are denied the right to organize, suffer unsafe and abusive working conditions, are forced to work overtime, or are paid less than a living wage, then they work in a sweatshop, regardless of how they came to take their jobs or if the alternatives they face are worse yet. (Miller 2003, 93)

For many years (until at least 1996) sweatshops were widely considered a non-issue—at least as far as wage compensation was concerned (Maitland 2013). Economists had argued that in fact we should *encourage* sweatshops in the developing world because they are a net benefit to those who work in them (Krugman 1997; Myerson 1997). This was despite the fact that the dire conditions inside these sweatshops had been well documented (Roberts and Bertstein 2000). However, more recently philosophers have argued that sweatshops constitute unjust employment conditions. Modern trade agreements such as the North American Free Trade Agreement have accelerated the creation of sweatshops in developing economies, rendering the issue more salient. The argument is that such trade agreements promote exploitation (Arnold and Bowie 2003; Arnold and Hartman 2003) even though workers line up to apply for the jobs produced by these agreements. The defense of sweatshops in light of these charges of exploitation is rooted in the assertion that workers not only consent to the employment provided by these factories but also often actively welcome the establishment of these factories and regard employment in them as mutually beneficial.

It is important to recognize that it is unclear how many factories established by multinational corporations in developing economies satisfy these conditions of voluntariness and mutual benefit. There are many cases in which it initially appears that employment is voluntary, but in fact the employment conditions were not as described in the initial agreement. In such cases, an element of fraud or coercion is involved, as in the well-known case of the Chinese factories that produced merchandise for Walmart, described in *Business Week* in 2000 (Roberts and Bertstein 2000). In another case, garment factories in Saipan, part of the Marianas Islands, were revealed to operate with deception, fraud, and coercion (including imprisonment, theft of documents, and forced abortion). In the 1990s the Commonwealth of the Northern Marianas Islands (CNMI) began to import workers from China, telling them they would be working in America, of which CNMI is a territory. Some politicians and lobbyists at the time touted CNMI as a "laboratory of liberty" and visited the islands, later testifying that working conditions did not fit the description of a sweatshop and claiming that the free market was raising up the (mostly) Chinese women who worked there. However, eventually human rights workers and American government investigators discovered that the women in those factories were not protected by American labor laws at the time.[1] It turned out that

> in fact, American authorities have discovered many Chinese workers are forced to sign secret agreements, known as shadow contracts, before they leave China, severely and, in some ways, illegally restricting their activities while on American soil. For example, in this agreement translated into English by American authorities, workers are forbidden to participate in

---

[1] In 2007, Congress intervened and superceded the CNMI minimum wage.

any religious or political activity or to ask for a salary increase or even to fall in love or get married, much as might be the case in mainland China. (Goodman 2006)

In practice, many women were forced to pay fees to gain employment, and some were coerced into prostitution once on the island of Saipan. Women who became pregnant were told that they must have an abortion or they would be banned from the factory. One Clinton administration official from the Department of the Interior, Allan Stayman, was tasked with investigating the conditions in these factories. He concluded that "to allow them to bring that on to U.S. soil is a very deep concern. We've now documented the fact that management coerces female workers who become pregnant into having abortions" (Goodman 2006).

So we ought not assume that all or even most sweatshops are the open and non-coercive arrangements that are truly mutually beneficial. Nonetheless, we ought to consider the moral status of sweatshops that *are* genuinely non-coercive, voluntary, and mutually beneficial—however rare they may be. The putative existence of such sweatshops has fueled interest in what has been called the "paradox of exploitation" (Ferguson 2016). Such sweatshops present a conflict between two things that both appear to be true. On the one hand, sweatshops take advantage of the weak bargaining position of workers to extract their labor at very low wages under poor working conditions; thus to many, *it seems wrong*. However, it also seems that *it cannot be wrong* to interact with others in a way that makes all parties to the transaction better off and is undertaken voluntarily—that is, without coercive threats on the part of those involved. Moreover, *it seems wrong* for third parties to interfere with such cases of exploitation. In situations of serious wrongdoing such as assault or murder, interference by third parties (when possible) appears obligatory; yet, here it is not clear that interference is even permitted. Thus, in cases in which workers voluntarily engage in sweatshop labor, the question arises: *how can such voluntary, mutually beneficial employment be wrongful exploitation?*

I argue that such sweatshops are a good example of transactions that may indeed be wrongful even if mutually beneficial and voluntarily undertaken, and even if third-party interference is unwarranted. Even if these exploitative transactions are morally impermissible, it does not follow (I argue) that we are permitted to stop them. In at least some cases, when an exploiter could interact on better terms with the exploited but refuses to do so, noninterference may be the morally best course of action. The issue of *wrongness* and the issue of *what third parties ought to do about such wrongness* involve two separate, albeit intimately related, questions. As Alan Wertheimer put it, there is a distinction between the *moral weight* of an action or situation and the *moral force* (Wertheimer 1996). The distinction between moral injury can help us understand how such transactions are seriously wrongful, even if we should not interfere with them. Thus this distinction promises to help us resolve the paradox and reject the commonsense intuition: a transaction could be both mutually beneficial and seriously wrong, and yet we might not be justified in interfering with it.

3. The Non-Worseness Condition

The idea that it cannot be seriously wrong to engage in unfair but mutually beneficial transactions is captured by what Alan Wertheimer called the "Non-worseness Claim" (NWC). As Wertheimer describes it in his book *Exploitation* (Wertheimer 1996), NWC is the claim that

> where A has a right not to transact with B, and where A's transacting with B is not worse for B than A's not transacting with B, then A's transacting with B cannot be seriously morally wrong, or at least cannot be morally worse than A's not transacting with B, even if the terms of the transaction are deemed unfair by some external standard. (Wertheimer 1996, 289)[2]

The idea here is that even if the benefits of the interaction are not evenly distributed between the parties, or are not distributed according to some other defensible metric of fairness, if no one is made worse off by a transaction, then

---

[2] This is somewhat different from Ferguson's formulation: "If a transaction is strictly Pareto improving and consensual, then engaging in the transaction is morally *better* than not transacting" (Ferguson 2016). Ferguson construes the paradox in terms of actions that are *impermissible despite being Pareto improving*. I argue that acts that are seriously wrong or even impermissible should, in some cases, be tolerated by third parties when less exploitative terms of interaction are not forthcoming. I agree with Ferguson that it is possible that even if interaction with another is not obligatory, there may be significant constraints on any interaction that is undertaken. This is easier to see when non-monetary conditions are in play: even if I am not obligated to open a factory in any particular part of the world, I may not make employment terms degrading: e.g., requiring workers to provide sex to managers, or to renounce their religion, or to labor under conditions at odds with their dignity. Even if employment under degrading conditions such as these is *preferred* by workers to the alternative of no employment at all, that ordering of preferences is not exonerating. Although I reach a very similar conclusion, I do not claim to solve Ferguson's formulation of the paradox.

it cannot be "seriously wrong." Wrongful exploitation is often understood as a species of unfair transaction. Wertheimer raises the question of whether we must accept NWC. Although he himself does not embrace it, others have explicitly done so in defense of sweatshops (Powell and Zwolinski 2012; Zwolinski 2007). Economists such as Paul Krugman and Jeffrey Sachs tacitly accept this principle. Others, including myself, have either explicitly rejected NWC or been critical of it (Arneson 2013; Faraci 2019; Meyers 2004; Sample 2003; Snyder 2008). If we accept NWC as a general moral principle, it would seem to follow that sweatshops are not "seriously wrong" because they benefit all parties to the transaction, all parties regard the interaction as preferred to their other options, and because none of the parties has a right (or obligation) to transact with any of the others in the first place—or so it is argued.

How can sweatshops be beneficial to all parties to the transaction, including exploited workers? There are many economic arguments to the effect that sweatshops reduce unemployment in the countries in which they occur, and that prohibiting sweatshops or even mandating OSHA-type safety regulations would either reduce total utility or harm the worst-off workers in the developing world (Powell and Zwolinski 2012). The benefits of these employment relationships are alleged to redound to both the participants in the immediate transaction and the surrounding community. There are also reasons to think that, to the contrary, even if they provide short-term gains, in the long run sweatshops do not advance the interests of those who work in them and may even undermine or harm their interests. Of course, the stipulated terms of employment might not be, in fact, what the employees find when they show up for work. One might also argue that the corporations who operate sweatshops do, in fact, have an obligation to interact with those in need of employment, and to interact on terms that would preclude sweatshops. However, I shall not examine all of those counterarguments here. Instead, I want to focus on the question of *whether the fact that an action is consensual and is not harmful— that it does not worsen the overall well-being of any of the agents involved— means that it cannot be "seriously wrong."* In order to do so, it is helpful to consider the relationship between harm and wrongdoing.

4. Harm and Wrongdoing

Jean Hampton was first among those philosophers who revived retributivism as a defensible theory of punishment, just when it appeared to be in decline. First in "Correcting Harms Versus Righting Wrongs: The Goal of Retribution" (Hampton 1992) and later in "Defining Wrong and Defining Rape" (Hampton 1999), Hampton considers the relationship between harm and wrongdoing. In jurisprudence, she notes, theorists make a distinction between a crime and a tort. Relying on the work of Jules Coleman, Hampton argues that a plausible way to understand the domains of criminal law and civil tort law is to focus on the kinds of justice appropriate to each: *retributive justice* (characterized by punishment) and *corrective justice* (characterized by compensation or correction). A crime is a type of morally wrong action; retributive justice directs itself at "annulling moral wrongs." On the other hand, a tort is a kind of wrongful harm or loss. While some crimes may be torts, it is possible to inflict a wrongful loss on another without that harm rising to the level of a crime (as in the case of a loss caused by criminal negligence). When one has harmed another in a tortious way, "corrective justice imposes on wrongdoers the duty to repair their wrongs and the wrongful losses that their wrongdoing occasions" (Coleman 1992, 325). What, then, counts as wrongful harm?

Hampton defines harm as "a disruption of or interference in a person's well-being, including damage to that person's body, psychological state, capacities to function, life plans, or resources over which we take this person to have an entitlement" (Hampton 1999, 120). Tort law concerns itself not with the wrongful (criminal) conduct but with the losses conferred by wrongful conduct. So "innocent harm"—harm incurred, but not as a result of any malfeasance or negligence—is not a tort. If I beat you in a tennis match, that loss may lower your well-being in a number of ways, but because it is not wrong for me to win in a competition, such harm is purely innocent and not within the domain of torts.

A further distinction within torts is the distinction between those harms that call for retribution and those that do not. A ship captain who destroys a dock owner's property (as in the famous case *Vincent v. Lake Erie Transportation Co.*) might rightfully be called upon to make reparations (corrective justice), but punishment (retributive justice) might not be called for if the action is overall "morally positive." Because in *Vincent v. Lake Erie* the captain was seeking shelter in a storm and the dock owner refused it, the action might have an element of wrongdoing in it, but the wrongdoing does not reach the threshold of retributive justice. Similarly, in the case of a negligent driver who causes an accident, corrective justice might be required, but not retribution. The driver might be liable for damages she has caused without being deserving of punishment. Hampton also argues that in the case of suicide, one might have wronged oneself (making corrective justice moot), but retribution is nonetheless not merited. These cases are quite different from cases where someone has, for example, defrauded another out of her life savings (Hampton 1999, 123). In those cases, corrective justice is simply insufficient; retributive justice is also warranted. Why? Under what circumstances is tortious action worthy of retribution? The answer, Hampton argues, is moral injury.

5. What Is Moral Injury?

Hampton's concept of moral injury is centered on the dignity of the victim of wrongful action. Certain wrongful actions do not merely cause harm in the sense defined above (a loss to one's interests) but instead constitute moral injury: "a particular kind of injury to a person's value" (127). On the anti-Hobbesian assumption that persons have intrinsic value (rather than mere "price"), it is possible to act in such a way that the value that a person possesses is not properly respected.[3] The Kantian theory of value used here is broad in that it is consistent not only with Kant's particular view of human value as located in rationality but also with the ancient view that all humans have indestructible, intrinsically valuable souls.

An individual is the subject of moral injury when that individual is the target of behavior whose meaning, appropriately understood by the members of the cultural community in which the behavior occurs, represents her value as less than the value she should be accorded (Hampton 1999, 126).

Moral injury is not, Hampton argues, the same as physical or even psychological harm to the injured person. It is important to distinguish Hampton's meaning from more recent uses of the term—for example, where it is used to describe the effects of wrongful action on the conscience of the perpetrator of wrongdoing (Sherman 2015). It is also distinct from what Joel Feinberg has called "the dubious notion of a moral harm" (Feinberg 1990, xx) and what Lisa Tessman has termed "moral damage," or "the damage that is done to [the agent's] character by institutionally embedded social forces" (Tessman 2005, 12). According to Hampton, a person could suffer a moral injury without

---

[3] The "value beyond price" of a person does not, however, mean that such a person cannot suffer estimable harm and be compensated for the lowering of their interests. Such compensation is the domain of civil tort law.

even being aware of it—as in the case of an Alzheimer's patient who is robbed of her savings (Hampton 1999, 126). A person could suffer a moral injury if they are the unwitting victim of an attempted murder. Moral injury is inflicted through *diminishment*—the appearance of degradation, rather than actual degradation, since on this Kantian view the intrinsic value of a person cannot literally be destroyed or degraded—at least as long as that person remains a person. Diminishment is an objective phenomenon; it depends not upon the subjective mental states of the diminished person but upon the objective meaning of the actions of the diminisher. Just as a person can be insulted without subjectively recognizing the insult, a person can be diminished by the actions of another without recognizing the diminishment. Even if there is no witness to recognize the diminishment, the diminishment is real. Diminishment is a denial of value.

Hampton says that there are two ways to diminish another. First, we may diminish another by damaging the *realization* of a person's value. Using a Gricean analysis of meaning, Hampton argues that by using certain words and/or actions, we can convey a "false message" about the person's value, when the bearer of that value is entitled to the recognition by another of her true value.[4] Second, we may diminish another by damaging the acknowledgment of a person's value. Through our words and/or actions, we may threaten the community's recognition of another's value. We can make it less likely (or perhaps even impossible) for others to accord the kind of value to another that a person deserves. Hampton illustrates how this could come about with a very graphic and disturbing description of a sexual mutilation, lynching, and burning of a Black man and his sons by the farmer who employed them and knew them for their whole lives (as told by the modern dancer Bill T. Jones) (Hampton 1999, 128). The details of the torture, mutilation, dismemberment, and lynching of the man and his sons are gruesome, and I shall not retell them here. Hampton's point in retelling them is that the farmer's actions allow us to *read off* an expression of the farm hands' worthlessness in multiple ways.

Hampton argues that in addition to, and quite distinct from, harming these men by assaulting, mocking, humiliating, traumatizing, and ultimately murdering them, the farmer also diminished them. The fact of diminishment

---

[4] Very briefly, Hampton relies on four kinds of Gricean meaning: natural meaning, word (conventional) meaning, speaker (or non-natural) meaning (such as pointing), and "conversational implicature" (1999, 130).

is what activates the requirement of retribution when the diminishment reaches a certain threshold. Oliver Wendell Holmes famously wrote in *The Common Law* that "even a dog distinguishes between being stumbled over and being kicked" (Holmes 1881, 3). Holmes foreshadowed Hampton's point that moral injury is distinct from harm and implicates an aspect of justice that mere harm cannot.

It is important to keep in mind that moral injury is not only distinct from harm (where harm is wrongful damage to one's interests or well-being) but also distinct from *offense*. This term has both non-normative and normative meanings. As with harm, a person can be offended in the non-normative or subjective sense without being wronged. Imagine, for example, a person who takes offense at being outbid at an auction. This person would *feel offended* by the fact that another has outbid her, but the bidding was legitimate and the action contained nothing wrongful. On the other hand, imagine a person who is called a racial slur and correctly apprehends that it is a racial slur. We would say that such a person has been genuinely, objectively, wrongfully offended. To make this distinction is to acknowledge that there is a difference between *feeling* offended and truly *being* offended. Although Feinberg considers offense a kind of harm (calling it a "mental state of a universally disliked kind"), he also argues that offending another might be a very narrow, limited kind of harm that, beyond the disliked mental state it engenders, does not create any further harm (Feinberg 1988, 2) and is thus in a sense "incommensurable" with interest-lowering harm. Offense is distinct from harm in that it requires that the offended person must experience a negative mental state, whereas a person's interests could be harmed without the person even knowing about it. For example, a real estate agent might accept one offer on my house knowing that another higher one is forthcoming, because her commission on the higher offer will only be marginally higher and will take up another two weeks of her time. Thus we can see that offense is distinct from moral injury in general, because moral injury can occur without the injured person knowing it. Perhaps offense may be best understood as a subtype of moral injury—a moral injury that is, by definition, recognized by the injured party. To "take offense" is to subjectively apprehend a moral injury.

6. How Is Moral Injury Possible?

How is moral injury possible? What must take place for moral injury to occur? Hampton considers the acts of murder, attempted murder, psychological or physical abuse of another, rape, castration, and lynching as "denials of value" (Hampton 1999, 133). All of these actions diminish another person in a way that involves severe wrongdoing. Diminishment, on her view, is not an all-or-nothing affair; some diminishment is worse than others. The extreme acts just listed constitute serious moral injury and are paradigmatic candidates for retribution. However, Hampton argues, public speech, words, and pictures can diminish as well: "The more a wrongdoing inflicts damage to value in either way [realization or acknowledgment], the more we object to it" (Hampton 1999, 132). There are other forms of diminishment that might be considered "minimally immoral" and unworthy of response, such as publishing a book proclaiming the intrinsic superiority of men over women, or whites over Blacks, but in such cases "that damage is negligible and society does not bother to respond. If people take them seriously, and come to believe these assertions of superiority, the books become much more dangerous. . . . Such materials denigrate people, not only by causing others to inflict harm on them, but simply by representing them as inferior" (Hampton 1999, 132). Hampton does not conclude that such words and actions ought to thereby be legally prohibited—there are other values hanging in the balance—but these forms of "denials of value" nonetheless count as moral injury.

Finally, actions that display *negligence* can diminish another person. For example, a "cavalier and reckless attitude," such as a negligent air traffic controller who fails to appreciate the value of the people whose lives are endangered by his negligence, also counts as moral injury. This is so even if the negligence of the air traffic controller does not lead to an accident causing harm (Hampton 1999, 133). Even if the air traffic controller does not express any mental content that denies the full value of the air travelers—either publicly or privately—he can still diminish them. His negligence can diminish them even if he is not thinking about the passengers at all. On Hampton's view, we can diminish another person even if we are not even thinking thoughts about their value. To be valuable is to be the kind of entity that others *should* care about, and they should care about it in a way that sufficiently respects the value that they have (Hampton 1999, 133). Moral injury is objective in the sense that it is not dependent upon the mental states of the injured, but *it is also not dependent upon the injurer explicitly denigrating the injured party.*

Suppose that Hampton is correct in her claim that the negligent air traffic controller has morally injured the passengers under his care. It is reasonable to ask whether such negligent moral agents are doing what could reasonably be described as "expressing content about the value of others." Does the negligent air traffic controller express anything about the value of the airline passengers as he plays Words with Friends on his phone? Hampton insists that he does. We can "read" the expressive content of his action from certain failures on his part, such as the failure to pay sufficient attention to the lives that are at stake. What is relevant to moral injury is not the effect on the psychological states of the passengers (who, in the event of an accident, might never know about this expressive content) but the nature of the expressive content we can "read off" of the actions of the air traffic controller (Hampton 1999, 135). Whereas in the most egregious cases the perpetrator is explicit and even brazen in expressing his contempt for his target, in this case the perpetrator may not be aware of his expressive content at the moment of his moral injury.

7. Moral Injury, Expressive Content, and Regard

This raises the question of whether the moral agent must be understood as having expressive content regarding those he morally injures. Expressions of contempt appear, on this view, sufficient for moral injury, but are they *necessary* for moral injury? Hampton considers another example that does seem morally injurious when she describes

> the persistent refusal of white apartment owners to rent apartments to prospective minority tenants; such discrimination is not just an injury to the particular people who are denied apartments, but also an injury to all members of the race being discriminated against. (Hampton 1999, 135)

Their actions, Hampton argues, express the content that "Your kind isn't the equal in worth of my kind" (Hampton 1999, 135).

The difficulty here is in determining the expressive content of the apartment owner's action. We do not have easy, transparent access to the mental states of others—indeed, we do not always have access to our own. Certainly, some discriminators do intend the expressive content described above. In such cases, the discriminator has some mental representation about the value of the minority group. Indeed, some such discriminators can be correctly called "strong racists." They acknowledge, or would acknowledge if asked, their view that some racial groups are less deserving of concern and respect than other groups. What should we make of cases where no such ideation is afoot? It seems at least plausible (although not conclusively so) that the air traffic controller expresses a lack of respect for his passengers in the sense that his negligent conduct occurs with an awareness that there are vulnerable people in flight. It is his job to keep them safe, even though he is not having any thoughts about them during his distraction. He does not think they are less deserving of care than he is; he simply fails to care about them in this particular case. Furthermore, he is at least within a framework where he takes himself to be responsible for their safety; he is an on-duty air traffic controller.

We should consider the case intermediate between the *negligent moral agent* (the inattentive air traffic controller) and the *active moral injurer* (the strong racist). What should we say about people who enact discriminatory policies that show less than equal concern and respect but *without* discriminatory intent? Such cases are part of what has come to be known as "systemic racism." Hampton does not consider this case, but it is worth considering. For example, an apartment owner might believe that it simply goes against his self-interest to rent to minorities, without intending any denial of value of the potential minority tenants. The white landlord might sincerely believe that if he rents to a minority tenant, it will tend to depress the rent that he can charge, as (racist) prospective white tenants will conclude that their neighborhood is thereby less desirable. The landlord's actions are aimed not at excluding minorities but at attracting higher-income tenants. Suppose that he recognizes the prevalence of racist attitudes in his neighborhood but he does not share them. The landlord could believe that excluding minorities will allow him to do this without believing that minority applicants have any less value than he does. Indeed, landlords make such judgments all the time in the case of potential renters who use Section 8 vouchers, students, renters with children, renters with pets, and so on, without necessarily harboring discriminatory intent against those groups as such. Consider the following counterfactual:

> The landlord would rent to the minority tenant provided that doing so would maximize his long-term profits.

It is, the landlord might say, "strictly a business decision." Although the result of iterating this decision over time and across many agents would result in unfair housing opportunities for minorities, *he has not issued any expressive content that would constitute diminishment*. He might, in fact, express admiration for any given racial minority, including people harmed by his business practices. And yet, making such a decision that any reasonable person would know will contribute to unfair housing opportunities does seem to diminish those discriminated against, but *not by virtue of its expressive content*. Hampton's understanding of diminishment in terms of expressive content would not allow us to see the self-interested landlord as guilty of moral injury—although he might be guilty of harming the interests of minority renters. Let us call this intermediate case the case of the *non-racist discriminator*.

What the case of the negligent, inattentive air traffic controller and the case of the non-racist, egoistic apartment owner have in common is a kind of failure. Neither intends to cause harm, and yet their actions fail to take the interests of the affected parties seriously in a way that may or may not lead to harm. Even if the flight lands safely, and even if the prospective minority tenants find comparable housing elsewhere, the agents in these cases fail to show appropriate respect for persons. The air traffic controller fails to respect the passengers because he lets himself be distracted by his game when he ought to be paying attention to the air traffic. And the landlord fails to respect the minority tenants when he chooses to prioritize maximizing his rental income over treating each prospective tenant fairly.

Recall that Hampton's account is supposed to be objective, in the sense that whether diminishment has occurred does not depend upon the diminished person perceiving herself as harmed, either psychologically or physically. It does not depend upon whether the diminished person is offended by the action, in Feinberg's sense of the word. The moral injury instead comes from objective features of the actions of the injurer. Here Hampton's Gricean analysis of the meaning of both words and actions allows us to assess whether an action is diminishing without relying on the subjective perceptions of the victim. Behavior itself, when properly interpreted in the context of the linguistic community of the actor, "can carry meaning with regard to human value" (Hampton 1999, 126).

On this analysis, although moral injury in general does not require determining the mental states of its target, it does require determining the subjective intentions of the injurer. Certainly, the determination of whether an action constitutes attempted murder, abuse, rape, or assault requires that we understand whether the action was intentional and what the actor intended to do. What counts as disrespectful behavior will depend upon the norms and shared meanings of the community. But in order to assess whether a person wrongs another, we need to know whether he took himself to be performing that action of diminishment, and indeed whether the actor was doing something on purpose at all. (Think of Holmes's distinction between kicking a dog and stumbling over it.) In the most egregious cases, moral injury occurs because an agent deliberately discounts the value of another person in the course of engaging in some sort of action. However, in the case of negligence, the moral injury occurs because the agent does not sufficiently attend to the interests of certain others. In such cases, the agent might even be described as intending nothing at all about the diminished person. It is his lack of specific intention, or the lack of a specific intention of a certain sort, that constitutes the moral injury. The (non-racist) discriminating apartment owner knows that by acting out of pure self-interest, but without racial malice, he is contributing to an unjust housing market that exploits the racism of others. It would be impossible to act in such a calculating manner *without* being aware that the reason renting to a minority tenant would tend to lower rental prices is because of the ambient racism of the housing market. Although there may be no intention to harm or even an intent to convey disrespect, this is nonetheless intentional behavior and has the capacity to wrong others, even if it cannot properly be described as an intention to wrong others.

The existence of such cases calls into question whether Hampton is correct to say that "expressive content" is the right way to understand the medium of moral injury. It is easy to identify the expressive content in the behavior of someone who, while passing by another on the sidewalk, deliberately spits on her. It also seems clear that the racist apartment owner acts in a way that disregards the value of prospective minority tenants. However, it is harder to characterize what the negligent air traffic controller is doing as a kind of expressive content. The air traffic controller acts in a way that does not attend to the interests of air travelers. But it is hard to say that his behavior allows us to read off expressive content about the value of the travelers since in this example it is stipulated that the air traffic controller is not thinking about them at all. Similarly for the non-racist but discriminatory apartment owner. This person does not have, and does not express, racist views that attribute less value to minorities. However, the non-racist discriminatory landlord fails to attend to the interests of minority tenants in a way that is commensurate with their value as persons. *We need a way of understanding moral injury that does not rely on attributing any animus toward another person or toward a group of other persons qua member of that group.* Although it is relevant whether a person acted intentionally, moral injury cannot depend upon a specific motivation to convey expressive content, although in many cases, it will contain such motivation. Someone who says the words "Why don't you go back to the country you came from?" is conveying the sentiment that the target's "kind" of people don't belong "here." In this case, the message sent is not contained in the literal words of the question. The person who says this often knows that the target is in fact American-born, or might well be. The person who says this is not really asking a question, either—even a rhetorical question. The speaker of this sentence is expressing the view that the target is less worthy of membership, rights, and privileges of citizenship.

Clearly, some moral injury involves a perpetrator intending to "send a message," but not all moral injury need do this. In many cases, the injurer has no intention of sending a message at all. The injurer might explicitly and even sincerely declare that she harbors no ill will toward the target and regards the target as worthy of equal concern and respect. And yet, I argue, it would be possible for such a person to behave in a way that diminishes the other. If the distinction between moral injury and harm is to be sustained in a way that includes negligent action, something other than expressive content is required. It has to be the case that a moral agent could participate in moral injury without intending to signal disvalue or contempt of others to others, including to the person who is morally injured.

For this reason, in order to understand cases of negligence as morally injurious, we might do better to think about moral injury not in terms of expressive content but in terms of *personal regard*. We can in many cases read off from a person's behavior—how she comports or orients herself—how she or he regards others. If a person properly regards others, she orients her behavior in a way that is appropriate for the value that those persons have. This need not be a set of conscious or unconscious mental states that could be expressed as propositions about the value of others. A person who regards others appropriately displays conduct that, within the cultural community she inhabits, displays the proper habits, attention, concern, and respect. The motivation for her behavior need not be specific, other than the fact that it *is* indeed behavior (as opposed to, say, reflex, or accidental motion). Thus, a person who does not adequately consider and weigh the fact that her renting practices will disadvantage members of minority groups shows through her behavior that she does not properly regard them. She does not consider the kind of harm imposed on members of such groups to warrant refraining from actions that would promote that harm. She ranks her own self-interest as a landlord higher than she ranks equitable treatment for minority tenants.

By acting this way, she displays a lack of sufficient regard for others whose value requires that she regard it. Morally injurious behavior may still be injurious even when there is no specific "target" of the action.

What, then, is the distinction between expressive content and regard? Expressive content implies having a certain attitude toward others, an attitude manifested in both words and actions. Expressive content is fundamentally active and explicit. Regard, on the other hand, includes comportment that is passive and implicit. Regard can be discerned from the way one attends to the interests of others, or fails to attend to them. It need not be accompanied by any particular specifiable propositions or speech acts. A person might regard another person as insignificant without having any mental states about that particular person (or the group to which that person belongs). On the other hand, to treat a person with disdain or contempt is to manifest expressive content as well. Expressive content is thus a subset of personal regard that is more explicit, active, and targeted. A person may regard another in a certain way without any expressive content, but all expressive content manifests a way of regarding others.

I propose an amended account of moral injury that goes something like the following:

> Morally injurious conduct occurs when an agent who is capable of acting in a way that reflects the value of other persons fails to do so. Such an agent may fail to respect another by virtue of the expressive content of her words or actions when the expressive content diminishes another. However, one may also diminish by not acting with the proper regard for relevant other persons, regardless of expressive content. Although the diminished persons may be the target of her actions, they need not be. An agent may morally injure another even if the agent does not materially harm the interests of another.

8. Exploitation as Moral Injury

Is mutually beneficial exploitation a kind of moral injury? My modification of Hampton's account suggests that it can be. Elsewhere (Sample 2003) I have offered an extended account of exploitation as degradation: interaction with another for the sake of advantage that fails to adequately respect the value of that person. This account of exploitation covers both exploitation that is harmful as well as exploitation that is beneficial. I explicitly leave room for the possibility that we can engage in wrongdoing even when we interact with another in a way that indisputably benefits them, and even when the interaction is consensual. Exploiting another does not necessarily involve expressive content central to Hampton's account, but it does capture the idea of moral injury as distinct from any harm—or benefit—that the exploiter might cause. In the case of sweatshop labor, the employer chooses to pay workers a lower wage than is compatible with meeting her basic needs, or in conditions that are unduly dangerous or otherwise onerous. Thus, merely offering employment in the context of the relevant background conditions may indeed be a kind of moral injury, and actual employment on such terms may be even more morally injurious. If an employer could interact with employees on terms that more adequately respect their intrinsic worth but instead offers those employees less, then the employer has committed a moral injury. Similarly, in the case of the asymmetrical friendship, continuing a relationship with another on significantly unequal terms is morally injurious.

If we recognize exploitation as a kind of moral injury, then the same considerations that arise in the case of torts are resurrected here.

- What kinds of mutually beneficial exploitation require retributive justice?
- What would retributive justice look like in such cases?
- Should exploitation be legally prohibited if it benefits those involved in the exploitative transaction?
- How should we respond to cases of mutually beneficial exploitation?

Before addressing these questions, we need to consider a few possible objections to any account of mutually beneficial exploitation as moral injury.

9. Moral Injury and Benefit

One objection might be the following: although harmful exploitation is a kind of moral injury, mutually beneficial exploitation is not. For in the cases of moral injury considered above, *the victim of the moral injury is also not benefited*. In sweatshops and in other cases, the "victim" is benefited. The victims of lynching and murder described by Bill T. Jones are in no way benefited; the victims of racist speech are in no way benefited; the victims of housing discrimination are in no way benefited; the airline passengers are in no way benefited; the targets of attempted murder are in no way benefited. In some cases, the targets of such behavior are also harmed as well as diminished. But in none of those cases are the targets benefited. So even if we grant the fundamental cogency of moral agency, the paradigmatic cases are not like the cases of mutually beneficial exploitation. The cases described by Hampton are seriously wrong in a way that sweatshops are not.

It is true that in the paradigmatic cases of moral injury described by Hampton, the target of moral injury is *not* benefited. We can concoct variations of those cases in which the targets *accidentally* benefit. The victim of attempted murder, for example, may have a sudden epiphany about how he should be living his life that he would not have had if he remained unaware of the plot against him. The victim of housing discrimination may end up renting in another part of town, leading her to make a deep and lasting friendship. An assault victim might go on to become a medal-winning Paralympian. And so on. Nonetheless, these cases all involve one party displaying a lack of regard for the value of the other in a way that, at the very least, tends toward harm. This is not the case with mutually beneficial exploitation. What makes such exploitation possible is the inducement of a benefit that makes the transaction attractive to both (or all) parties.

A couple of points are relevant here. First, cases of putatively mutually beneficial exploitation may nonetheless "tend toward harm." Let us return to the case of sweatshop employment. Even if I have benefited you "globally" in the sense that you prefer the sweatshop employment to the available alternatives, I may have harmed you "locally" in the sense that accepting this employment may require you to compromise important elements of your well-being that no one should have to compromise. For example, you may have to accept risks to your health and safety that no one should have to make, but because the nature of risk is stochastic, and the paycheck is (almost) certain, it is your overall best choice to accept those terms of employment. The possibility of, say, lung disease in the future is too remote and uncertain to make turning down employment with a weekly paycheck the rational option. Similarly, the job may require you to work hours that require you to compromise your family obligations or religious practices. In the very worst situations, you may have to tolerate sexual harassment or even sexual assault and rape in order to keep your job—and yet you may rightly conclude that the job is better than the alternative. The fact that the alternatives available to you are even worse does not gainsay the fact that the employer uses dire circumstances as a means of inducing her into employment on terms that are, in specific respects, degrading. The all-in judgment of overall benefit may mask the nature of the harms, and some of those harms may be related to moral injury. This is not to deny that sweatshop labor may be the worker's best employment option. Rather, it highlights that the overall benefit might serve to disguise important costs that it is wrong to impose on anyone, or even to induce them into choosing it. Similarly, the fact that the attempted murderer did not succeed, or that the drunk driver did not kill anyone, does not undermine the fact that those actions also tend toward harm, even though the outcome may be neutral or even positive. Mutually beneficial exploitation may in fact tend toward harm, and that may be part of why we object to it. It may not be beneficial in the long run, and it may not even be benign. The fact that the exploitation at least immediately benefits the worker relative to his prior situation does not mean that the offer cannot tend toward harm, and it does not show that such a transaction does not involve moral injury—even if it does not involve harm.

10. Moral Injury and Consent

A second and related objection involves the role of consent. Because we are considering non-coerced, voluntary transactions, it might be thought that the consent precludes the charge of moral injury. Very briefly, I regard a coerced choice to be one made in response to a threat of harm that one would be wrong to impose. So, for example, I have no right to harm you if you do not hand me your wallet; therefore your choice to do so in light of a threat of violence would be coerced. However, I do have a right to withdraw my friendship if you act abusively, so your non-abusive behavior is not coerced. There may be disagreement about what kinds of threats are wrongfully coercive, but my general point is that I am not always wrong when I threaten to worsen your situation. Some threats, however, are wrongful to make. Given this assumption, in the absence of wrongfully coercive threats, does consent show that moral injury is not a worry for mutually beneficial exploitation? Can moral injury occur when the interaction is consensual, and when my actions have made you better off?

One of the reasons why consent is considered relevant in decision-making is that it is often used as the primary evidence that a transaction is beneficial to the person who consents to it and therefore one that we can recognize as rational for that person. Making choices that advance one's overall well-being is a hallmark of prudentially rational action. On the assumption that rational agents are capable of being responsible for making their own choices, when such agents make a choice voluntarily, it is often assumed that the agent regards the choice as their best option, or at least as good as any other option they might have. In the absence of any coercive threat, the fact that someone voluntarily engages in an enterprise is some (although not decisive) proof that they regard it as beneficial. Clearly it is not decisive evidence, because there are many situations in which a decision-maker must choose between multiple options that are all harmful. In such cases, the agent is choosing the least worst option. Thus, engaging in a consensual transaction is prima facie evidence that the choice is preferred to all others, or at least as good as all others. But the voluntary nature of the choice does not actually indicate that the agent believes the option improves her situation ex ante. Imagine, for example, that a person has run out of food, and is offered several foods to choose from, all of which are contaminated and are likely to make her sick. If she eats nothing, her health will worsen, but that will not be as bad for her as eating the contaminated food. Whatever choice she makes will worsen her health, but eating nothing appears to be the least bad option. Her voluntary choice, in this situation, is to eat nothing, and that will overall lower her health relative to what it is at the time of choice. In such cases, the agent makes a voluntary, uncoerced choice, but we cannot conclude that whatever she chooses makes her better off. It is reasonable, however, to assume ceteris paribus that she regards it as the least harmful—or at least no worse than the other options available to her. Her action appears rational in that, while it does not improve her overall well-being, it seems most likely to lower her well-being the least. It is her least harmful option.

Thus, while consent (again, ceteris paribus) is an indicator that an action is prudentially rational and choiceworthy, consensual interaction does not tell us whether choosing that action will benefit or harm the agent. Consent cannot tell us whether an interaction is potentially tortious because it cannot, first and foremost, tell us whether an offer of interaction is harmful *or* beneficial to either of the interactors. It may, however, be able to tell us something about whether the offer of interaction, or the interaction itself, was wrongful. For it is commonly argued that if an interaction is between consenting adults, then the interaction is not wrong—or at least not, as Wertheimer's NWC puts it, "seriously wrong." And if it is not seriously wrong, then it is hard to see how it would be a kind of moral injury.

Now, there is no doubt that many (if not most) take the other side of this question. Offering a consenting adult dangerous and/or addictive drugs, offering a consenting adult money in exchange for sexual services, and offering a consenting adult money in exchange for a vote in an election are acts that are widely regarded as seriously wrong.[5] A defense of the NWC by appealing to consent has a strong libertarian flavor, which, though currently popular, is not universally savored. Why should we accept it?

I think its appeal lies in the fact that one idea adjacent to condemning such acts as morally injurious is that if an act is so "seriously wrong" that it should be morally proscribed, then that act should also be legally proscribed. This would appear to entail criminalizing these exploitative but consensual acts; it would also appear to entail assigning criminal penalties to the violation of the law. Many otherwise liberal democracies criminalize prostitution, the sale of one's own organs, and much recreational drug use. However, this criminalization is often at odds with liberal ideology. John Stuart Mill famously argued that the only good reason to punish, either by "moral opinion" or by law, the conduct of another is that such conduct *harms* another—famously known as the "harm principle" (Mill 1978). His modification of this principle, in the face of the objection that virtually *any* action a person performs has some (albeit indirect) effect on others, is not dispositive. He argues that the kind of harm that we may sanction must violate a "distinct and assignable obligation" that we have not to harm in some very specific way (Mill 1978, 79). What these obligations are is, of course, one of the longest ellipses in modern history.[6] The phrase "between consenting adults" is thus regularly used to defuse any objections to a transaction.

When two or more people engage in a consensual interaction that is mutually beneficial, it might seem that Mill has a ready answer to the question of whether it is morally permissible. But moral permissibility is not really his focus; he is interested in when it is legitimate to interfere with another person's conduct. In fact, Mill does not even have a ready answer to the question of whether it would be acceptable to sanction mutually beneficial exploitation. It might seem as though he does, because it is hard to see how such an interaction would violate the harm principle. It is true that many cases of

---

[5] That has not deterred people from engaging in such acts, or at least endorsing them. In a recent poll, one-third of those surveyed said they would give up their right to vote—for life—for a 10 percent annual pay raise (Calfas 2018).

[6] Joel Feinberg wrote four volumes trying to answer this question, and concluded that only harm and possibly some forms of offense could justifiably limit individual liberty. It is a masterly work, and yet does not substantially upend Mill's conclusion in the very succinct *On Liberty*.

such exploitation have effects on others, but do they have effects that would violate a "distinct and assignable obligation" against that particular harm?

The examples used by Mill are not terribly illuminating. Consider the issue of "free trade." Are market transactions between consenting adults off-limits, or may society regulate them? Mill calls trade a "social act" and says that, as such, it "comes within the jurisdiction of society in general." He goes on to criticize prices that are set by the government because setting prices, he points out, is counterproductive; they "do not really produce the results which it is desired to produce by them." And yet, he says, "restrictions on trade, or on production for purposes of trade, are indeed restraints; and all restraint, qua restraint, is an evil." He concludes that, nevertheless, the principle of liberty is not involved in

> the doctrine of free trade, so neither is it in most of the questions which arise respecting the limits of that doctrine, as, for example, what amount of public control is admissible for the prevention of fraud by adulteration; how for sanitary precautions, or arrangements to protect workpeople employed in dangerous occupations, should be enforced on employers ... that they may legitimately be controlled for these ends is in principle undeniable. (Mill 1978, 94–95)

Thus it seems that free trade may legitimately be restricted after all—*so long as the reason for doing so is not paternalistic*. Restrictions on free trade must not "second-guess" what the parties involved regard as conducive to their own well-being. Mill concludes that if the justification for the restrictions on trade appeals to the well-being of the persons involved in the transactions, then that trade can be regulated. In the case of the buying and selling of "stimulants," for example, Mill says that these transactions may not be taxed or discouraged because society does not approve of their use. This makes it seem as though Mill thinks that the well-being of society can be the basis of restrictions, but not the well-being of the people involved in the transaction, insofar as the people involved regard the transactions as productive. The idea seems to be that paternalistic restrictions on trade would be a tax on individuality—on freethinking or otherwise experimental lifestyles that we all need to be able to at least contemplate. Although we must not interfere with the flourishing of individuality, we may restrict transactions on other grounds. Gambling may not be prohibited, he argues; nor shall "fornication," because that would be a liberty-restricting tax on individuality. The state may not sanction houses of gambling and fornication if those establishments are limited to members, but the state may prohibit gambling open to the public. It may seem that this would lead Mill to conclude that selling oneself into slavery is permissible, but he argues that this is not so: "It is not freedom to be allowed to alienate [one's] freedom" (Mill 1978, 101).

What we can conclude is that for Mill, the one principle that may *not* be invoked in order to justify interference with a putatively exploitative transaction is paternalism—concern for the good of the own agent—except in the limiting case of self-slavery. Unless exploitative interactions constitute self-slavery, they can only be regulated for non-paternalistic reasons.

There are many reasons to think that criminalizing such acts would be dangerous, harmful, or simply pointless. People who do benefit from such acts are, after all, highly motivated to continue to engage in them, and their consenting counterparts will help to ensure that they do so. And even if many violators were caught and many others deterred, there might be good reasons to not legally sanction consensual acts, even when they are morally injurious.

However, it is a mistake to think that we ought to legally prohibit all morally injurious actions or transactions. Hampton explicitly says that there might be insufficient reason to prohibit morally injurious speech that is manifestly racist. Hampton suggests instead that when an action involves moral injury that reaches a certain *threshold*, retribution is warranted.

She argues that some wrongful actions cause harm (murder), but others do not (attempted murder; negligent driving that does not cause an accident). In addition, some harmful actions involve no wrongdoing whatsoever (purely accidental injury to another). However, there are also actions that are wrongful but do not call for retributive justice (using another person's dock in a storm without permission and damaging it; suicide). What do the wrongful actions have in common, then, given that the harm itself is not what makes the action wrong? Hampton located the source of the wrongdoing in moral injury. The moral injury is conveyed by the expressive content of the action, but acts of negligence, she argues, convey the requisite expressive content for moral injury to occur. Expressive content that misrepresents, denies, or simply does not honor the value that persons have is morally injurious. Does mutually beneficial exploitation contain such morally injurious expressive content? Or, alternatively, does mutually beneficial exploitation display a lack of regard for the value that persons have? If, as I have argued, it does, then we have an account of how such exploitation could be wrongful, despite the fact that it cannot be understood to harm either of the parties.

Hampton's account allows for harmless wrongdoing, but does it allow us to develop an account of mutually beneficial wrongdoing? I think it might. If so, it helps us to see our way toward a resolution of the paradox of exploitation.

References

Arneson, R. 2013. "Exploitation and Outcome." *Politics, Philosophy and Economics* 12, no. 4: 392–412.

Arnold, D. G., and N. E. Bowie. 2003. "Sweatshops and Respect for Persons." *Business Ethics Quarterly* 13, no. 2: 221–242. https://doi.org/10.5840/beq200313215.

Arnold, D. G., and L. P. Hartman. 2003. "Moral Imagination and the Future of Sweatshops." *Business and Society Review* 108, no. 4: 425–461. https://doi.org/10.1046/j.0045-3609.2003.00173.x.

Calfas, J. 2018. "Here's What Americans Would Sacrifice for a 10% Pay Raise." *Money*, April 5, 2018. https://money.com/lendedu-survey-lose-voting-rights-pay-raise/.

Coleman, Jules. Risks and Wrongs. Cambridge: Cambridge University Press, 1992.

Faraci, D. 2019. "Wage Exploitation and the Nonworseness Claim: Allowing the Wrong, to Do More Good." *Business Ethics Quarterly* 29, no. 2: 169–188. https://doi.org/DOI: 10.1017/beq.2018.28.

Feinberg, J. 1988. *The Moral Limits of the Criminal Law, Volume 2: Offense to Others*. New York: Oxford University Press. https://doi.org/10.1093/0195052153.001.0001.

Feinberg, J. 1990. *The Moral Limits of the Criminal Law, Volume 4: Harmless Wrongdoing*. New York: Oxford University Press. https://doi.org/10.1093/0195064704.001.0001.

Ferguson, B. 2016. "The Paradox of Exploitation." *Erkenntnis* 81, no. 5: 951–972. https://doi.org/10.1007/s10670-015-9776-4.

Goodman, A. 2006. "Forced Abortions and Sweatshops: A Look at Jack Abramoff's Ties to the South Pacific Island of Saipan and How Tom DeLay Became an Advocate for Sweatshop Factory Owners." *Democracy Now*, January 1, 2006. https://www.democracynow.org/2006/1/4/forced_abortions_sweatshops_a_look_at.

Hampton, J. 1992. "Correcting Harms Versus Righting Wrongs: The Goal of Retribution." *UCLA Law Review* 39, no. 6: 1659–1702.

Hampton, J. 1999. "Defining Wrong and Defining Rape." In *A Most Detestable Crime: New Philosophical Essays on Rape*, edited by K. Burgess-Jackson, 118–156. New York: Oxford University Press.

Holmes, O. W. 1881. *The Common Law*. Boston: Little, Brown.

Krugman, P. 1997. "In Praise of Cheap Labor." *Slate*, March 21, 1997, 1–6.

Maitland, I. 2013. "The Great Non-Debate over International Sweatshops." In *Ethical Theory and Business*, 9th edition, edited by D. G. Arnold, T. L. Beauchamp, and N. E. Bowie, 553–562. Boston: Pearson Education.

Meyers, C. 2004. "Wrongful Beneficence: Exploitation and Third World Sweatshops." *Journal of Social Philosophy* 35, no. 3: 319–333. https://doi.org/10.1111/j.1467-9833.2004.00235.x.

Mill, J. S. 1978. *On Liberty*. Edited by E. Rapaport. Indianapolis: Hackett.

Miller, J. 2003. "Why Economists Are Wrong About Sweatshops and the Antisweatshop Movement." *Challenge: The Magazine of Economic Affairs* 46, no. 1: 93–122.

Myerson, A. R. 1997. "In Principle, a Case for More 'Sweatshops.'" *New York Times*, June 22, 1997.

Powell, B., and M. Zwolinski, M. 2012. "The Ethical and Economic Case Against Sweatshop Labor: A Critical Assessment." *Journal of Business Ethics* 107: 449–472. https://doi.org/10.1007/s10551-011-1058-8.

Roberts, D., and A. Bertstein. 2000. "Inside a Chinese Sweatshop: 'A Life of Fines and Beating.'" *Business Week*, October 2, 2000.

Sample, R. J. 2003. *Exploitation: What It Is and Why It's Wrong*. Lanham, MD: Rowman & Littlefield.

Sherman, N. 2015. *Afterwar: Healing the Moral Wounds of Our Soldiers*. Oxford: Oxford University Press.

Snyder, J. C. 2008. "Needs Exploitation." *Ethical Theory and Moral Practice* 11, no. 4: 389–405.

Tessman, L. 2005. *Burdened Virtues: Virtue Ethics for Liberatory Struggles*. Oxford: Oxford University Press.

Wertheimer, A. 1996. *Exploitation*. Princeton, NJ: Princeton University Press.

Zwolinski, M. 2007. "Sweatshops, Choice, and Exploitation." *Business Ethics Quarterly* 17, no. 4: 689–727. https://doi.org/10.5840/beq20071745.

8
Exploitation Across Time
Climate Change, Public Debt, and Resource Depletion

Nicola Mulkeen

> The past is a foreign country.
> —L. P. Hartley, *The Go-Between*

1. Introduction

Can we exploit future people? It has been argued that identifying exploitation is especially important in policy domains with an extended timeframe. This includes proposals made within climate policy for passing the costs of climate action on to future generations, or governments accruing public debts on a long-term basis, with the repayments falling on subsequent generations. But how can we exploit future generations? More specifically, how can we exploit future generations when we do not live at the same time?

In this chapter I examine three answers to this question and argue that all three answers are flawed. I then develop and defend the *intergenerational account*. Here, I appeal to structural approaches to exploitation that identify exploitation in global relations, particularly sweatshop labor contracts. I argue that in the same way that structural exploitation can be identified *globally*, it can also be identified *intergenerationally*. I argue that just as our background institutions and structures cross national boundaries, such that people face a limited set of options (for example, entering sweatshop contracts), they can also cross intergenerational boundaries, such that future generations face a limited and morally troublesome set of options. I argue

---

Thank you to Brian Berkey, Benjamin Ferguson, Johannes Kneiss, Hillel Steiner, Andrew Walton and audience members at ToonFest (Newcastle University) and the Zicklin Centre Normative Business Ethics Workshop (Wharton School, University of Pennsylvania) for their insightful and helpful comments.

that the intergenerational account provides a more philosophically satisfying explanation of exploitation across time and explains how exploitation between generations not only is possible but also is likely to arise in our world. To make this case, I examine key contexts involving resource depletion and long-term public debt in the context of climate change. In the latter context, I show how exploitation between generations is possible, where the earlier generations do the exploiting. However, in the former context of resource depletion, I show how earlier generations can give rise to preconditions that facilitate the exploitation of later generations.

2. Exploiting the Future

In this section, I examine three different accounts of exploitation across (non-overlapping) generations that have been suggested in the literature. I argue that all three suffer from various deficiencies, and so fail to capture exploitation across time.

2.1. The Distributive Account

According to Matthew Rendall, we exploit future people when we unfairly take advantage of our temporal position by depriving them of their just inheritance (Rendall 2011, 243). We determine a future generation's share of just inheritance depending on our theory of distributive justice. For Rendall, this means that there will inevitably be different accounts of exploitation depending on what justice requires. Rendall notes that when it comes to exploitation, what is important is the fact that earlier generations can abuse their temporal position and take unfair advantage of their distant descendants (Rendall 2011, 243). Similarly, Hallie Liberto argues that earlier generations exploit later ones when they deplete future generations' resources. On Liberto's understanding, exploitation has two features: first, that an agent is vulnerable, and second, that another agent benefits from that agent's vulnerability (Liberto 2014, 76–79). Liberto argues that depleting resources meets the first of these conditions because distant future generations have no alternative but to live with the amount and quality of resources left to them by the current generation (Liberto 2014, 77). Moreover, in choosing to deplete resources, the current generation is enjoying advantages by using more than their fair share of these resources, whereas future generations will have less than their fair share (Liberto 2014, 78).

The problem with the distributive account is that it wrongly describes acts of theft as exploitation. Suppose I take all worldly possessions from Albert because he is too sick to stop me. This case satisfies the criteria for exploitation on the distributive framework. On Rendall's account I gain from depriving Albert of his just possessions. On Liberto's account I gain benefits from Albert's vulnerability. However, it is obvious that I am stealing from Albert, not exploiting him. Theft and exploitation are two different concepts. In the case of a theft, goods travel in one direction from the victim to the thief—there is no reciprocation. Theft is not consensual and, typically, makes the victim worse off. Exploitation, on the other hand, involves a morally troublesome exchange with goods and services traveling in both directions.[1] Unlike theft, exploitative transactions can also be mutually beneficial and consensual.[2] For example, sweatshop labor contracts improve people's situation relative to a non-transaction baseline insofar as they move workers out of starvation and employers benefit from labor inputs. Workers also choose to enter these contracts to the extent that they choose to move from their status quo in which they are subject to dire poverty to another situation in which they are spared such hardship. Victims of theft, however, do not typically choose to move from their status quo to another situation in which they have been robbed. Thus, in identifying acts of theft as exploitation, the distributive account stretches our ordinary understanding of exploitation too far. I conclude that the account fails to provide us with an adequate account of exploitation across time.

2.2. The Reciprocity Account

A plausible way to deal with the conceptual overstretch worry might be to redefine intergenerational exploitation as a breach of fair reciprocity. A reciprocity-based definition captures our sense in which exploitation involves an unfair exchange. This type of view is held by Christopher Bertram (2009), who argues that when people are linked together in cooperation there

---

[1] See Steiner 1984, 233.
[2] See Berkey 2019, 2021; Goodin 1987; Ferguson 2016; Sample 2003; Steiner 1984; Valdman 2009; Wertheimer 1996; Zwolinski, 2007.

is exploitation when the distribution of rewards from that cooperation fails to be roughly proportional to the distribution of effortful contribution. He argues that the possibility of intergenerational exploitation arises because cooperative schemes may span a number of generations. Just as within a group of contemporaries, shirkers exploit their counterparts, this is also the case in long-term intergenerational cooperation (Bertram 2009, 156). For example, if one generation neglects to invest in the maintenance of infrastructure and pushes these costs onto future generations, then on Bertram's view this generation would be described as exploiting future people (Bertram 2009, 156).

However, there are several problems with the reciprocity-based definition. First, it is difficult to understand how a breach of fair reciprocity has occurred unless we can identify an exchange between future people and their ancestors who have ceased living. This problem is outlined by Nicholas Vrousalis (2023). Vrousalis asks us to imagine there are n generations, $G_1, G_2, \ldots, G_n$, such that G_1 overlaps with G_2 but not with G_3, G_2 overlaps with G_3 but not G_4, and so on. Vrousalis argues that G_1 cannot exploit G_3. He accepts that G_1 undoubtedly has power over G_3.[3] But G_1 cannot extract unequal exchange from G_3—G_1 cannot have G_3 unilaterally serve G1—because G_1 is not around when G_3 is around, and vice versa. So G_1 cannot exploit G_3.

Second, a lack of reciprocity is insufficient for exploitation. For example, gifts are non-reciprocal and involve knowingly imposing disproportionate burdens or benefits on those engaged in cooperation. But in the case of gift giving, we do not want to say that people are exploited because the distribution of rewards fails to be roughly proportional (Goodin 1987, 175–176; Risse and Wollner 2019, 85). In the intergenerational context, if an earlier generation transfers resources to a later generation—without hope or expectation of a return—we do not want to say that the interaction is exploitative. Third, there is a danger of swamping later generations with duties of reciprocity, especially if unintentionally produced benefits give rise to the same range of duties as intentionally produced benefits. Here, there are also issues surrounding the involuntary receipt of benefits. According to Nozick (1974, 90–95), foisting benefits on others without their consent can never generate obligations to pay the benefactors because this would implausibly subject us to other people's will. For these reasons it seems that we need to look elsewhere for the moral basis of how future people can be exploited.

---

[3] This is assuming that G_3 will exist.

2.3. The Extortion View

The above objections might lead us to an entirely different approach that we can call the extortion view. Extortion is a form of coercion in which one party intentionally attempts to secure goods by threatening to commit an injury or harmful action against the victim. The extortion account avoids one of the key objections that afflicts the distributive and reciprocity accounts: it is not necessary to identify an exchange because extortion involves a unilateral interaction with benefits traveling from the victim to the extortioner. This view has recently been advocated by Stephen Gardiner (2017). According to Gardiner, extortion is a threat to intergenerational relations and the threat is manifest in some existing proposals in climate policy.

Gardiner's account is directed against John Broome's "efficiency without sacrifice" proposal, which favors passing on the costs of climate action to future people. Broome's view, roughly, is that adequate climate action can be achieved if the current generation undertakes robust mitigation at the expense of future generations. As an example, Broome proposes that we reduce our individual emissions to zero through offsetting—that is, by investing in activities that absorb greenhouse gases. This implies that present people may leave fewer resources (artificial and natural) to future people, as these people will be better off on balance than they would have been if emitters had not emitted less carbon (Broome 2012, 44–45). According to Gardiner, Broome's proposal constitutes extreme intergenerational extortion. To make his case, Gardiner draws parallels between Mafia protection rackets and Broome's proposal. Both practices are thought to involve the principle that the vulnerable should pay *because* they are vulnerable. Mafia organizations demand protection money in exchange for "ensuring the security of their victims" by not violently attacking them. This protection money becomes "compensation" for not exercising that threat. Similarly, Broome's proposal requires that the most vulnerable (future generations) should "compensate" or pay off the less vulnerable (their predecessors and especially the current generation) to induce them to restrain their emissions (Gardiner 2017, 371, 374, 376). Gardiner says that in both cases, the threat is created by those who must be paid off, so compensation looks more like money for menaces (Gardiner 2016, 377).

Although the extortion view avoids one of the key objections that afflicts the distributive and reciprocity accounts, it does suffer from two fundamental problems. First, there is difficulty conceptualizing extortion between non-overlapping generations. Extortion is a coercive relationship between two agents in which one agent issues a threat, the second agent deliberates and responds, and the first agent acts based on the second agent's decision. But this kind of conversation does not exist between non-overlapping generations. You cannot extort if the other party cannot be influenced by the threat. This is rather like my sending a threatening email, but the victim cannot see the threat because they do not have access to the account. Second, existing climate policy proposals (passing the costs of climate action on to future generations) do not meet the intentionality condition for extortion. Extortion involves one party *intentionally* attempting to secure goods by threatening to commit a future injury against the victim. For the extortion charge to hold, we would need to identify a group-level intention—from existing generations—to use fear to threaten future people. However, applying extortion to the climate change context does not consider that climate change is a threat that we have inherited, along with a myriad of background institutions and social structures that involve people necessarily releasing pollutants to satisfy their basic needs. What the extortion approach misses is the restrictive background conditions that some members of current generations face in the context of climate change. The phenomenology of extortion and the intentionality condition it advocates do not fit with the issues facing current generations because of institutional and social structures that restrict the actions and choices of the world's people. Unless we can find such an intention, we should resist the conclusion that current generations are guilty of extorting future people.

3. Structural Exploitation

As a solution to the deficiencies in the accounts considered in the previous section, I argue that exploitation in the intergenerational terrain is best explained by closely examining how our background social structures function across time. Drawing on prominent structural accounts of exploitation, I argue that institutional structures matter for intergenerational exploitation.

Structural accounts of exploitation have a shared understanding that exploitation can be a structural phenomenon that is built into our political, legal, and economic systems and that it can occur between groups. For example, in the context of sweatshop labor contracts, we might consider exploitation as hinging on the problematic exchange between the sweatshop owner and the worker. A structural account recognizes that sweatshop owners can struggle to raise the wages of workers because they are living in perpetual fear of being driven out of business. Supply chains force businesses to compete and select manufacturers that put forward the lowest price. At the same time, developing countries lower taxes to encourage multinational companies to work within their country because they know their citizens desperately need the work. So, what we have is a race to the bottom between developing countries and sweatshops to win these contracts and supply chain status. Focusing on the discrete transactions between individuals misses how the operations of many of our domestic and global institutions and practices can be the site of exploitation—by constraining the choices of some people and at the same time enabling others to take advantage of these constraints.

Prominent accounts of structural exploitation derive from Iris Marion Young and, more recently, from Mathias Risse and Gabriel Wollner.[4] On Risse and Wollner's view exploitation consists in "power-induced failure of reciprocity," which generates an unfair distribution of the benefits and burdens associated with trade relationships.[5] They argue that an individual is an *exploiter* if her position within the structure compels her to take unfair advantage of others to optimize revenue. An individual is *exploited* if her position compels her to be taken advantage of to maximize revenue. Structural exploitation occurs where constraints or rewards no individual can alter make it rational for some to exploit, or for others to subject themselves to exploitation (Risse and Wollner 2019, 100). On Young's account, most of us participate in structural processes that harm or have unjust consequences for others because of our jobs or purchasing choices (shopping in Primark, buying Apple products, etc.). We therefore share political responsibility to fix structural injustice. Political responsibility involves working collectively to prevent future harms on the grounds that we are connected by our own actions to the processes that cause injustice for others, along with our relative power and privilege. Very simply, more powerful individuals and institutions have more responsibility to change unfair processes. Those who acquire privileges by virtue of the structures have special responsibilities to correct

---

[4] For discussions on the significance of structural exploitation, see Berkey 2019, 2021; Gray 2020; Kuch 2020; McKeown 2016; Mulkeen 2020, 2023; Sample 2003; Wollner 2019; Zwolinski 2012.

[5] For other fairness-based accounts of exploitation, see Berkey 2019, 2021; Cohen 1979; Goodin 1987; Ferguson 2016, 2020; Roemer 1986; Sample 2003; Steiner 1984; Valdman 2009; Wertheimer 1996; Wood 1995.

them. According to Young, our political responsibilities must be discharged if we are to mitigate exploitation created by our social structures.

I argue that in the same way that structural exploitation can be identified *globally*, it can also be identified *intergenerationally*. Just as our background institutions cross national boundaries, such that people face a limited set of options (for example, entering sweatshop contracts), they can also cross intergenerational boundaries, such that succeeding generations face a limited set of options.

What structural accounts take seriously is the implications of constrained agency generated by our social structures and the fact that most agents must choose what to do from a limited set of options. I contend that structural exploitation, identifiable on a global scale, is equally discernible on an intergenerational scale. Much like how our foundational institutions traverse national borders, constraining people to a restricted set of choices (like resorting to sweatshop employment), these institutions can span across generational lines, similarly limiting the choices available to future generations. What we need is a structural and intergenerational account to identify intergenerational exploitation.

Importantly, there are two different ways in which our institutional structures can be the site of intergenerational exploitation. On the one hand, our structures and institutions can constrain the options of later generations and enable earlier generations to take advantage of these constraints. In this kind of case, we can see how it is possible for an earlier generation to exploit a future non-overlapping generation. On the other hand, our institutions can constrain the options of some future people and at the same time enable other future people to take advantage of these constraints. In this kind of case, our institutional structures create the preconditions for future exploitative relationships. In the following sections, I examine key contexts involving resource depletion and long-term public debt in the context of climate change to show these two types of exploitation at work.

4. Exploiting Future People

Earlier generations can be accused of exploitation when they design and/ or maintain institutions and processes that allow them to take out huge debts and pass on the costs to future generations. In this kind of case, earlier generations use structural and institutional processes to enjoy benefits of expenditures while imposing the costs upon future people. An example, discussed by Gardiner, involves recent policy proposals suggesting that we take out large-scale public debts to cover the costs of climate mitigation and adaptation.[6] These massive debts will be passed on to future taxpayers who are not yet born. Typically, public debt takes the form of government bonds, where governments induce domestic or foreign investors to loan money by guaranteeing a payout when the bond matures. This payout is greater than the amount lent, as it includes interest payments, and the interest payments can be paid in increments or when the loan matures.

To see how it is possible for earlier generations to exploit later generations, let us begin by first imagining that in a society, generation 1 (G_1) borrows £500 billion at time t_1 to cover the costs of climate mitigation and adaptation. Suppose that t_2 is the point in time at which all members of generation 1 have died, and this massive debt continues to bind generation 3 (G_3), so they pay a significant proportion of the costs. In such a case, G_1 has been able to use political, economic, and legal structures to impose disproportionate costs on G_3 that are binding. For example, G_3 can be forced to honor the massive debts due to the disastrous consequences of refusing to pay back the money owed: being excluded from further credit, being subject to high interest rates on subsequent borrowing, turmoil in international trade, recession, and economic upheavals.

So, what we have is a situation in which G_1 takes out a loan from L and this is passed on to G_3. Because G_3's bargaining position is worse than G_1's—because they are not yet born when the loan is taken out—then G_1 can issue a repayment schedule in which G_3 pays the bulk of the bill. However, to get this argument off the ground and show this is a case of exploitation and not another type of injustice such as theft (whereby G_1 steals from their successors), then we need to ensure that this case meets the conditions for exploitation that I described earlier. Specifically, we need to ensure that there is a mutually beneficial and consensual exchange taking place. We also need to ensure that the exchange has the same wrong-making features identified in the structural accounts.

Let's first consider the matter of a *mutually beneficial exchange*. Here, it is helpful to draw on James Madison's argument contained in a letter he sent to

---

[6] Mitigation involves a duty to cut back on activities that cause climate change (for example, activities that cause emissions of greenhouse gases) and to have a decarbonized economy. Adaptation involves a duty to devote resources to protect people from the ill effects of climate change (for example, spending money on seawalls, inoculating people against infectious diseases).

Thomas Jefferson in the year in which Congress proposed the Bill of Rights. Madison famously argues that when it comes to public debts, such debts may be incurred for purposes that interest younger generations as well as the unborn. This includes debts for repelling a conquest and debts for the benefit of posterity. According to Madison, what we need to do is ensure that the debts against succeeding generations do not exceed the advances made by earlier generations.

If we apply Madison's reasoning to our case, then we might say that G_3 engages in a beneficial exchange with both L and G_1. This is because L receives interest payments from the loan, G_3 receives benefits of posterity (the effects of a climate mitigation program such as a decarbonized economy, adaptation advancements, etc.) in exchange for servicing the loan. G_1 also receives these benefits (but they might also receive additional benefits in the form of fiscal stimulus generated by climate mitigation and adaptation initiatives). So, what we can see is a mutually beneficial exchange of goods and services taking place between G_1, G_3, and L.

Let us now turn to the matter of consent. How does G_3 consent to this kind of interaction if generations do not overlap? Here, I think that we can draw on a Lockean answer to this concern. According to Locke (1980), at the age of majority, later generations come to be bound—by their tacit consent—to obey the laws of their ancestors by inheriting, or residing on, the land of their ancestors. This explains how later generations consent to these laws and the paying of public debt in our case. G_3 offers morally binding tacit consent to the loan by continuing to remain on the soil of their ancestors and taking the benefits provided by the loan.

However, some might question the consensual nature of this type of exchange. A familiar objection pressed against Locke concerns the freedom of tacit consent. Can later generations really be said to consent to the state if they have nowhere else to go? States have discretionary control over migration: they erect walls, detain people in camps, ship people back home, and so on. Thus, if leaving one's country is the alternative, how can these agreements be consensual? In response, it is helpful to consider Robert Nozick's (1997) framework for distinguishing threats from offers. Nozick maintains that threats consist of coercion and offers do not. What is key is that the structure of an exploitative interaction closely resembles what Nozick describes as a restricted offer. For Nozick, a proposal is an offer if a person would rationally choose to move from the pre-offer situation to the offer situation. This can be contrasted with a threat where people do not prefer to make this move—if

I were to force you to hand over your wallet at the point of a gun, then I would be moving you from a status quo to another situation in which you would not have chosen to put yourself (Nozick 1997, 41). In the case of an offer, my intervention involves moving you from a status quo to another situation that you would prefer. For Nozick, the threat/offer distinction is also marked by the fact that compliance with a threat will leave a person worse off than she was in the pre-threat situation. By contrast, accepting an offer makes a person better off than she was in the pre-offer situation—for example, by helping the person or reducing the harm she faced. If we consider this framework in the context of sweatshop labor contracts, workers in developing countries are moved from their status quo to another situation in which they are better off. Indeed, these workers desperately want and compete for sweatshop contracts because they benefit workers, moving them out of extreme poverty. Similarly, in our public debt example, we can identify a mutually beneficial and consensual transaction: earlier generation G_1, later generation G_3, and L all gain benefits from the loan. We might also say that G_3 tacitly consents to the loan by accepting the benefits it provides (e.g., by accepting benefits from a climate mitigation program, such as a decarbonized economy). To ensure that benefits are not being foisted on G_3 (due to a lack of any reasonable alternative), we can appeal to Nozick's distinction between threats and offers. In our example, it seems plausible that G_3 prefers to move from the pre-proposal situation, in which they are subject to the harmful impacts of climate change, to the proposal situation, in which these harmful impacts have been mitigated.

So, these transactions might be mutually beneficial and consensual. To show that they are exploitative, we now need to identify the wrong-making features. I'll begin with structural constraints and unfairness. What is key is that in the same way that our political, economic, and legal structures and institutions can restrict the options of workers and give factory owners the power to impose sweatshop contracts, our structures and institutions can also restrict the options of later generations and give earlier generations the power to impose binding debts and unfair deals on their successors. Exploitation occurs when earlier generations that receive more than their fair share of the relevant benefits and/or shoulder less than their fair share of the relevant burdens employ the power they possess over succeeding generations involved in trading relationships with them to ensure such an unfair outcome. Earlier generations are under an obligation to refrain from using the power they might possess over succeeding generations subject to our institutions and structures in ways that will generate an unfair distribution of the benefits and burdens associated with cooperative trading activities in which they are engaged.[7]

To return to our case involving G_1 and G_3, because the institutional structure of society can restrict the options of later generations, this gives G_1 power over G_3. G_1 can then use this power to get G_3 to agree to a repayment plan that involves G_1 unfairly benefiting more than G_3 from the loan. For example, imagine G_1 takes out large-scale public debt to protect its members from the ill effects of climate change. This involves procuring a vast number of cooling technologies for its buildings so that members can continue working despite increasing global temperatures. G_3 gains some benefits in the sense that they learn how to develop cooling technologies, but let us also imagine that (i) a large proportion of the debts to cover G_1's cooling technologies is passed on to G_3 and (ii) G_1's cooling technologies contribute to increasing global temperatures in G_3's lifetime. Here, we can see how the financial operations of our institutions and practices can constrain the choices of some future people and at the same time enable earlier generations to use their power to take advantage of these constraints.[8] In this kind of case, we can identify a fairness-based wrong in the exchange if the debts against later generations exceed the benefits made by former generations.

Now let us turn to the matter of political responsibilities. Following Young's framework, we might reason about our political responsibilities along the parameters of (i) connection, (ii) power, and (iii) privilege. We might call these our *intergenerational political responsibilities*.

To flesh out this framework in the context of public debt, earlier generations might trace connections between their own actions and later generations potentially affected by these activities. For example, they might first consider whether they have contributed to the release of emissions (driving cars, international travel, working for and receiving wages from companies that release harmful pollutants, etc.) that can harm their successors. They might also consider whether they have authorized debts to fund mitigation and adaptation programs where the debts restrict the choices of later generations and the costs of covering the debt exceed the advances that future

---

[7] Note here, that this closely assimilates Risse and Wollner's (2019) account of exploitation generated by our global structures and institutions.

[8] This relates to my earlier point that institutions and practices can constrain future people in the context of debt because future people can be forced to honor the massive debts due to the disastrous consequences of refusing to pay back the money owed.

generations receive. Tracing these connections helps us to understand the structural processes that mediate between generations.

More powerful agents within our institutions and structures have more responsibility to change unfair processes and their outcomes, and those with relatively less power (but some ability to influence the powerful members) can take on the responsibility of actively pressuring the more powerful to take responsibility for change. Equally, people who acquire relative privileges because of our institutions and structures have special responsibilities to correct them. Here we might argue that the beneficiaries of activities that cause climate change have special responsibilities not to impose huge debts on their successors—if the debts exceed the advances made by former generations. In such circumstances, these beneficiaries should shoulder the principal financial and other costs associated with implementing policies designed to prevent or reduce human disadvantage arising from climate change.[9] This is not because the more privileged are to blame, but because they have more resources and are able to instigate changes without suffering serious deprivation. Building on the proposal above, it follows that the intergenerational political responsibilities of earlier generations should be discharged if they are to mitigate intergenerational exploitation created by our social structures.

What this section has shown is how it is possible for members of an earlier generation to exploit members of a later one in the case of public debt. So far, I have argued that earlier generations can exploit when they design and/or maintain institutions and processes that allow them to take out huge debts and pass on the costs to future generations. Exploitation occurs when (i) earlier generations use structural and institutional processes so that debts against a later generation exceed the advances/benefits made by the former generation and (ii) members of the former generation fail to honor their intergenerational political responsibilities. In the intergenerational context, our intergenerational political responsibilities are grounded in how we are connected by our own actions to the processes that cause unfairness to later generations, along with our relative power and privilege. Importantly, I'm not arguing that taking out long-term debt and putting costs on the future is ipso facto exploitative. Governments loan money to invest in productive things.[10]

---

[9] This coheres with a general beneficiary-pays principle relating to how the costs of climate mitigation and adaptation ought to be distributed. See Caney 2010; Page 2012.

[10] Smith (2021) has recently argued that states are often more likely to undermine substantive justice by taking on too little debt rather than by taking on too much.

The aim is to identify the conditions in which long-term debt exploits our successors and when it does not.

Next, I show how our institutions can constrain the options of some future people and at the same time enable other future people to take advantage of these constraints. In this kind of case, our institutional structures create the preconditions for future exploitative relationships. I first examine the impacts of climate change and resource depletion to show this type of exploitation at work.

5. Creating the Preconditions for Future Exploitative Relationships

Natural resource depletion is increasing due to anthropogenic activities. When we use fossil fuels, release pollutants, generate hot or cold air, drive a car, travel on trains and planes, and so on, our individual actions accumulate. This results in environmental changes that affect distant others. The actions of individuals engaging in these types of activities in one part of the world can subject spatially distant people in other parts of the world to extreme disadvantage, including the harsh effects of hurricanes, rising sea levels, flooding, radical temperature increases, disease, droughts and water scarcity, and loss of home and livelihood. In the same way, these activities will also have profound and long-lasting impact on temporally distant future people who will be facing environmental dangers throughout their lifetime.

Earlier we considered how the distributive and reciprocity accounts hold that earlier generations can exploit distant future ones by depleting natural resources. However, these accounts are problematic because they fail to identify cooperation between non-overlapping generations. Because these accounts fail to identify cooperation, resource depletion constitutes theft, not exploitation. In this section, I argue that resource depletion does not consist in exploitation where earlier generations (as a group) exploit future generations. Instead, exploitation features in a different way. Specifically, by drawing on a structural account of exploitation, we can see how our institutional and social structures can give rise to preconditions that facilitate the exploitation of future people by their own contemporaries.

Recall that on a structural account many of our domestic and global institutions and practices can be the site of exploitation, by constraining the choices of some people and at the same time enabling others to take advantage of these constraints. The fact that a person is in a constrained position gives others the power to impose unfair deals and extract terms that he or she would not ordinarily contemplate accepting.

It is possible for earlier generations to set the preconditions for exploitation when institutions and social structures are designed or maintained in such a way that they make some members of succeeding generations vulnerable in their trade relations with future others. More specifically, exploitation occurs when some members of future generations that receive more than their fair share of the relevant benefits and/or shoulder less than their fair share of the relevant burdens employ the power they possess over other members involved in trading relationships with them to ensure such an unfair outcome.

To see this type of exploitation, let us consider recent studies showing that some countries are considerably poorer than they would have been without global warming, while other countries are benefiting from global warming (Diffenbaugh and Burke 2019, 9808–9813). Between 1961 and 2010, warming temperatures have significantly slowed economic growth in tropical countries such as India and Nigeria, while aiding economic growth in Canada, Russia, and the United Kingdom. Some communities are bearing the brunt of famine, drought, flooding, and other climate-related horrors. And these problems are set to worsen. But for places such as Canada, melting ice caps could bring economic prosperity by opening major shipping lanes and granting access to vast quantities of natural gas beneath the Arctic Circle. It is predicted that Canada's GDP is set to grow by 242 percent by 2050 (Diffenbaugh and Burke 2019, 9808–9813). If these trends continue, then our carbon-emitting actions will be creating and reinforcing a fundamentally unequal distribution of opportunities, resources, welfare, and power between members of succeeding generations. This can have huge implications when members interact; it can allow those who have more to exercise unacceptable forms of power over victims of the effects of climate change. Consider the following example.

Future Society: Imagine a future society comprised of two groups. Both have been impacted by anthropogenic climate change, but one group (G_3N) situated in the global North has found it easier to adapt. Land that had previously been half buried by snow has become fertile. New plants have appeared, and the group has plenty of fresh water, food supplies, and access to renewable energy sources. People in this group are generally flourishing. On the other hand, many members of the other group (G_3S), situated in the global

South, died during the harsh summer. Drought ravages the landscape. Plants and animals have disappeared, and food supplies are scarce. The remaining members of the group build a boat and set off in search of help or a better climate. After months of sailing, G_3S finds habitable land but discovers that it is occupied by G_3N. Members of G_3N then approach G_3S with this proposal: "Come work long hours in our sweatshop factory and we won't let you starve."

So, exploitation in this case arises when background structural processes restrict the choices of some members of succeeding generations but not others. The fact that some future people are in a restricted position (while others are more advantageously placed) means that others are then able to use the restricted circumstances as leverage to extract unfair terms. Thus, in the same way that people are choosing to enter sweatshop contracts because of global background structures, G_3S is choosing to enter exploitative contracts because historical institutions and structures have restricted their choices. Here, we can identify various wrongs in the above interaction. First, if institutions are being designed and maintained by earlier generations (G_1) so that G_3S faces highly restrictive conditions—leaving the safety of the global North will subject them to climatic horrors—then this puts G_3S in a situation of vulnerability. This means that G_3N can offer sweatshop employment. Here, we might claim that members of G_1—in consenting to and maintaining political, social, and economic institutions—put G_3S in a restrictive condition such that G_3N can exploit G_3S. This is because G_3N can use their power over G_3S to push an unfair deal. In this case, we might say that G_1 acts unjustly if they do this, but it does not follow that G_1 exploits G_3S; they act unjustly perhaps because G_1 does not discharge their political responsibilities and makes G_3S vulnerable to exploitation by others.

Importantly, some members of G_1 might feel constrained by institutions and structures in their own decisions and outcomes. While G_1's activities contribute to this outcome, it seems odd to say that they intend to produce hurricanes, rising sea levels, crop failures, droughts and water scarcity, and so on, which cause devastation in the global South. For example, some members of G_1 might themselves live in developing countries in the global South, where they need to use cheap fossil fuels because this is their only means of avoiding poverty and taking care of their own families. It is therefore important to work with a forward-looking account of intergenerational political responsibilities. Again, these responsibilities might be determined along the parameters of connection, power, and privilege. More specifically, earlier generations might trace connections between their own actions and members of future generations potentially affected by these activities. More powerful members (whether that be states, firms, or individuals) have more responsibility to change unfair processes and their outcomes, and those with relatively less power (but some ability to influence the powerful members) can take responsibility actively to pressure the more powerful to take responsibility for change. Equally, members who acquire relative privileges by virtue of the structures have special responsibilities to contribute to organized efforts to correct them. Again, this is not because the more privileged members are to blame, but because they have more resources and are able to adapt to changed circumstances without suffering serious deprivation. It follows that our intergenerational political responsibilities should be discharged if we are to mitigate the exploitation of our successors created by our institutions and social structures.

6. Conclusion

I have argued that it is possible for individual members of an earlier generation to exploit (non-overlapping) future people, and I hope to stimulate thinking on this type of wrongdoing as a fundamental concern. First, I argued that we should reject the most prominent accounts of exploitation across time: the distributive account, the reciprocity account, and the extortion account. Second, I developed and defended the intergenerational account of exploitation. On this view, exploitation occurs when we design and maintain our background structures so that they put future people in a restricted choice situation in which others (earlier generations or their own contemporaries) can take advantage of their power over victims and impose unfair deals. We do this, I argued, when we transfer public debts to future generations or when we deplete the resources of future generations in the context of climate change.

References

Berkey, B. 2021. "Sweatshops, Structural Injustice, and the Wrong of Exploitation: Why Multinational Corporations Have Positive Duties to the Global Poor." *Journal of Business Ethics* 169: 43–56.

Berkey, B. 2022. "Exploitation, Trade Justice, and Corporate Obligations." *Moral Philosophy and Politics* 9, no. 1: 11–29.

Bertram, C. 2009. "Exploitation and Intergenerational Justice." In *Intergenerational Justice*, edited by A. Gosseries and L. H. Meyer, 147–166. New York: Oxford University Press.
Broome, J. 2012. *Climate Matters*. New York: Norton.
Caney, S. 2010. "Climate Change and the Duties of the Advantaged." *Critical Review of International Social and Political Philosophy* 13, no. 1: 203–228.
Cohen, G. A. 1979. "The Labour Theory of Value and the Concept of Exploitation." *Philosophy and Public Affairs* 8: 338–360.
Diffenbaugh, N. S., and M. Burke. 2019. "Global Warming Has Increased Global Economic Inequality." *Proceedings of the National Academy of Sciences of the United States of America* 116: 9808–9813.
Ferguson, B. 2016. "The Paradox of Exploitation." *Erkenntnis* 81, no. 5: 851–872.
Ferguson, B., and S. Köhler. 2020. "Betterness of Permissibility." *Philosophical Studies* 177, no. 9: 2451–2469.
Gardiner, S. M. 2017. "The Threat of Intergenerational Extortion: On the Temptation to Become the Climate Mafia, Masquerading as an Intergenerational Robin Hood." *Canadian Journal of Philosophy* 47, nos. 2–3: 368–394.
Goodin, R. 1987. "Exploiting a Situation and Exploiting a Person." In *Modern Theories on Exploitation*, edited by A. Reeve, 166–200. London: Sage.
Gray, D. 2020. "Rethinking Micro-Level Exploitation." *Social Theory and Practice* 46, no. 3: 515–546.
Kates, M. 2019. "Sweatshops, Exploitation, and the Case for a Fair Wage." *Journal of Political Philosophy* 27, no. 1: 26–47.
Kuch, H. 2020. "The Market, Competition, and Structural Exploitation." *Constellations* 27, no. 1: 95–110.
Liberto, H. 2014. "The Exploitation Solution to the Non-Identity Problem." *Philosophical Studies* 167, no. 1: 73–88.
Locke, J. 1980. *Second Treatise of Civil Government*. Edited by T. I. Cook. New York: Hafner.
McKeown, M. 2016. "Global Structural Exploitation: Towards an Intersectional Definition." *Global Justice: Theory, Practice, Rhetoric* 9, no. 2: 155–177.
Mulkeen, N. 2020. "Exploitation: Bridging the Gap Between Social Egalitarianism and Distributive Egalitarianism." *Political Studies* 6: 954–972.
Mulkeen, N. 2023. "Intergenerational Exploitation." *Political Studies* 71, no. 3: 756–775.
Nozick, R. 1974. *Anarchy, State and Utopia*. New York: Basic Books.
Nozick, R. 1997. *Socratic Puzzles*. Cambridge, MA: Harvard University Press.
Page, E. 2012. "Give It Up for Climate Change: A Defense of the Beneficiary Pays Principle." *International Theory* 4, no. 2: 300–330.
Roemer, J. 1986. *Value, Exploitation and Class*. London: Routledge.
Rendall, M. 2011. "Non-Identity, Sufficiency and Exploitation." *Journal of Political Philosophy* 19, no. 2: 229–247.
Risse, M., and G. Wollner. 2019. *On Trade Justice: A Philosophical Plea for a New Global Deal*. New York: Oxford University Press.
Sample, R. 2003. *Exploitation: What It Is and Why It's Wrong*. Lanham, MD: Rowman and Littlefield.
Smith, P. T. 2021. "Intergenerational Justice and Debt." In *The Oxford Handbook of Intergenerational Ethics*, edited by S. M. Gardiner. Oxford: Oxford University Press.
Steiner, H. 1984. "A Liberal Theory of Exploitation." *Ethics* 94: 225–241.
Valdman, M. 2009. "A Theory of Wrongful Exploitation." *Philosophers' Imprint* 9, no. 6: 1–14.

Vrousalis, N. 2023. *Exploitation as Domination*. New York: Oxford University Press.
Wertheimer, A. 1996. *Exploitation*. Princeton, NJ: Princeton University Press.
Wollner, G. 2019. "Anonymous Exploitation: Non-Individual, Non-Agential, and Structural." *Review of Social Economy* 77, no. 2: 143–162.
Wood, A. W. 1995. "Exploitation." *Social Philosophy and Policy* 12, no. 2: 136–158.
Young, I. M. 2004. "Responsibility and Global Labor Justice." *Journal of Political Philosophy* 12: 365–388.
Young, I. M. 2006. "Responsibility and Global Labor Justice: A Social Connection Model." *Social Philosophy and Policy* 23: 102–130.
Zwolinski, M. 2007. "Sweatshops, Choice and Exploitation." *Business Ethics Quarterly* 17: 689–727.
Zwolinski, M. 2012. "Structural Exploitation." *Social Philosophy and Policy* 29, no. 1: 154–179.

PART III
APPLIED ISSUES IN EXPLOITATION THEORY

9
Unequal Exchange and International Justice

Roberto Veneziani and Naoki Yoshihara

La première des servitudes, c'est la frontière. Qui dit frontière, dit ligature. Coupez la ligature, effacez la frontière, ôtez le douanier, ôtez le soldat, en d'autres termes, soyez libres.

—Victor Hugo, 1869

1. Introduction

The last few decades have been characterized by the progressive removal of barriers to international trade and capital flows, as well as by an increasing integration of national economies, a phenomenon often labeled "globalization." In this period, some areas of the world have experienced an unprecedented growth, but large inequalities in income and standard of living among countries have persisted and, at least according to some indices, actually worsened. Actually, inequalities within advanced nations seem to pale compared to the inequalities between nations. Yet there is no consensus in contemporary political philosophy that such inequalities raise significant moral issues for the citizens of the affluent countries.

There are in fact several views about what constitutes international justice. Among the major writers, Rawls (1999) and Nagel (2005) argue, in different ways, that international justice does not require the maximization of a joint social welfare function; rather, countries engage in some form of

---

We would like to thank Ben Ferguson for useful feedback and suggestions. Special thanks go to Gil Skillman for combing through the paper with his usual care, and for sending us long, detailed and insightful comments. We have done our best to incorporate them but we doubt that the final version of the paper does full justice to them. The usual disclaimer applies.

bargaining over international norms and institutions.[1] More specifically, Rawls (1999) devises a two-stage procedure whereby individuals first meet in the original position to decide principles of justice within each country (leading, inter alia, to the adoption of the difference principle). Then each nation sends a representative to a new round of negotiations in an international original position. According to Rawls, in this second round only the customary rules of international law will be chosen, but no principle of global justice.

Part of Rawls's hesitation to endorse a cosmopolitan extension of his theory of justice derives from the acknowledgment of significant heterogeneity across countries. Not all societies are "well-ordered": in this case, the necessary requirements of justice are unmet, and societies lack the material and other conditions necessary to develop just institutions. Well-ordered societies may have a duty to provide "assistance" to burdened societies to achieve well-ordered status, but the second principle of justice does not apply here. Indeed, Rawls's necessary conditions for a people to participate in the original-position thought experiment are violated in the case of burdened societies. Even among "well-ordered" societies, Rawls allows for the possibility that some countries are not liberal, and therefore do not accept liberal or democratic principles of distribution of the sort expressed in the second principle.

But, and perhaps more surprisingly, a significant part of the anticosmopolitan thrust of the *Law of Peoples*, and of many liberal egalitarians more generally, does not depend on this heterogeneity. *Even in a (counterfactual, ideal) world with liberal societies, national boundaries imply a discontinuous break in our normative thinking*, according to these authors.

Other egalitarians—and in particular socialists—have long condemned international relations and the structure of international trade because of their asymmetric effects on developed and less developed countries.[2] Many authors support a cosmopolitan approach to global justice and raise doubts about the possibility of holding justice important domestically but not internationally.[3] Thomas Pogge (1994) aptly asks:

---

[1] Roemer and Veneziani (2007) analyze the implications of different views about international justice, including the bargaining view and the cosmopolitan approach, for intergenerational equity and environmental sustainability.

[2] The literature is too vast for a comprehensive list of references. See the classic contributions by Emmanuel (1972) and Frank (1978), which sparked extensive debate, and the surveys by Griffin and Gurley (1985) and Howard and King (1999).

[3] The literature is vast here too. A representative but far from comprehensive sample includes Pogge (1989, 1994, 2002); Beitz (2000); and Nielsen (2003).

How can Rawls justify the enormous distributional significance national boundaries now have, and in a Rawlsian world would continue to have, for determining the life prospects of persons born into different states? How can he justify that boundaries are, and would continue to be, associated with ownership of, full control over, and exclusive entitlement to all benefits from, land, natural resources, and capital stock?

This chapter addresses these questions in the context of a thought experiment in ideal theory that focuses on exploitation and unequal exchange between countries, and international justice. We do not try to provide a comprehensive defense of the philosophical foundations of a cosmopolitan approach to international inequalities. Rather, we examine objections to cosmopolitanism in the context of a highly stylized model that captures some of the key characteristics of the current global economy, including the free movement of capital and significant barriers to migration, but at the same time abstracts from differences between burdened and well-ordered societies and, within the latter, between liberal and hierarchical societies.

By examining the structure of the interaction between countries in global markets and identifying some of the root causes of international inequalities in a rather abstract context, we raise doubts about some of the key theoretical objections against a cosmopolitan approach to inequalities. In particular, we show that differences in inherited productive endowments—which citizens are not responsible for—are one of the key determinants of international inequalities in well-being. Considering these inequalities as fundamentally different from inequalities within a country creates some tensions within liberal anti-cosmopolitan approaches. According to all of the main liberal egalitarian views, unequal standards of living generated by morally arbitrary inequality in initial endowments call for redress within country borders. If, once all contingent empirical features are abstracted away and the bare bones of the structure of the global economy are examined, the differences in living standards across country borders are entirely due to differences in inherited per capita endowments, then the anti-cosmopolitan position is hardly tenable from a liberal egalitarian perspective. "For where one is born is a morally arbitrary personal feature, and equality of opportunity mandates compensation to those born into societies with low standards of living" (Roemer 1994, 115). And such inequalities appear all the more arbitrary, and the anti-cosmopolitan view all the more difficult to support, if the compensation required by the equality of opportunity ethic has no supererogatory quality, as we shall argue.

To be sure, one may object that in reality the contingent empirical features that we abstracted from *are* relevant, and unequal living standards do not arise only from morally arbitrary factors and may be perfectly justified at the bar of justice. Even assuming this claim to be correct, it makes no difference to our key conclusions. For our aim is not to argue that justice requires all inequalities between countries to be removed. Rather, our point here is that *at least some* international inequalities in well-being likely arise from morally arbitrary factors—specifically, morally objectionable inequalities in inherited per capita endowments—and, perhaps more importantly, that inequalities *between countries* should be subject to the same normative scrutiny as inequalities *within a country*. Some international inequalities may be justified, but the question about their legitimacy cannot be rejected offhand.

While part of our analysis lies squarely within a liberal egalitarian perspective, a second contribution of our chapter is a discussion of Roemer's (1982, 1983) theory of exploitation, and classes in the international context. Roemer's theory is interesting for two main reasons. First, although it focuses on the notion of unequal exchange (Emmanuel 1972; henceforth UE), it is strictly related to modern theories of equality of opportunity, given its emphasis on the distribution of productive assets. Thus it provides interesting insights on Marxian *and* on liberal egalitarian approaches to international inequalities. Second, unlike much of the economic literature on international trade and justice, it identifies UE in mutually beneficial transactions and competitive markets. From a normative viewpoint, even if UE emerges from voluntary market interactions, it may still be condemned on normative grounds, and international relations can be unjust independently of any non-competitive distortions. Thus Roemer's approach is suitable to analyze international justice at the level of ideal theory—or pure morality, as opposed to practical morality—at which many empirically relevant features of the international economy, such as non-competitive distortions, can be set aside. In this abstract framework, Roemer's theory identifies differences in per capita endowments as the main culprit in generating UE exploitation and classes.

Roemer's general theory of exploitation has generated a vast literature, mostly focused on its methodological foundations,[4] but its application to the international context has received much less attention.[5] Yet, Roemer's approach provides interesting insights on global distributive justice, and it

---

[4] For a survey, see Veneziani 2013.
[5] Notable exceptions include Schweickart 1991, van Parijs 1992, Yoshihara and Kaneko 2016, Veneziani and Yoshihara 2017, and Kaneko and Yoshihara 2019.

contributes to modern debates on globalization and inequalities. Strikingly, we prove that there exists a correspondence between global inequalities, a division of countries into classes, and international UE-exploitative relations. *All* of these phenomena are fundamentally driven by international disparities in per capita productive endowments, which makes the anti-cosmopolitan objections of liberal egalitarian theorists even more puzzling.

Finally, unlike in Roemer (1983), we explicitly apply the game-theoretic definition of exploitation (Roemer 1982), thus formalizing a concept of *citizenship exploitation* different from that first proposed by van Parijs (1992). We prove, again, that capitalist exploitation arises in the global economy due to differential endowments. Not only does this provide further support to our cosmopolitan approach by confirming the relevance of morally arbitrary factors in the emergence of international inequalities and various forms of exploitation. It also allows us to dispel some standard—pragmatic, rather than theoretical—objections against cosmopolitan egalitarian approaches.

To be specific, our results suggest that a mixture of capital transfers and measures ensuring freer (if not completely free) movement of people may go a long way toward redressing international injustices. On the one hand, this provides ethical foundations for relaxing border restrictions as a policy that various stripes of egalitarians should support. On the other hand, this forcefully shows that there exist some reasonable, and realistically implementable, policies to address the massive inequalities that characterize the current global economy.

It is worth stressing at the outset that our aim is not to develop a comprehensive policy analysis taking into account the costs and benefits of different approaches. Therefore, our conclusions should not be taken as unreservedly supporting an open-border approach or massive international transfers of capital. Ours is an exercise in ideal theory, and we only focus on distributive justice: there may be "non-ideal" reasons, or trade-offs between distributive concerns and other fundamental goods (for example, health), suggesting to restrict movement across borders (Roemer 2006). Subject to this important caveat, our basic point stands: the reduction of inequalities and the mitigation of UE exploitation do not entail massive strains of commitment, the creation of a world state, or the socialization of assets at a world scale.

The rest of the chapter is structured as follows. In section 2, the model of the international economy is set up. Section 3 analyzes international inequalities in equilibrium. In section 4, the concepts of UE exploitation and class are defined and the full class and UE exploitation structure of international relations is characterized. Section 5 analyzes the game-theoretic notion of capitalist exploitation, and some policies to tackle international inequalities. Section 6 concludes.

2. The Model

We consider a dynamic generalization of Roemer's (1982, 1983) economies with a credit market. Roemer's models can be interpreted as describing either a single period or a sequence of identical periods, but in either case agents' savings decisions and the intertemporal trade-offs they face are not explicitly considered. As shown by Veneziani (2007), Veneziani and Yoshihara (2017), and Kaneko and Yoshihara (2019), this assumption is not innocuous, and an explicit consideration of the dynamic dimension of agents' decisions is important from both a positive and a normative viewpoint.

The economy consists of a set of countries $\aleph = \{1, \ldots, N\}$ in which a sequence of non-overlapping generations exists, each generation living for $T + 1$ periods and indexed by the date of birth $k(T + 1)$, $k = 0, 1, 2, \ldots$ In what follows, we shall lay out the model focusing on the first generation ($k = 0$): the notation can be extended to subsequent generations ($k > 0$) with obvious adaptations.

Capital can freely migrate across borders seeking the highest return, whereas labor is immobile. The economy produces one consumption good that is also used as a productive input.[6] Technology is freely available to all countries: in every period t, capitalists in each country can operate any activity of the fixed coefficient technology (A, L), where $0 < A < 1$ and $L > 0$ are, respectively, the amounts of produced input and labor necessary to produce one unit of the good.[7]

Unlike in Roemer (1982, 1983, 1988), agents (countries) produce, consume, and exchange over several periods. In every t, p_t and r_t denote, respectively, the (international) price of the produced good and the interest rate. It is assumed that agents are identical within each country, so the superscript v denotes both a country and its representative agent. This can be interpreted

---

[6] Assuming a single good allows us to avoid a number of unnecessary technicalities. All of our basic insights can be extended to general m-good economies.

[7] In order to abstract from unnecessary technicalities, we assume that technology remains constant over time. For an analysis of the effects of technical change on exploitation and class, see Cogliano, Veneziani, and Yoshihara 2016.

as a simplifying assumption to focus on international market exchanges, or—perhaps more significantly—as reflecting Rawls's two-stage approach, whereby agents first agree on principles of justice within each country, including the difference principle, and then meet in the international original position. Because effort is nugatory, justice requires complete equality within borders.[8] This means that we can take our model as providing a stylized description of a world economy with liberal peoples who interact on a global capital market (interdependence) and where the first-stage original position guarantees justice (equality) within each country. According to Rawls (1999, §16.3), no global redistribution will, or should take place in this context.

In every t, each agent (country) is endowed with a certain amount of the good, ω_t^v—where ω_0^v denotes the endowments inherited at birth—and labor, l^v, which is assumed to be time-invariant, reflecting the immobility of labor.[9] At the beginning of each period, an agent v can engage in three types of economic activities: she can activate production either with her own capital, x_t^v, or with borrowed capital, y_t^v, and she can lend capital abroad, z_t^v. $\Lambda_t^v = Lx_t^v + Ly_t^v$ is the amount of labor v performs in productive activities at t. At the end of the period, any (net) income obtained from economic activities can be devoted either to consumption c_t^v or to (net) savings s_t^v.

Unlike in Roemer (1982, 1983), where agents minimize labor or maximize revenue, we assume that countries maximize the discounted present value of lifetime consumption streams. There are several reasons for this choice. First, while it is reasonable to suppose that agents minimize labor in subsistence economies, it seems less plausible in the global economy with a credit market and savings. Furthermore, the assumption that agents minimize labor creates an immediate link between welfare inequalities and exploitation as the unequal exchange of labor. In our analysis, however, we want to distinguish these phenomena and explicitly analyze the relations between them.

Second, given our focus on countries and the one-good assumption, it is appropriate to assume that agents maximize consumption rather than utility. Furthermore, given our focus on exploitation and liberal theories of equality of opportunity, it may be argued that it is preferable to have an objective measure of well-being—which may also be interpreted as a simple index of

---

[8] We follow standard practice in economics and interpret Rawls's second principle of justice as the adoption of the maximin social welfare function (see, for example, Roemer 1996).

[9] If each v is a representative of her people, then l^v can be interpreted as the country's population, e.g., a continuum of agents living in the country.

primary goods—instead of a subjectivist neoclassical utility function. It is worth stressing, however, that all of our key conclusions continue to hold—albeit with a substantial increase in technicalities—if one assumes that countries maximize discounted utility, rather than consumption.[10]

Last, but definitely not least, we aim to abstract from any heterogeneity in preferences: different cultural traits feature prominently in Rawls's (1999, §16.2) explanation of international inequalities, and his normative conclusions crucially depend on the assumption that cultural differences play a key role in differential outcomes across countries. This, however, is an empirical postulate that may or may not be valid. It is therefore theoretically apt to abstract from such differences in the analysis of international inequalities among liberal peoples emerging in the second stage of the original position.

Let $c^v = \{c_t^v\}_{t=0}^T$ denote v's lifetime consumption plan; likewise for $x^v, y^v, z^v, s^v, \Lambda^v$, and ω^v. Let $(p, r) = \{p_t, r_t\}_{t=0}^T$ denote the path of the price vector during the lifetime of a generation. Let $0 < \beta \leq 1$ be the time preference factor.[11] Each agent chooses a plan $\xi^v = (x^v, z^v, y^v, c^v, s^v)$ to maximize the discounted present value of lifetime consumption streams subject to the constraint that in every t, (1) national income is sufficient for consumption and savings; (2) wealth is sufficient for production and lending; (3) labor performed does not exceed the endowment; and (4) the dynamics of capital is determined by net savings. Furthermore, (5) resources should not be depleted.[12] Formally, countries solve the following intertemporal optimization program:

---

[10] For an analysis of exploitation when agents have general utility functions depending on consumption and leisure, see, for example, Veneziani and Yoshihara (2017).

[11] We consider the possibility that $\beta < 1$ because it allows us to further differentiate welfare inequalities (where time preference *may* play a definitional role in the sense that $\beta < 1$ can be part of the definition of individual welfare) and exploitative relations (where it should arguably *not*; that is, $\beta < 1$ should not be part of the definition of exploitation, at least from a Marxian perspective). The introduction of time discounting is far from uncontroversial in normative theory in general (Rawls 1971), and we have argued elsewhere that time preference should not play a key role in the analysis of the necessary and sufficient conditions for persistent exploitative relations (Veneziani 2007, 2013; Veneziani and Yoshihara 2017). Yet our purpose here is not to identify the appropriate definition of exploitation, and we are not trying to establish whether exploitation theory reduces to a concern for asset inequalities. In order for our conclusions to hold, all that is required is that asset inequalities play a causally primary role—we need not maintain their normatively primary relevance, let alone their exclusive relevance. (Observe, further, that our arguments are conditional on the existence of welfare inequalities and UE exploitation; the bone of contention between cosmopolitans and their adversaries is not the *existence* of international inequalities but their *relevance* for egalitarians.)

[12] Constraints (1) and (2) are assumed to be binding without loss of generality. Observe that in a one-good economy the notation might be simplified by expressing all magnitudes in physical terms and dropping the price p_t. However, we follow the literature and keep prices in the model for

$$MP^v : V(\omega_0^v) = \max_{\xi^v} \sum_{t=0}^{T} \beta^t c_t^v$$

subject to

$$p_t(1-A)x_t^v + [p_t - (1+r_t)p_t A]y_t^v + r_t z_t^v = p_t c_t^v + p_t s_t^v \quad (1)$$

$$p_t A x_t^v + z_t^v = p_t \omega_t^v \quad (2)$$

$$\Lambda_t^v = L x_t^v + L y_t^v \leq l^v \quad (3)$$

$$\omega_{t+1}^v = \omega_t^v + s_t^v \quad (4)$$

$$\omega_{T+1}^v \geq \omega_0^v \quad (5)$$

Let E_0 denote the economy with technology (A, L), time preference factor β, and distribution of endowments $((\omega_0^1, \omega_0^2, ..., \omega_0^N), (l^1, l^2, ..., l^N))$. Let $x_t = \sum_{v \in \aleph} x_t^v$; and likewise for $y_t, z_t, s_t, \Lambda_t, \omega_t$, and c_t. Let $l = \sum_{v \in \aleph} l^v$. Following Roemer (1982, 1983), the equilibrium concept can now be defined.[13]

Definition 1. *A reproducible solution (RS) for E_0 is a path of price vectors (p, r) and an associated set of actions such that*

  (i) *ξ^v solves MP^v, for all v;*
  (ii) *$(x_t + y_t) \geq A(x_t + y_t) + c_t + s_t$ for all t;*
  (iii) *$A(x_t + y_t) \leq \omega_t$, for all t;*
  (iv) *$p_t A y_t = z_t$, for all t;*
  (v) *$\omega_{T+1} \geq \omega_0$.*

In other words, at an RS, (i) every agent optimizes. Moreover, in every t there are enough resources (ii) for consumption and saving plans and (iii) for production plans, and (iv) the international credit market clears. Finally, (v) every generation is required not to deplete resources.[14]

It is immediate to prove that in equilibrium, in every period, the price of the commodity is strictly positive, net revenues must be non-negative,

---

conceptual clarity and because it suggests how to generalize the framework to economies with n goods (Roemer 1988).

[13] For the sake of notational simplicity, we write "for all t" instead of "for all $t, t = 0, ..., T$."

[14] Because at the solution to MP^v, $\omega_{T+1}^v = \omega_0^v$, all v, it follows that if (p, r) is an RS for E_0, then it is also an RS for E_{T+1}. Hence, our focus on generation $k = 0$ yields no loss of generality.

170 EXPLOITATION

and if they are strictly positive, every country works up to the maximum amount, l^ν.[15]

In the next sections, we devote particular attention to equilibria in which agents do not save ($s_t^\nu = 0$, all ν, t), which we call *interior RS's* (henceforth IRS). We focus on such stationary equilibria because we do not aim to describe the dynamics of capitalist economies; ours is a normative thought experiment on international justice, and growth is unnecessary to analyze our concerns. Moreover, at a general RS where agents save, inequalities and exploitation status may change over time depending on the dynamic paths of consumption, savings, and capital due to optimal choices. These changes do not necessarily convey any morally relevant information.

Finally, it can be proved that *even though there exists no international labor market*, in equilibrium wages are equalized across countries in each period. Formally, there is a non-negative sequence $\{w_t\}_{t=0}^T$ such that $p_t = (1 + r_t) p_t A + w_t L$, all t. The possibility of equilibria with $w_t = 0$, some t, is due to the stark specification of the model, which gives no weight to leisure. Therefore, with no loss of generality, in what follows only RS's with $w_t > 0$, all t, are considered and prices are normalized, setting $w_t = 1$, all t.[16]

3. International Inequalities Among Liberal Peoples

In this section we analyze the inequalities that emerge in the global economy where countries interact on the goods and credit markets. The aim is to determine, in our stylized framework, the root causes of such inequalities.

Let $r_\beta \equiv (1 - \beta)/\beta$ and let $p_\beta = L[1 - (1 + r_\beta)A]^{-1}$.[17] Proposition 1 shows that if (p, r) is such that $r_t = r_\beta$ and $p_t = p_\beta$, all t, then it is optimal for agents not to save.[18]

---

[15] Formally, at an RS, at all t: $p_t > 0$; if $c_t + s_t > 0$, then $p_t \geq (1 + r_t) p_t A$; and if $p_t > (1 + r_t) p_t A$, then $\Lambda_t^\nu = l^\nu$, all ν. By Definition 1(i) and (iv), this implies that at an RS with strictly positive net revenues at all t, $\Lambda_t = l = LA^{-1}\omega_t$ at all t: in every period the total labor demand of the global economy is equal to the total supply of labor.

[16] Essentially, this condition rules out the possibility that labor is absolutely abundant in the economy. Because $w_t > 0$ implies $p_t > (1 + r_t) p_t A$, the argument in footnote 14 implies that an RS with $w_t > 0$, all t can only be interior and $\omega_0 = \frac{A}{L} l$ is a necessary condition for its existence. For an analysis of exploitation when labor is abundant in equilibrium, see Cogliano, Veneziani, and Yoshihara (2016). (The proof of existence of an RS is available from the authors upon request.)

[17] In the rest of the chapter, we assume that $\beta > A$, which guarantees a strictly positive wage rate if $r_t = r_\beta$.

[18] It is also possible to prove that (i) there exists a unique IRS with $(p_t, r_t) = (p_\beta, r_\beta)$, all t; and (ii) if (p, r) is an IRS, then $(p_t, r_t) = (p_\beta, r_\beta)$ must hold at all t. Given the arguments in footnotes 14 and 15, it

Proposition 1 *If $r_t = r_\beta$ and $p_t = p_\beta$, all t, then $s_t^v = 0$, all t, solves MP^v for all v. Furthermore, for all agents v: if $\beta < 1$, then $V(\omega_0^v) = \frac{(1-\beta^T)}{p_\beta}\left[\frac{l^v}{(1-\beta)} + \frac{p_\beta \omega_0^v}{\beta}\right]$; if $\beta = 1$, then $V(\omega_0^v) = T\frac{l^v}{\lambda}$.*

In order to interpret Proposition 1, let $K_t^v = \frac{p_t \omega_t^v}{l^v}$: K_t^v is country v's wealth per capita, and it can be interpreted as the main proxy for a country's level of development. A higher K_t^v is associated with more advanced countries; less developed countries are characterized by a lower K_t^v, and pre-capitalist economies have $K_t^v = 0$. Proposition 1 highlights the centrality of the distribution of endowments since it shows that, unless $r_\beta = 0$, per capita wealth is the main determinant of a people's welfare and for all agents $v, \mu \in \aleph$, $\frac{V(\omega_0^v)}{l^v} \gtreqless \frac{V(\omega_0^\mu)}{l^\mu}$ if and only if $K_0^v \gtreqless K_0^\mu$.

In other words, inequalities in wealth per capita drive inequalities in welfare per capita. In equilibrium, the amount of per capita productive resources inherited by countries at birth determine inequalities in per capita welfare in each and every subsequent period and over the lifetime of each generation. Once one abstracts from empirically contingent and highly debatable factors such as differences in cultural traits or attitudes, inequalities are driven by factors that are arguably beyond the control of any one agent or country, such as inherited resources.

Of course, one may argue that resources inherited by one generation are the product of previous generations' choices and that these are *not* morally arbitrary. This argument would indeed be persuasive within, say, an entitlement theory of justice. It is much less cogent, however, within a liberal egalitarian framework. In particular, it is unclear why one should deem inequalities in inherited wealth morally arbitrary when considering individual agents but not at a country's level. Indeed, one advantage of our abstract modeling framework is to highlight the striking formal similarity between the world economy with N countries and a national economy with N independent producers interacting on a credit market. In either case, there seems to be no compelling ground to consider agents entitled to any and all resources bequeathed to them by their predecessors.

Another objection is that the dynamics of accumulation in the real world would be quite different from the steady-state equilibrium depicted in the

---

follows that there exists a unique RS with $w_t > 0$, all t, if and only if $\omega_0 = \frac{A}{\lambda}l$ holds, and this RS is the IRS with $(p_t, r_t) = (p_\beta, r_\beta)$, all t. This provides a further reason to focus on IRS's.

model, and welfare would also be determined, in general, by factors such as preferences, social norms, knowledge and human capital, institutions, political culture, and so on. This is certainly true but it is not relevant to assess the nature of the inequalities in our thought experiment: we have abstracted from all these factors in order to examine the interaction of liberal peoples in a highly stylized framework. Our exercise is theoretically relevant and raises significant doubts about the claim that international welfare inequalities are normatively irrelevant, at least from a liberal egalitarian perspective.

Suppose, then, that, knowing the structure of the equilibria of the economy, the representatives of liberal peoples met in the second stage of the original position in order to decide the most appropriate arrangements for the international economy. Why should their interaction be characterized by bargaining? Why should one not assume that they would adopt the same procedure as in the standard Rawlsian original position? As we have argued above, once one strips away all unnecessary complications, there are sound *normative* arguments to support the extension of the Rawlsian thought experiment to the international context.

But even if one considers decision-making in the original position from the viewpoint of choice under uncertainty, it is quite unclear that—once placed under the veil of ignorance—the representatives of different countries would adopt a dramatically different criterion to deal with international inequalities than in the national context. Suppose the representatives of each country know the basic characteristics of E_0, including preferences, the distribution of productive endowments, and technology, but they do not know their identity.[19] They can compute, in advance, the equilibrium of the economy and the welfare level of each country. If an argument based on extreme risk aversion justifies the adoption of the difference principle, shouldn't the same hold in our context too? If, instead, liberal peoples are assumed to be indifferent to global inequalities among them, as suggested by Rawls (1999, §16.3), then this may be interpreted as implying that in the second-stage original position they would opt for allocation rules that maximize expected utility. In this case, however, they would not advocate international redistribution or a global difference principle but rather utilitarianism, as is well known. This seems at odds with liberal egalitarianism in general, and directly in contradiction with Rawls's (1971) general theory of justice.

---

[19] Pogge (1989, 1994) argues that it is illegitimate to assume that the second-stage representatives will not care about their own people's welfare. This is not inconsistent with their being placed under a veil of ignorance, of course.

4. Unequal Exchange and Cosmopolitan Justice

This section analyzes international justice from a different perspective—namely, John Roemer's (1982, 1983) theory of exploitation as the UE of labor. In this context, the theory of UE is interesting because it also focuses on asset inequalities, consistent with the Marxian tradition, and because it is the intellectual antecedent of Roemer's theory of equality of opportunity, which emphasizes the role of morally arbitrary factors—of which, as we have argued in the previous section, inherited productive endowments seem a clear example.

In a dynamic context, there are two criteria to define UE exploitation, based on the unequal exchange of labor performed either in each period or during the lifetime of a generation. Generalizing Roemer (1983), country v is UE exploited (exploiting) if and only if labor embodied in its consumption bundle is less (more) than the labor expended by its population, either in t or during its lifetime. Let $\lambda = \lambda A + L$ denote embodied labor: this is the amount of labor directly and indirectly necessary to produce one unit of output. Given our assumptions, $\lambda = L(1 - A)^{-1} > 0$.

Definition 2 *At an IRS for E_0, country v is UE exploited within period t if and only if $\Lambda_t^v > \lambda c_t^v$ while it is an UE exploiter if and only if $\Lambda_t^v < \lambda c_t^v$. Similarly, country v is UE exploited during its whole life if and only if $\sum_{t=0}^{T} \Lambda_t^v > \sum_{t=0}^{T} \lambda c_t^v$, while it is an UE exploiter if and only if $\sum_{t=0}^{T} \Lambda_t^v < \sum_{t=0}^{T} \lambda c_t^v$.*

The two definitions incorporate different normative concerns. The whole-lives (henceforth WL) definition reflects the intuition that, from a single country's viewpoint, to be exploited in every period is certainly worse than being exploited only in some periods. An analysis based on the within-period (henceforth WP) definition captures the idea that the existence of exploitation is morally relevant per se, and a global economy where countries switch their exploitation status over time is not necessarily just. This distinction, however, is not central to the main thread of this chapter, and since both criteria convey normatively relevant information, both are considered below.[20]

Let $K^* \equiv \frac{p_\beta - \lambda}{r_\beta \lambda}$. Theorem 1 proves that at an IRS, the WL and WP definitions of exploitation are equivalent, the UE status of each v is a function of its per

---

[20] For a thorough discussion of the WP and WL perspectives, and a defense of the relevance of the WP approach, see McKerlie (1989); Veneziani (2007, 2013).

capita wealth, and K^* represents the cutoff value of initial per capita wealth that identifies exploitation status.

Theorem 1 *Let (p, r) be an IRS for E_0 such that $r_t > 0$ all t. Then, v is UE exploited within period t, all t, and UE exploited during its whole life if and only if $K_0^v < K^*$; while v is an UE exploiter within period t, all t, and an UE exploiter during its whole life if and only if $K_0^v > K^*$.*

Theorem 1 states that international relations are characterized by a transfer of labor from less developed countries, with low per capita wealth, to developed countries, with high per capita wealth. Next, the international class structure is derived, where "classes of countries can be defined with reference to the use of the credit market" (Roemer 1983, 54), which explains the mechanism through which the transfer of labor takes place. Let (a_1, a_2, a_3) be a vector where $a_i \in \{+, 0\}$, $i = 1, 2, 3$, and "+" means a non-zero value in the appropriate place; let $X^v \equiv \Sigma_{t=0}^{T} x_t^v$, and likewise for Z^v and Y^v. There are two dynamic extensions of Roemer's definition of classes.

Definition 3 *At an RS for E_0, country v is a member of WP class (a_1, a_2, a_3) in t, if there is an optimal ξ^v such that (x_t^v, z_t^v, y_t^v) has the form (a_1, a_2, a_3) in t. Similarly, v is a member of WL class (a_1, a_2, a_3), if there is an optimal ξ^v such that (X^v, Z^v, Y^v) has the form (a_1, a_2, a_3).*

There are eight conceivable classes (a_1, a_2, a_3) for each definition, but only four are theoretically relevant.[21] Generalizing Roemer (1982, 1983), the four main WL classes can be defined as follows.

$C^1 = \{v | v \text{ is a member of } (+, +, 0), \text{ but not of } (+, 0, 0)\}$,
$C^2 = \{v | v \text{ is a member of } (+, 0, 0)\}$,
$C^3 = \{v | v \text{ is a member of } (+, 0, +), \text{ but not of } (+, 0, 0)\}$,
$C^4 = \{v | v \text{ is a member of } (0, 0, +)\}$.

WP classes $C_t^1 - C_t^4$ are similarly specified. Countries in C^1 (C_t^1) must lend capital abroad to optimize; countries in C^2 (C_t^2) can optimize without using the capital market; countries in C^3 (C_t^3) must borrow foreign capital to optimize; countries in C^4 (C_t^4) must borrow all their operating capital. This

---

[21] Classes $(0, 0, 0)$ and $(0, +, 0)$ can be ignored at an RS with $w_t > 0$, all t.

definition of classes based on credit relations conveys the intuition that a country's position in the credit market affects its international status.

Theorem 2 generalizes Roemer's theory of classes: at an IRS, WL and WP class structures coincide, WP and WL classes are pairwise disjoint and exhaustive, class status depends on a country's wealth per capita, and the *Class-Exploitation Correspondence Principle* (Roemer 1982, 78ff.) holds, according to which exploitation and class status are correlated.

Theorem 2 *Let (p, r) be an IRS for E_0. (i) For all $1 \leq i < j \leq 4$, $C_t^i \cap C_t^j = \{\emptyset\}$ and $\cup_{i=1}^{4} C_t^i = \aleph$, all t. (ii) For all j, if $v \in C_0^j$ then $v \in C_t^j$, all t, and $v \in C^j$; conversely, if $v \in C^j$ then $v \in C_t^j$ all t. (iii) (Class-Exploitation Correspondence Principle) Let $r_t > 0$, all t. If $v \in C_0^1$, and thus $v \in C^1$, then v is an UE exploiter within period t, all t, and an UE exploiter during its whole life; whereas if $v \in C_0^3 \cup C_0^4$, and thus $v \in C^3 \cup C^4$, then v is UE exploited within period t, all t, and UE exploited during its whole life.*

Theorems 1 and 2 characterize the class and exploitation structure of the global economy. Theorem 1 derives the structure of exploitive international relations, in which developed countries exploit and less developed countries are exploited. Theorem 2 characterizes the international capital market, in which the former emerge as net lenders and the latter as net borrowers, and it proves the WP and WL correspondence between a country's position in the credit market and its exploitation status. This confirms the positive and normative importance of inequalities in capital/labor ratios: international relations characterized by UE emerge from differences in development and wealth and a perfectly competitive (short-term) international capital market.

It is important to note that Theorems 1 and 2 are not corollaries of Proposition 1. UE exploitation theory and liberal cosmopolitan egalitarianism provide alternative criteria to evaluate international justice. In the latter, inequalities are measured in terms of the discounted value of the *consumption* stream that a country obtains. In the former, the normative focus is on *labor* flows and consumption matters only indirectly, as it allows one to measure the amount of labor "received" by agents in exchange for the labor performed.[22]

A priori, there is no reason to suppose that the two normative approaches will render the same verdict when analyzing a given allocation. Unlike in

---

[22] Furthermore, in measuring WL exploitation status, labor flows are not discounted, as time preference arguably plays no normative role in UE exploitation theory.

Roemer's (1982, 1983) models with labor-minimizing agents, the relation between UE exploitation and welfare inequalities is not obvious. Theorem 1 partitions the set of agents into three subsets and evaluates each agent's position with respect to its membership in one of such subsets, but it does not take account of inequalities within each class. Nonetheless, strikingly, it immediately follows from Proposition 1 and Theorems 1 and 2 that at an IRS welfare inequalities exist if and only if UE exploitation exists and countries are partitioned into classes, and countries with higher (lower) per capita welfare levels tend to be exploiters (exploited) and net lenders (borrowers).

This provides a further argument in favor of cosmopolitan views. For UE exploitation and divisions into classes are morally problematic,[23] and in our economy with a credit market and restrictions to the movement of people, a country's status in terms of class, exploitation, and welfare in each period of their life is driven by the level of per capita productive endowments they inherited, which, as we have argued, is morally arbitrary.[24]

To be sure, the equivalence between a normative approach focusing on UE exploitation and classes, on the one hand, and a liberal egalitarian criterion, on the other, will likely fail to hold under more general assumptions, and the two theories will return different verdicts on the justice of different allocations. This is not relevant for our conclusions, however. For we are not trying to prove that the two approaches are equivalent in general. Rather, our thought experiment is meant to highlight a theoretical inconsistency of anti-cosmopolitan approaches such as Rawls's (1999) and the normative relevance of exploitative relations and welfare inequalities in a context where a number of confounding factors are abstracted away.

5. Cosmopolitan Justice and Citizenship Exploitation

One of the key insights of Roemer's theory concerns the relevance of differences in per capita endowments in generating UE exploitation. Yet, asset inequalities are only indirectly relevant in the UE approach, whose primary focus is on labor flows. Roemer (1982) has therefore suggested an alternative game-theoretical definition of exploitation that is meant to generalize the UE

---

[23] For a thorough discussion of the foundations of UE exploitation theory, see Veneziani and Yoshihara (2018).
[24] It is worth stressing that classes, exploitation, and inequality do not arise from market failures. A global credit market makes mutually beneficial trades possible, but it is also the institutional mechanism that allows transfers of labor across borders and creates class divisions among countries.

approach while directly focusing on its essential normative core—namely, differential ownership of productive assets. This approach has led Roemer to define a whole range of exploitation phenomena, including feudal and socialist exploitation. Yet, interestingly, he has never applied it to the analysis of international relations. The main reason is that, according to Roemer (1983, 57), unlike in the national case, "it is unclear that justice would require the socialisation of capital among nation-states." This objection is interesting, as it echoes some criticisms leveled against cosmopolitan egalitarianism—namely, that redressing inequalities would entail massive strains of commitment, or the creation of a world state, or the socialization of assets at a world scale.

While relevant, these objections are pragmatic rather than theoretical, and there is no a priori reason not to explore the implications of Roemer's (1982) game-theoretic definition when extended to the international context—which is what we do in this section. Our analysis yields interesting insights that raise doubts precisely about standard pragmatic objections to cosmopolitan approaches.

Let $\Im$ be a generic coalition—a group of agents—which is part of a larger society $\aleph$. Let $\Im' = \aleph - \Im$ be the complement to $\Im$ in $\aleph$: all of the agents in society not included in coalition $\Im$. Let $(V^1, \ldots, V^N)$ be the payoffs of the members of society $\aleph$ at the existing allocation: this can be thought of as the vector describing the payoff (utility, income, wealth, opportunities) of each member of society at the status quo. Let $P(\aleph)$ be the set of all possible subsets of $\aleph$ and let $\Psi: P(\aleph) \to \mathbb{R}_+$ be a characteristic function that assigns to every conceivable coalition $\Im$ an aggregate payoff $\Psi(\Im)$ if it withdraws: it is a function that defines the *counterfactual* benefits that would accrue to a group of agents if they seceded from the society they belong to. The property relation definition of exploitation can be stated as follows.

Definition 4 *(Roemer 1982, 194–195) Coalition $\Im$ is exploited at allocation $(V^1, \ldots, V^N)$ with respect to alternative Ψ if and only if (i) $\Sigma_{v \in \Im} V^v < \Psi(\Im)$, and (ii) $\Sigma_{v \in \Im'} V^v > \Psi(\Im')$.*

The type of exploitation involved depends on the function Ψ chosen to identify the hypothetical alternative to $(V^1, \ldots, V^N)$: different withdrawal rules identify different types of exploitation. For instance, a coalition is *feudally exploited* at an allocation if it would improve "by cooperative arrangements on its own, availing itself of the private endowments of its members" (Roemer 1982, 219). Feudally non-exploitive allocations coincide with the *private ownership core* of E_0, and it can be proved that there is no feudal exploitation in E_0. From this perspective, the familiar propositions on mutual gains from trade can be understood as proving the absence of a specific form of exploitation in a competitive international economy. From an egalitarian viewpoint, though, the absence of non-competitive distortions—and of feudal exploitation—is insufficient to guarantee the fairness of international relations, and a different specification of Ψ is necessary.

In the context of the global economy, the status quo payoffs are given by each country's per capita welfare $\left(\dfrac{V(\omega_0^v)}{l^v}\right)_{v \in \aleph} = \left(V^1, \ldots, V^N\right)$ at the RS, and the characteristic function Ψ captures the welfare that a coalition of countries $\Im$ can obtain if they withdraw with a share of the world endowments (ω_0, l) of material assets and population corresponding to $\left(\omega_\Im^E, l_\Im^E\right)$, where $0 < l_\Im^E < l$ and $\omega_\Im^E \equiv \frac{l_\Im^E}{l}\omega_0$. In other words, the countries in coalition $\Im$ receive their per capita share of the initial endowment of produced assets, but the withdrawal rule allows for migration—and thereby a variable population—as $l_\Im^E = \Sigma_{v \in \Im} l'^v$ is not required. This specification of the characteristic function explicitly incorporates the idea that borders have limited normative significance: the counterfactual scenario is constructed in such a way that neither capital nor labor is necessarily tied to a specific location, and therefore—when used to evaluate a given, existing allocation—it is meant to identify injustices that occur because of the geographical distribution of productive endowments.

A coalition $\Im$ can communally block an RS by $\left(\omega_\Im^E, l_\Im^E\right)$ if there is a profile of (not necessarily optimal) actions $(\xi'^v)_{v \in \Im}$ and an allocation of the coalition's population to the various countries that form it, $(l'^v)_{v \in \Im}$ such that (i) the coalition's endowments $\left(\omega_\Im^E, l_\Im^E\right)$ are all distributed to its members; (ii) all countries in $\Im$ obtain a higher per capita welfare; (iii) production plans are feasible in every period; (iv) aggregate net output is equal to consumption and net savings; (v) labor employed in production does not exceed the endowment; (vi) capital accumulation is determined by net savings; and (vii) the reproducibility constraint is satisfied, and countries in $\Im$ leave to their successors at least as much capital as they started with. Formally:

Definition 5 *A coalition $\Im$ can communally block an RS $(\xi^v)_{v \in \aleph}$ by $\left(\omega_\Im^E, l_\Im^E\right)$ if there is a $(\xi'^v, l'^v)_{v \in \Im}$ such that* (i) $\Sigma_{v \in \Im} \omega_0'^v = \omega_\Im^E$ *and* $\Sigma_{v \in \Im} l'^v = l_\Im^E$; (ii) $\dfrac{\Sigma_{t=0}^T \beta^t c_t'^v}{l'^v} > \dfrac{\Sigma_{t=0}^T \beta^t c_t^v}{l^v}$, *for all* $v \in \Im$; (iii) $A\Sigma_{v \in \Im} x_t'^v \leq \Sigma_{v \in \Im} \omega_t'^v$, *all* t; (iv) $(1-A)\Sigma_{v \in \Im} x_t'^v = \Sigma_{v \in \Im} c_t'^v + \Sigma_{v \in \Im} s_t'^v$, *all* t; (v) $Lx_t'^v \leq l'^v$, *for all* $v \in \Im$ *and all* t; (vi) $\Sigma_{v \in \Im} \omega_{t+1}'^v = \Sigma_{v \in \Im} \omega_t'^v + \Sigma_{v \in \Im} s_t'^v$, *all* t; (vii) $\Sigma_{v \in \Im} \omega_T'^v \geq \omega_\Im^E$.

Definition 5 generalizes the notion of communal blocking in Roemer (1982), which only allows for a redistribution of capital. Based on this more restrictive definition, Roemer (1982) defines a coalition to be capitalistically exploited if it can communally block the allocation, and an allocation non-exploitative if no coalition is capitalistically exploited. However, in the analysis of international relations, Definition 5 seems preferable because, *in principle*, both capital and labor endowments may be redistributed, unlike in the single-country model. We call the associated injustice *citizenship exploitation*.[25] Thus, we are conceptualizing international exploitation differently from van Parijs (1992), according to whom citizenship exploitation is a form of feudal, not capitalist, exploitation, and it derives from both labor and capital being immobile (which prevents factor price equalization).

Theorem 3 proves that UE and citizenship exploitation coincide at an IRS for E_0.

Theorem 3 *At an IRS for E_0, there is no UE exploitation if and only if no coalition is citizenship exploited.*

Theorem 3 further strengthens our argument in support of a cosmopolitan egalitarian approach. Observe, again, that there is no a priori reason to believe that the three criteria based on citizenship exploitation, UE exploitation, and welfare inequalities should coincide. Yet, our previous results demonstrate that, under certain conditions, they do, and show that international relations are marred by citizenship exploitation, as well as welfare inequalities and UE exploitation, due to morally arbitrary differential ownership of productive assets (per capita).

Theorem 3 and the notion of citizenship exploitation actually bring the central relevance of asset inequalities into focus. If international relations are characterized by citizenship exploitation, then this requires an analysis of the ethical basis for the "annihilation of differential capital-labor ratios among countries" (Roemer 1983, 57). From a Marxian, or even liberal (opportunity-)egalitarian approach, it is indeed possible to argue that morally arbitrary inequalities in productive endowments (per capita) should indeed be eliminated.

Nonetheless, Roemer (1983, 57) argues that "it is not immediately clear that the argument [for the socialization of capital within a country] applies as well to the socialization of capital among nation-states." Although he does not discuss this issue in any detail, Roemer does not seem to question the

---

[25] Furthermore, it may be argued that the structure of the interaction between countries is different from that between workers and capitalists.

cosmopolitan approach at the theoretical level. Rather, he seems to consider the implications of his theory as unrealistic and thus he is skeptical about its application at the global level. The socialization of capital among nation-states may indeed seem far-fetched, but this is hardly true for redistributive policies that transfer capital to poor countries as a matter of justice. Moreover, if massive international transfers of capital may be deemed to entail severe strains of commitment, in our (admittedly simplified) framework a less restrictive approach to international migrations people may also be an effective policy to enhance global distributive justice.

Indeed, through less stringent border restrictions, if agents from countries with relatively low capital/labor ratios tend to move to countries with higher ratios, as is typical in the reality, that would in turn tend to decrease inequalities in per capita productive endowments.[26] In other words, policies favoring a higher degree of labor mobility across borders may be an effective complement to policies promoting capital transfers to poorer countries.

But if this is true, then it means that rather reasonable policies can be found that reduce international inequalities *and*, at the same time, mitigate exploitation but which do not entail massive strains of commitment, especially if implemented gradually (see, for example, the wealth taxation and redistribution schemes proposed by Piketty (2014)). Nor does the implementation of gradual policies of capital transfers or the relaxation of migration restrictions entail the creation of a world state, let alone the socialization of capital at the global scale.

The existence of reasonable, implementable policies to mitigate morally arbitrary inequalities makes it even more obvious that the existence of international inequalities is entirely human-made, as there are feasible changes in policies and political institutions that would remove them. In turn, this reinforces—in the process of reaching a reflective equilibrium—our criticism of Rawls's inconsistency in the treatment of international justice, by showing a feasible politico-institutional scheme that improves justice *and* is consistent with liberal principles.

---

[26] Observe that this is true even if agents are allowed to move their per capita share of capital with them when they migrate.

6. Conclusions

We have analyzed international inequalities and exploitation in a global economy characterized by the free movement of capital and barriers to migration. We have proved that both international inequalities in primary goods (or well-being) and exploitative and class relations arise from morally arbitrary differential ownership of productive assets per capita. We have argued that this raises doubts on the criticisms of cosmopolitanism advanced by prominent liberal egalitarian writers. We have shown that there exist feasible policies that mitigate international injustices and do not entail massive strains of commitment, such as capital transfers and more welcoming migration policies.

In closing this chapter, it is worth briefly discussing three features of our analysis that may raise some concerns, and which suggest some avenues for further research. First of all, our description of welfare inequalities and UE between countries is derived based on the assumption that each nation can be conceived of as a single representative agent. While we think that this simplifying assumption is analytically appropriate in order to focus purely on the international dimension of distributive justice and unequal exchange, it is clear that, both descriptively and normatively, abstracting from inequalities and class divisions within countries is not innocuous. If both wealthier and less wealthy nations have capital and labor classes, for example, then one may argue that the position of capitalists in relatively endowment-poor countries is akin to capitalists who operate production processes with comparatively low compositions of capital in Marx's transformation analysis in chapter 9 of *Capital III*. As Marx notes, prices of production based on an economy-wide rate of profit serve to transfer labor from these sectors to those with comparatively high compositions of capital. Are these capitalists exploited by those in more advanced countries? This is not obvious. More generally, opening the black box of the individual countries is clearly crucial in order to provide a more comprehensive normative evaluation of international arrangements.[27]

Second, our formal analysis has focused on a specific set of equilibria in which welfare (and opportunity) inequalities and UE coincide. This has allowed us to provide the starkest case in favor of the extension of distributive concerns to the international context. One may wonder, however, whether welfare (and opportunity) inequalities and UE always coincide,

---

[27] We are grateful to Gil Skillman for pointing out this important issue to us.

for in that case the concepts of class and exploitation would seem at best redundant. As we have shown elsewhere (see, for example, Veneziani (2007); Veneziani and Yoshihara (2017)), welfare inequalities and UE do *not* coincide in general: they incorporate different normative intuitions and yield different insights on the fairness of economic allocations. It is an open question how to evaluate (both national and international) allocations when the two criteria diverge.

Finally, it may be argued, following Rawls (1999), that a key dimension of heterogeneity across countries—namely, differences in political culture and institutions— is crucial in explaining international differences in the accumulation of physical as well as human capital and population growth; this, in turn, may explain international differences in productive endowments. By assumption, such heterogeneity is set aside in our model, and our focus on stationary equilibria rules out the analysis of accumulation.

As we have already noted, this does not cast any serious doubts on our conclusions. Ours is a thought experiment, and we have abstracted from a number of empirically relevant features of the global economy in order to make a precise theoretical point. It is worth noting, however, that there are other aspects of international relations that we have abstracted from in the chapter that are normatively relevant and pull in a direction exactly opposite to that suggested by Rawls's (1999) argument.

By focusing on perfectly competitive markets (including perfect information and perfect contracting) and on stationary solutions, we have managed to highlight the role of differential ownership of productive assets in generating international inequalities and various forms of exploitation. Nonetheless, as we have argued at length elsewhere,[28] under capitalist relations of production, asset inequalities are relevant not only for their direct effect on well-being but also because of the *bargaining power* that higher holdings of productive assets confer upon their owners, which in turn allows them to reap higher benefits from economic interactions, thus further increasing their advantage. This is one of the key lessons of exploitation theory, and it provides yet another reason to doubt the moral neutrality of international inequalities, to be skeptical about the idea that international

---

[28] Veneziani (2013), Veneziani and Yoshihara (2017), and Yoshihara and Kaneko (2016) show that competitive markets and differences in capital/labor ratios are sufficient to generate UE exploitation and welfare inequalities, but not necessarily their persistence, and argue that power is a key ingredient for any explanation of the persistence of exploitative relations.

justice can be reached by having the representatives of different countries bargain in the second stage of the original position, and to support a cosmopolitan approach.

References

Beitz, C. R. 2000. "Rawls's Law of Peoples." *Ethics* 110: 669–696.
Cogliano, J., R. Veneziani, and N. Yoshihara. 2016. "The Dynamics of Exploitation and Class in Accumulation Economies." *Metroeconomica* 67: 242–290.
Emmanuel, A. 1972. *Unequal Exchange*. New York: Monthly Review Press.
Frank, A. G. 1978. *Dependent Accumulation and Underdevelopment*. New York: Monthly Review Press.
Griffin, K., and J. Gurley. 1985. "Radical Analyses of Imperialism, the Third World, and the Transition to Socialism: A Survey Article." *Journal of Economic Literature* 23: 1089–1143.
Howard, M. C., and J. E. King. 1999. "Whatever Happened to Imperialism?" In *The Political Economy of Imperialism*, edited by R. M. Chilcote, 19–40. Boston: Kluwer.
Kaneko, S., and N. Yoshihara. 2019. "On the General Impossibility of Persistent Unequal Exchange Free Trade Equilibria in the Pre-Industrial World Economy." Working Paper 2019-05, UMass Amherst Economics Papers.
McKerlie, D. 1989. "Equality and Time." *Ethics* 99: 475–491.
Nagel, T. 2005. "The Problem of Global Justice." *Philosophy and Public Affairs* 33: 113–147.
Nielsen, K. 2003. *Globalization and Justice*. Amherst, NY: Humanity Books.
van Parijs, P. 1992. "Citizenship Exploitation, Unequal Exchange and the Breakdown of Popular Sovereignty." In *Free Movement*, edited by B. Barry and R. Goodin, 155–165. Hemel-Hemstead: Harvester.
Piketty, T. 2014. *Capital in the 21st Century*, Cambridge, MA: Harvard University Press.
Pogge, T. W. 1989. *Realizing Rawls*. Ithaca, NY: Cornell University Press.
Pogge, T. W. 1994. "An Egalitarian Law of Peoples." *Philosophy and Public Affairs* 23: 195–224.
Pogge, T. W. 2002. *World Poverty and Human Rights: Cosmopolitan Responsibilities and Reforms*. Cambridge, UK: Polity Press.
Rawls, J. 1971. *A Theory of Justice*. Cambridge, MA: Harvard University Press.
Rawls, J. 1999. *The Law of Peoples*. Cambridge, MA: Harvard University Press.
Roemer, J. E. 1982. *A General Theory of Exploitation and Class*. Cambridge, MA: Harvard University Press.
Roemer, J. E. 1983. "Unequal Exchange, Labor Migration, and International Capital Flows: A Theoretical Synthesis." In *Marxism, Central Planning and the Soviet Economy*, edited by P. Desai, 34–60. Cambridge, MA: MIT Press.
Roemer, J. E. 1988. *Free to Lose*. Cambridge, MA: Harvard University Press.
Roemer, J. E. 1994. *A Future for Socialism*. Cambridge, MA: Harvard University Press.
Roemer, J. E. 1996. *Theories of Distributive Justice*. Cambridge, MA: Harvard University Press.
Roemer, J. E. 2006. "The Global Welfare Economics of Immigration." *Social Choice and Welfare* 27: 311–325.

Roemer, J. E., and R. Veneziani. 2007. "Intergenerational Justice, International Relations, and Sustainability." In *Intergenerational Equity and Sustainability*, edited by J. E. Roemer and K. Suzumura, 228–251. London: Macmillan.

Schweickart, D. 1991. "The Politics and Morality of Unequal Exchange." *Economics and Philosophy* 7: 13–36.

Veneziani, R. 2007. "Exploitation and Time." *Journal of Economic Theory* 132: 189–207.

Veneziani, R. 2013. "Exploitation, Inequality, and Power." *Journal of Theoretical Politics* 25: 526–545.

Veneziani, R., and N. Yoshihara. 2017. "Globalisation and Inequality in a Dynamic Economy: An Axiomatic Analysis of Unequal Exchange." *Social Choice and Welfare* 49: 445–468.

Veneziani, R., and N. Yoshihara. 2018. "The Theory of Exploitation as the Unequal Exchange of Labour." *Economics and Philosophy* 34: 381–409.

Yoshihara, N., and S. Kaneko. 2016. "On the Existence and Characterization of Unequal Exchange in the Free Trade Equilibrium." *Metroeconomica* 67: 210–241.

Appendix: Proofs of Formal Results

Proof of Proposition 1

Proof. Plugging constraints (4) and (2) into (1), and noting that at any solution to MP^v, $\Lambda_t^v = l^v$ all t, one obtains $c_t^v = \frac{l^v}{p_\beta} + (1 + r_\beta)\omega_t^v - \omega_{t+1}^v$, all t, v. Substituting the latter expression into the objective function of MP^v, and noting that $\beta(1 + r_\beta) = 1$, one obtains $\Sigma_{t=0}^{T} \beta^t c_t^v = (1 + r_\beta)\omega_0^v - \beta^{T-1}\omega_T^v + \Sigma_{t=0}^{T-1} \beta^t \frac{l^v}{p_\beta}$. Therefore $s_t^v = 0$, all t, solves MP^v for all v and the second part of the statement immediately follows.

Proof of Theorem 1

Proof. Using the same argument as in Proposition 1, and noting that at an IRS, $\omega_t^v = \omega_0^v$ all t, v, we derive $c_t^v = \frac{l^v}{p_t} + r_t\omega_0^v$ all t, v. Therefore, noting that $r_t > 0$ all t, it follows that for all t, $\lambda c_t^v \leq \Lambda_t^v \Leftrightarrow \lambda \frac{l^v}{p_t} + \lambda r_t \omega_0^v \leq \Lambda_t^v$. The desired result then follows, noting that $\Lambda_t^v = l^v$ all t, v and if (p, r) is an IRS for E_0 such that $r_t > 0$ all t, then $(p_t, r_t) = (p_\beta, r_\beta)$ all t.

Proof of Theorem 2

Proof. Let $\Gamma^v \equiv \{(X^v, Z^v, Y^v) \mid \xi^v \text{ solves } MP^v\}$ and $\Gamma_t^v \equiv \{(x_t^v, z_t^v, y_t^v) \mid \xi^v \text{ solves } MP^v\}$.

Part (i). 1. First of all, at all t, $v \in C_t^4$ if and only if $K_t^v = 0$. Next, consider v with $K_t^v > 0$. We shall prove that at all t: $p_t A y_t^v < z_t^v$ all $(x_t^v, z_t^v, y_t^v) \in \Gamma_t^v$ if and only if $K_t^v > (p_t A / L)$; there is a $(x_t^v, z_t^v, y_t^v) \in \Gamma_t^v$ with $p_t A y_t^v = z_t^v$ if and only if $K_t^v = (p_t A / L)$; $p_t A y_t^v > z_t^v$ all $(x_t^v, z_t^v, y_t^v) \in \Gamma_t^v$ if and only if $0 < K_t^v < (p_t A / L)$. First, suppose there is a

$(x_t^v, z_t^v, y_t^v) \in \Gamma_t^v$ with $p_t A y_t^v = z_t^v$; without loss of generality, set $x_t^v = 0$. By optimality $L y_t^v = l^v$ and $z_t^v = W_t^v$; hence $p_t A y_t^v / L y_t^v = K_t^v$, as desired. Conversely, if $p_t A / L = K_t^v$, then there exist $y_t^v > 0$ and $z_t^v > 0$ such that $L y_t^v = l^v$, $z_t^v = W_t^v$, and $p_t A y_t^v = z_t^v$ which belong to an optimal solution for v at t. A similar argument holds for the other two cases.

2. Finally, as in Roemer (1982, Theorem 2.5, p.76), we have that at all t: $v \in C_t^1$ if and only if $p_t A y_t^v < z_t^v$ for all $(x_t^v, z_t^v, y_t^v) \in \Gamma_t^v$; $v \in C_t^2$ if and only if there is a $(x_t^v, z_t^v, y_t^v) \in \Gamma_t^v$ with $p_t A y_t^v = z_t^v$; $v \in C_t^3$ if and only if $p_t A y_t^v > z_t^v$ for all $(x_t^v, z_t^v, y_t^v) \in \Gamma_t^v$.[29] Then part (i) follows from step 1 of the proof.

Part (ii). The result follows immediately from steps 1 and 2, noting also that, at an IRS, $v \in C_0^4$ implies $v \in C_t^4$, all t, and therefore $v \in C^4$, and, conversely, $v \in C^4$ implies $v \in C_t^4$, all t.

Part (iii). The result follows immediately noting that at all t, $p_t A / L = (p_t - \lambda) / r_t \lambda$.

Proof of Theorem 3

Proof. 1. (Sufficiency) Suppose agent v is UE-exploited. By Theorem 1, $p_\beta \omega_0^v < l^v K^* = l^v \frac{p_\beta \omega_0}{l}$. Therefore by Proposition 1,

$$\frac{V(\omega_0^v)}{l^v} = \frac{(1-\beta^T)}{p_\beta}\left[\frac{1}{(1-\beta)} + \frac{K_0^v}{\beta}\right] < \frac{(1-\beta^T)}{p_\beta}\left[\frac{1}{(1-\beta)} + \frac{K^*}{\beta}\right] = \frac{(1-\beta^T)}{p_\beta}\left[\frac{1}{(1-\beta)} + \frac{p_\beta \omega_0 / l}{\beta}\right].$$

As $p_\beta \omega_{\{v\}}^E = \frac{l^v}{l} p_\beta \omega_0$ for the singleton coalition $\mathfrak{J} = \{v\}$, it follows that

$$\frac{V(\omega_0^v)}{l^v} = \frac{(1-\beta^T)}{p_\beta}\left[\frac{1}{(1-\beta)} + \frac{K_0^v}{\beta}\right] < \frac{(1-\beta^T)}{p_\beta}\left[\frac{1}{(1-\beta)} + \frac{\frac{1}{l^v}p_\beta \omega_{\{v\}}^E}{\beta}\right] = \frac{V(\omega_{\{v\}}^E)}{l^v}.$$

Hence, $\mathfrak{J} = \{v\}$ can communally block the IRE by $(\omega_{\{v\}}^E, l_{\{v\}}^E)$ with $l_\mathfrak{J}^E = l'^v$.

2. (Necessity) Suppose there is no UE exploitation. If $r_\beta = 0$ then the result immediately follows. Therefore, suppose $r_\beta > 0$. Then $K_0^v = K^*$ and $\frac{V(\omega_0^v)}{l^v} = \frac{(1-\beta^T)}{p_\beta}\left[\frac{K^*}{\beta} + \frac{1}{1-\beta}\right]$, all v. Under the communal withdrawal rule, it follows that for any possible coalition $\mathfrak{J}$ with $(\omega_\mathfrak{J}^E, l_\mathfrak{J}^E)$, there is an assignment $(\omega_0'^v, l'^v)_{v \in \mathfrak{J}}$ such that (i) $\Sigma_{v \in \mathfrak{J}} \omega_0'^v = \omega_\mathfrak{J}^E$, $\Sigma_{v \in \mathfrak{J}} l'^v = l_\mathfrak{J}^E$, and $\frac{\omega_0'^v}{l'^v} = \frac{\omega_\mathfrak{J}^E}{l_\mathfrak{J}^E}$ and (ii) $\frac{V(\omega_0'^v)}{l'^v} = \frac{(1-\beta^T)}{p_\beta}\left[\frac{(p_\beta \omega_\mathfrak{J}^E / l_\mathfrak{J}^E)}{\beta} + \frac{1}{1-\beta}\right] = \frac{(1-\beta^T)}{p_\beta}\left[\frac{K^*}{\beta} + \frac{1}{(1-\beta)}\right] = \frac{V(\omega_0^v)}{l^v}$ for every $v \in \mathfrak{J}$.

Therefore, there is no other assignment $(\omega_0'''^v, l'''^v)_{v \in \mathfrak{J}}$ such that $\Sigma_{v \in \mathfrak{J}} \omega_0'''^v = \omega_\mathfrak{J}^E$, $\Sigma_{v \in \mathfrak{J}} l'''^v = l_\mathfrak{J}^E$, and $\frac{V(\omega_0'''^v)}{l'''^v} > \frac{V(\omega_0^v)}{l^v}$ for all $v \in \mathfrak{J}$. This result holds for any population withdrawing $l_\mathfrak{J}'^E$. Therefore, if there is no UE exploitation, then there is no citizenship exploitation.

---

[29] This implies that in every t, WP classes (+, +, +), or (0, +, +) are redundant.

10
Exploitation, Children and Childhood, and Parental Responsibilities

Samantha Brennan

On one popular account of the obligations of parenthood, parents are charged with bringing children into the world and delivering them safely to the threshold of adult life. You can hold a minimalist version of this view, where a child merely making it to the adult years, unharmed and intact, meets the obligations of parenthood. Or you can hold a maximalist version of the view, where success entails bringing about the best possible adult person, and the obligations of parenthood entail maximizing the child's potential to excel as an adult.

Note that this way of describing the obligations of parenthood is neutral about the standards by which we judge adult success. It might be that we think that what is most important for leading a good adult life are rich and rewarding friendships and family relationships. Or it might be that we think financial and career achievement matter more. But both versions, and all of the possibilities in between, discount childhood itself as a site of value and obligation. On this broad view, childhood friendships are valuable and useful only insofar as they contribute to flourishing adult friendships and relationships. Childhood achievements in school may be judged for their contribution to financial well-being and career success. Childhood art is only valuable as a developmental stage on the way to producing great adult art, and the same thing is thought to be true for childhood athletic achievements.[1] Only parents and grandparents (and possibly coaches and talent scouts) watch children's sporting competitions. Even the best teams are rarely watched by others. On a common view of childhood and the obligations of

---

[1] For an exception, see the fascinating documentary *My Kid Could Paint* (2007) by director Amir Bar-Lev. The documentary tells the story of Marla Olmstead, a young girl who was thought to be a child prodigy painter of abstract art, but is later the subject of controversy concerning whether she actually completed the paintings in question by herself or had help.

parenthood, childhood goods are seen as having no value in their own right, and as not grounding parental obligations to protect or nurture them. It is worth noting that this popular view has its philosophical defenders. In *Goods and Virtues* (1983) Michael Slote defends the view that even an extremely unhappy childhood may be made up for by successful, happy adult years, but no amount of childhood happiness can outweigh bad adult years. Slote thinks that the prime of life matters more than either childhood or old age when it comes to overall life assessments.

There are a variety of ways in which this popular account—the threshold account of parental obligations—might be thought to go wrong. We might believe that parents have obligations to children as children, not just as future adults. We might also believe that parental obligations, at least the ethical obligations of parenthood, do not end when a child reaches adulthood. Although I think both criticisms are correct and that some parental obligations to a child continue past that child reaching maturity, that is a topic I plan to write about in the future. This chapter is going to focus on the first set of worries, on the moral obligations that parents have regarding childhood and childhood goods. It is also worth noting that I am offering this story about the way the threshold account of parental obligations goes wrong not to entirely replace other sets of criticisms, but instead to show what they leave out. It is my hope that thinking in terms of exploitation adds to the conversation.

Consider the example of how we might justify constraints on parental behavior, such as constraints on physically disciplining children. Both advocates of physical discipline and its critics point to developmental accounts of childhood, adolescence, and adulthood. The justification for any constraints placed on parental behavior, for example, is often that the behavior in question will lead to unhealthy development—that is, bad outcomes. For example, in the case of corporal punishment, those who advocate its abolition as a practice or the removal of clauses in the criminal code that exclude it from the category of assault do so using studies that point to negative adult outcomes. (Those who are physically disciplined as children are more likely to engage in violent or aggressive acts themselves and they are more likely to suffer from mental illness. See, for example, Turner 2002.) You might think that this mode of reasoning follows from consequentialist accounts of constraints and liberties. But note that in the case of children, even rights theorists base their arguments on the outcomes of childhood. Joel Feinberg's classic paper "A Child's Right to an

Open Future" (1980) argues for children's rights largely on the basis of the adults they are to become.

Many philosophers writing about the moral significance of children and childhood—see work by Anca Gheaus, Daniel Weinstock, Colin Macleod, Patrick Tomlin, and Anthony Skelton—argue that childhood well-being matters for its sake. While these theorists' work differs both in the details and in the justification, what they have in common is the central claim that the right approach to including children in moral and political philosophy cannot be one that completely discounts childhood and the goods it contains. Patrick Tomlin (2018) argues that the simple contrast I have set up here—childhood goods either have some intrinsic value or they are purely instrumentally valuable—is too simple and misses out on a range of questions one might ask, and views one might have, about the value of childhood. I will not rehearse the arguments or respond here. I will note that I am open to a wide range of views about how much and why childhood goods matter. All I want to claim here is that the very strong view that childhood goods can only have instrumental value is false.

If it is true that childhood and childhood goods matter and that we also have obligations to the development of the child into a happy and successful adult (remaining neutral here about the standard by which this is judged), then parents are charged with weighing childhood goods against adult goods in the life of the person their child will become. Note, though, that not all childhood goods are separate from adult goods. Sometimes things are good both for the child now and for the adult they will become. One editor of this volume, Benjamin Ferguson, reports that he enjoyed hiking as a child and it gave him an appreciation of the outdoors that benefits him now as an adult. No doubt for most academics, childhood reading is both good for the child who is read to and learns to read on their own and good for the adult's lifetime enjoyment of reading. The point I want to make is that even if reading to children produced no tangible adult benefits, it might be something parents are required to do, as it produces a childhood good. As a side benefit, parents reading to children likely also benefits the parent-child relationship.

Often, though, there are trade-offs to be made between what is good for the child now, as a child, and what is good for the child in the future, for the adult he or she will become. Decisions about how to weigh goods that occur in childhood against goods for the adult the child will become are often made by parents. An important question facing parents is how we, as agents who act on behalf of children, balance things that are good for the child-as-child with the things that are good for the child-as-future-adult. It is my hope that seeing the obligations that parents have toward children in this way demonstrates what a complex task parenting can be. I have argued elsewhere that while parenting has become more demanding than the old-fashioned "deliver them safely to the threshold of their adult years" approach, the ways in which it is more demanding show how engaging, creative, and enjoyable an endeavor parenthood can be (Brennan 2014).

While there is a wide range of ways to parent correctly, this paper argues that there is one way that certainly gets it wrong. I argue that parents *exploit* childhood and children when they view childhood as merely a resource to be mined for developmental goods and parent in ways that reflect those values. This chapter looks at the concept of exploitation in the context of childhood and childhood goods and argues that parents have obligations not to promote their own good at the expense of their child and, more controversially, not to promote their child's future good too much at the expense of current childhood goods. I argue that parents have an obligation not to exploit childhood even when the beneficiary of the act of exploitation is the adult person that the child becomes. Exploitation in this case involves getting the balance wrong, giving too much weight to adult goods and discounting excessively the goods of childhood.

The end of this chapter suggests, much more controversially, that parents may have obligations not to allow children to view their own childhoods as of no moral significance and make all of their decisions on a future-directed basis. That is, sometimes parents may have to intervene in order to ensure that children appreciate the goods of childhood and do not make the mistake of putting all their eggs in a future-directed basket. Parents may need to prevent children from exploiting their own childhoods.

Talk about the exploitation of children and people often assume that you are referring to child labor or the sexual abuse of children. While child labor is often wrong and child sexual exploitation always so, here I focus on a less clear area of moral concern. This chapter focuses on the exploitation of children by their parents in areas that at least at the outset look as if they could be in the best interests of the child. I am interested in looking at the treatment of children by those charged with promoting the interests and protecting the rights of children—namely, their parents.

Often the contrast with exploitation is treatment to which a person properly consented, and exploitation marks the absence of the conditions under which free consent is possible. Note that with children the situation is more complicated. At least in the case of very young children, consent does not play a normative role. Yet children are not like cats, which presumably can be harmed but not exploited. Even in the case of older children consent is complicated, especially when it comes to consent to the wishes of parents. If exploitation consists in the "wrongful behavior [that violates] the moral norm of *protecting the vulnerable*," as Robert Goodin writes (Goodin 1987, 187), then the failure to protect a child's current interests looks to be a paradigmatic case of exploitation.

Some people might resist the use of the language of "exploitation" in this context. Let me say a little bit more about why I think this is the right moral concept to capture the phenomena and to motivate the discussion that follows. Sometimes we talk about exploitation when we use a thing, or simply view a thing, purely in terms of its instrumental benefits. We exploit relationships with wealthy, well-connected relatives when we view those relationships entirely in terms of the benefits they offer us and not in terms of the value of the relationships in their own right. We might exploit an environmental object when we see it and make use of it in ways that consider just its instrumental benefits and not its intrinsic value. For example, we exploit old-growth forests when we fail to appreciate their significance or beauty and instead use them as raw materials to turn into paper or plywood. Instead of awe, we just make a calculation of what we can get from the forest. Another example is when we think about rainforests just in terms of the medicinal ingredients they might contain and not in terms of their own diversity and beauty.

You do not need to agree here that it's *correct* to talk about exploiting environmental objects. You might disagree that environmental objects have intrinsic value, and that is fine. All I need is for you to see the conceptual sense in which exploitation talk is used here. That is the sense of childhood exploitation I am interested in, when we view childhood solely in terms of its instrumental benefits, either for the adult person the child is to become or, more worryingly, in terms of goods for the adult who is doing the choosing on behalf of the child. Exploitation consists in both an attitude toward childhood goods and a mistaken distribution of goods either between parents and their children or between life stages (the person as child and the person as adult). Like Benjamin Ferguson (2021), I think that exploitation has both an attitudinal component and a distributive component.

There are at least two ways parents might go wrong when it comes to making decisions that are justified in terms of the interests of parents and the interests of their children, and one of these ways involves exploitation.

First, parents might promote their own good instead of the good of the child, substituting their own interests for the interests of the child to a degree that is morally unacceptable. That is, we might allow that some parental decisions can give weight to parental interests over children's interests, but there is a point at which parents must pay attention to the interests of the child and at which their decisions must reflect those interests.

Second, and more controversially, parents might sacrifice the goods of childhood and the interests the child has in the person she is now in favor of the goods for the person the child is to become. They do so because they think the goods of childhood have no significance. If childhood goods have value, it is because of the goods they contribute to the life of the adult person the child becomes. This is a less familiar version of exploitation in which the current child is exploited for their future interests.

Let me be clear about what I am not claiming and about the scope of my claims. First, I am not claiming that exploitation is the only way in which parents go wrong in the cases I discuss. Often the wrongness of the parents' actions is overdetermined. Their actions may be wrong for many reasons. For example, the parents' actions might violate the rights of the child. The parents' actions might also bring about worse consequences. I am not claiming that these factors are not also part of the explanation of wrongness. I am merely claiming that exploitation is *a* morally significant factor and that exploitation is part of the explanation. I know some moral philosophers want to isolate one factor that makes for wrongness—consequences or rule-breaking or intentions—but it is my view that ethical life is rarely that simple and that most things that are wrong are wrong for a myriad of reasons. Morality is messy and complicated. Again, my claim here is simply that exploitation is one significant factor and that paying attention to exploitation helps us understand the wrongs parents sometimes commit.

To get started, let us consider an extreme case of child abuse and exploitation which combines two of the ways parents can get parenting wrong.[2]

In the book *Breaking Away: A Harrowing True Story of Resilience, Courage and Triumph* (2008), hockey player Patrick O'Sullivan tells his story of a childhood of physical abuse and emotional cruelty at the hands of his father, who hoped to shape his son into a star professional hockey player. One might think of O'Sullivan's case as extreme, but I am with O'Sullivan in worrying that this happens more often than you might think. In an interview with

---

[2] Thanks to Sarah Hinchcliffe for this particularly brutal example.

Canadian Press, O'Sullivan says, "I think it's a story that is far too common—maybe not as extreme as mine—but there's a lot of people, parents or even coaches that think they're going to be the difference-maker in their kid making it, whether it sports or music or whatever. You do a lot more harm than you do good."[3]

O'Sullivan was Ontario Hockey League and Canadian Hockey League rookie of the year in 2002, and the American Hockey League's top rookie in 2005. He was the all-time leader in games, goals, assists and points for the Mississauga/Niagara IceDogs franchise. He played 334 National Hockey League (NHL) games over eight seasons with Los Angeles, Edmonton, Carolina, Minnesota, and Phoenix. He played in three world junior championships, scoring the winning goal to lift the United States over Canada for gold in 2004.

O'Sullivan's book tells the story behind this athletic career. His father, himself a failed hockey player, was determined that his son would make it. His training methods were unorthodox and cruel. For example, he force-fed his son, and when the boy threw up, he made him eat the meal again; this started when Patrick was just eight years old. There were nights Patrick was locked outside until morning to toughen him up or to punish him for a bad game. He was forced to run, weighed down by his sweaty equipment, behind his dad's van after games. He was woken up in the night to do "pushups until my arms gave out ... situps until my stomach cramped" (O'Sullivan 2008, 68).

"When I came off the ice after practice or a game, I never knew exactly what was next, but I knew it was going to be bad," O'Sullivan writes.

> I'd be looking at an hour or two or more of my father's conditioning program, running the steps in the arena stands like a hamster on a treadmill or chasing after the van for two or three miles. If he didn't think that was toughening me up, he'd slap me around. Every year he was ramping it up: slap in the face when I was eight; a slap with more force and a kick in the ass when I was nine; a punch when I was 10; a big right hook on my jaw and a kick in the gut or ribs until I was gasping when I was eleven, twelve and thirteen. (O'Sullivan 2008, 70)

---

[3] See Michael Shulman, "'It Was Never Good Enough': Former NHLer Patrick O'Sullivan Opens Up About Abusive Father," CTV News, October 21, 2015, https://www.ctvnews.ca/sports/it-was-never-good-enough-former-nhler-patrick-o-sullivan-opens-up-about-abusive-father-1.2621680.

At the age of sixteen, O'Sullivan fought back against his father. He eventually got a restraining order, and when he attended the 2003 NHL draft—which saw him fall from a projected top-five talent all the way down to fifty-sixth overall—he was flanked by two security guards.[4]

Now, I take it to be uncontroversial that the father was a bad parent and that he performed acts that are by many standards morally wrong. In O'Sullivan's case, the father acted immorally, and even in terms of achieving his own goals, he was not successful. His son claims to have been scarred for life by the treatment he received at his father's hands. He is not a good example of a successful outcome. But we can imagine a less extreme version of the story, one in which O'Sullivan has a successful athletic career and his father used more conventional, less controversial techniques to achieve that outcome. Suppose the father's milder parenting techniques worked and his son became a successful hockey player. Would his parenting techniques then be justified? I suspect most of us would think not, and our rejection of his parenting methods will be based on more than the failure of the outcome.

Such stories are not hard to find. Indeed, they are common enough that a parent might wonder if aggressive parenting—whether violent or merely psychologically demanding—is a necessary path to ensure that one's child has a successful athletic career.

Andre Agassi's story, to consider another example, is familiar to many of us.[5] Agassi is a world champion tennis player who has also written a memoir detailing an awful childhood. Agassi's book *Open* (2010) tells of a pushy father who was determined that his son would succeed at tennis. Agassi succeeded but says he has always and continues to hate tennis. Tennis ruined his life, says Agassi. Again, his father was a violent individual who kept axe handles in the car and who tried to beat critical thinking out of his son, since he believed that a good tennis player relies only on instinct. Thought gets in the way of the game, according to Agassi's father.

Here's one more tennis story from Kevin Kinghorn's paper "Authoritarian Tennis Parents: Are Their Children Any Worse Off?" (2010). (An aside: Tennis parents seem to be bad enough that they merit their own subfield in sports ethics.)

---

[4] Source: Canadian Press, https://www.ctvnews.ca/sports/it-was-never-good-enough-former-nhler-patrick-o-sullivan-opens-up-about-abusive-father-1.2621680.
[5] Thanks to Colin Macleod for the Agassi example.

Here are the quick details about Jan, who was born in November, 2001. He showed such aptitude as a—well—toddler that he was attracting media attention by the age of three. At the ripe old age of four, his parents quit their jobs and moved the whole family (Jan has two siblings) from Sacramento to France so that Jan could attend the prestigious Mouratoglou Tennis Academy. The Academy provides Jan with a cadre of coaches and physio advisors; and his scholarship to the Academy covers the family's living expenses—reportedly to the tune of $140,000 a year. The Academy's founder, Patrick Mouratoglou, estimates that, all told, he'll probably invest 2 to 3 million dollars in Jan's career.

Such stories are not reserved for athletes, of course. Many successful musicians have a love/hate relationship with their instrument, never fully endorsing the source of their own talent and achievement. As children, they were pressured to practice in ways that made it very hard to love their instrument even as their talents grew and developed. Just as there are successful tennis players who hate tennis, there are also successful pianists and violinists who hate the piano and the violin. Likewise, there are successful dancers, actors, and chess players who hate dance, acting, and chess. It is a phenomenon worth noting that we sometimes tell people to do what they love, yet it is not uncommon among the greats in any given field to hate the things at which they excel. Further, for many, the very process that resulted in their excellence also resulted in the hatred.

The story philosophers know best, of course, is that of John Stuart Mill, who was pressured by his father, James Mill, to become an intellectual genius. While James Mill arguably succeeded, it seems to me that his parenting techniques also involved exploitation. Following the advice of Jeremy Bentham, James Mill shielded his son from all contact with other children. Instead, he was instructed in Greek beginning at the age of three. Latin followed at eight along with a hefty dose of mathematics and history. At the age of twelve, he began studying logic and composing poetry. But most of us reading know how this story ends. At the age of twenty the younger Mill suffered a nervous breakdown and a severe bout of depression. While he recovered and went on to a happy and productive life, did James Mill do wrong as a parent?

In answering this question, I want to start by noting that it might not matter how Mill, O'Sullivan, and Agassi view the actions of their fathers. You can imagine versions of these life stories in which each thanks his father for his success. In some cases, this might be because the person regards the sacrifice of their childhood as justified in achieving the outcome, but sometimes, of course, this will happen for what we would impartially regard as bad reasons: children are overly forgiving of their parents, people rationalize their experiences for the sake of maintaining a certain self-image, no one wants to think of their own childhood as lacking, et cetera.

Someone might defend this style of aggressive parenting as justified when it produces a good outcome. There are two standards you might use to argue that the outcome is a good one. You might argue, using the perfectionist account of the good, that sufficient achievement is enough to make the outcome a good one. Suppose that Agassi or O'Sullivan or Mill achieved enough; then you might think that this method of parenting was justified. Their personal misery does not matter. On a perfectionist account of the good, human perfection in the realm of athletic, artistic, intellectual, or musical endeavor might be enough to outweigh childhoods that are lacking in childhood goods. A perfectionist might think that a world without extremely talented musicians and the music they produce is worse than a world in which children are abused for the sake of producing great music. I do not share this view and I am not going to engage here with arguments for a perfectionist theory of the good.

I am going to focus instead on theories of the good that include a subjective component such as desire, satisfaction or happiness. I suspect most of us are going to reject a perfectionist account of the good in favor of one that includes subjective components. So, the other way one might think that these life stories turned out well is if the person's life on balance is happier than it would have been without these parenting methods. Or you could hold a mixed view, in which what is good is both some object—such as music, dance, math, art, athletic achievement—and an endorsement by the person whose good it is. Music is good, but the human good consists in the joint condition of making music and loving it.

However, it seems to me that this too is the wrong standard. Why? Return to the case of O'Sullivan. Success might not be enough to justify the way O'Sullivan was parented. Likewise, success that includes happiness might not be enough. Arguably O'Sullivan's father failed by putting his own interests ahead of those of his child. More controversially, the father also failed by denying his child the goods of childhood, sacrificing childhood goods at the doorstep of adult outcomes. Let me say a little bit about both these kinds of failures and then the ways in which parenting can go wrong.

If I am right and the negative conception of childhood is false, then a common view of parenting, that our main obligations consist in shepherding our children safely to the threshold of adulthood, well prepared for autonomous adult lives, is incorrect. On my view, one of the most important and difficult tasks of parenting consists in balancing things that are good for the child-as-child with the things that are good for the child-as-future-adult.

Returning to the O'Sullivan case, the wrongness of it is overdetermined. The first way in which O'Sullivan's father went wrong is in putting his own interests ahead of those of his child. He wanted his son to excel at hockey to make up for his own failed attempt. He also used methods that clearly violated the rights of his child, even the very basic rights such as the right not to be harmed. Such rights protect children even if the long-term outcome is good, though in this case it was not.

Imagine now a scenario in which O'Sullivan does become a successful hockey player and the methods employed by his father are milder though still focused on the singular goal of producing a star hockey player. It might even be the case that the adult child is happy with the outcome, though it is still true that the parent got it wrong. How so? It might have cost O'Sullivan his childhood, and doing so could be exploitative regardless of the overall good produced.

There are three reasons for thinking we do not get to maximize goods across a life span, discounting childhood altogether. First, there is a significant gap between the child we were and the adult we become. When I make sacrifices now to benefit retirement-age me, I do so knowing that I will appreciate it. I am not here referring just to financial sacrifices, which are easy to explain because of the fungibility of money. Other sacrifices might include giving up playing aggressive sports so that older me can enjoy hikes. Fifty-year-old me is the same person as seventy-year-old me in ways that five-year-old me is not the same person as twenty-year-old me. The changes in identity through childhood are much more profound and make sacrificing early goods for later goods tricky. Second, it may be that there are goods only possible in childhood. It is controversial, but I think certain types of imaginative play are only possible in childhood. (For the counter view, see Gheaus 2015.) If we miss those goods in childhood, then we can never attain them. People may talk about rediscovering their inner child as an adult, but that is not the same as actually being a child. Third, in the case of children the trade-offs are made by other people. There are reasons to be extra careful when we are making decisions that affect other people.

Although the O'Sullivan case is about hockey, it's true as well for those of us anxious to see our children excel in music or the arts. What is interesting is that if I am right and we can exploit childhood both for our own good, if we are parents, and for the good of the adult person the child is to become, then not all exploitation consists in the harm of one person for the benefit of others. We can exploit a person's particular life stage when we do not value it for its own sake.

Some people, on hearing about the incredible cost in terms of childhood goods in the production of certain adult talents, are moved to think that we are not morally justified in bringing about this outcome. Childhood exploitation is part of the story of what constrains our treatment of children. Still, others are not convinced. They ask, "But what if the only way to produce the best musicians and the best athletes were to exploit children and ruin their childhoods? What would need to be the case for that to be justified?"

Here are some responses to this line of questioning:

1. What do we mean by the best? If we were constrained in our production of musicians and athletes by ethical imperatives about the way children ought to be treated and the way childhood ought to be valued, then "the best" would be "the best that can be produced by ethical means." We do not think about mistreating adult athletes and musicians for better results. Suppose, counterfactually, that torturing symphony musicians before a performance produced better concerts. We would not think that this is the standard by which to judge symphony performances.
2. It would be justified if music and athletic performance had a certain kind of objective value, in addition to the subjective value of those who appreciate it, and if that value trumped the value of childhood goods, the rights of children, and the subjective experiences of the children involved. Still, I think most of us either believe that art and sports do not have objective value or believe that if they do, that objective value does not trump the rights of persons.
3. The exploitation of childhood in the production of athletes and musicians is also, importantly, a life-changing course of action. They are transformative experiences that cannot be undone. Imagine being the best at some sport, with everything in you being used to produce that outcome, and then just walking away from the sport. At a certain point it is not just a lost childhood. It is also a kind of shaping that

makes it very hard to choose anything else. Some Olympic athletes at the end of their athletic careers express relief that finally it's over and they can do other things.

We do not need to turn to science fiction or thought experiments for cases in which the exploitation of childhood to produce a certain kind of result crosses the intuitive barrier of impermissibility for most people. Consider the case of castrati, the historical phenomenon most modern minds find appalling. In the 1700s, musical audiences preferred the castrato singing voice, which is achieved by castrating young men before the age of puberty. Though the endocrinological condition also happens very occasionally naturally, due to illness, disease, or accident, most castrati were surgically castrated. There is no other way to prevent puberty from transforming a boy's larynx into one that produces sounds in the lower register. At the peak of the popularity of this style of music thousands of boys were castrated annually. Most of the boys were poor and were offered up by their parents to be forcibly castrated, though some stories exist of boys who requested the operation to prevent their voices from changing.

Again, the wrongness of such actions is overdetermined. The children were harmed, they did not consent, and even if they did consent, arguably they were too young for that consent to be morally binding. What mattered to those who thought this course of action not wrong was the beautiful music it produced. But how beautiful the music is seems irrelevant. Children were tortured and lives were ruined as a result. I am using this case to show that there are some ways of treating children that are clearly wrong, no matter how good the outcomes that are produced.

Now, one might wonder what all of this has to do with modern parenting methods. Surely, we all agree that aggression and physical violence towards children break certain moral rules. Surely, we all also agree that no aesthetic outcome is so good that it justifies torturing children. No amount of beautiful music or world-class tennis makes it okay to hurt children and take their childhoods away. Yes, but I am suggesting that this way of thinking about children and childhood remains part of the contemporary ethos of parenting. Many of us still view parenting as focused on an outcome and view childhood as a period of time and potential to be exploited in pursuit of adult goods.

Let us conclude by considering, in turn, parents' choices and children's choices, in the context of childhood development.

Parents' choices: Parenting well requires a lot of balancing. Parents play an active role in moving from protecting and promoting children's interests to respecting and promoting their rights to make their own choices. A second sort of balancing occurs when parents must determine how to weigh the interests children have in being children with the interests they have in being happy, successful adults. This suggests two ways parents can get it wrong. First, a child's developmental readiness might speak to protecting their choices, but instead, parents continue to think about protecting only the child's interests. (Or they could promote the child to choice rights too early.) Second, parents might give too much weight to the interests of the future person the child is to become and not enough to the interests the child has now. Conversely, parents might weigh childhood goods too heavily and not care enough about the future person.

You can get the balance wrong in a number of different ways. But I think it's helpful to reserve talk of "exploitation" for cases in which parents completely discount childhood goods and treat childhood purely as having instrumental value. Return to the environmental case with which we began this paper. If we assigned some intrinsic value to mountains, rivers, and trees, we would not be exploiting nature even if we were wrong about the amount of intrinsic value versus instrumental value. Likewise, parents can assign too little value to childhood without being guilty of exploiting childhood goods for adult gains.

Children's choices: Note that when it comes to balancing interests between current and future selves, adults get to do this, and we make mistakes much of the time. But children can also get it wrong. One important difference between children and adults is that it is legitimate in the case of children for others to help correct them and guide their choices. If we are imagining one kind of bad parent being those who fail to pay proper attention to their children's interests and childhood goods and weigh them appropriately, a second kind of bad parent might be those who let children themselves make this mistake. If the parents in the first group are making the kid practice tennis or play the piano, parents in this second group may be failing to tell the child to "put down that violin and go outside and play." Though the error here on the child's part is failing to give enough weight to childhood and childhood goods, I do not think it is helpful to think of this mistake in terms of exploitation. Parents can exploit children and their childhoods. Parents can also fail to require children to give enough weight to childhood goods. But only the first is helpfully thought of in terms of the concept of exploitation.

References

Agassi, A. 2010. *Open: An Autobiography*. New York: Vintage Books.
Brennan, S. 2014. "The Goods of Childhood, Children's Rights, and the Role of Parents as Advocates and Interpreters." In *Family-Making: Contemporary Ethical Challenges*, edited by F. Baylis and C. McLeod, 29–45. Oxford: Oxford University Press.
Feinberg, J. 1980. "A Child's Right to an Open Future." In *Whose Child? Parental Rights, Parental Authority and State Power*, edited by W. Aiken and H. LaFollette, 124–153. Totowa, NJ: Littlefield, Adams.
Ferguson, B. 2021. "Are We All Exploiters?" *Philosophy and Phenomenological Research* 103, no. 3: 535–546.
Goodin, R. 1987. "Exploiting a Situation and Exploiting a Person." In *Modern Theories of Exploitation* edited by Reeve, 166–200. London: Sage.
Gheaus, A. 2015. "Unfinished Adults and Defective Children." *Journal of Ethics and Social Philosophy* 9: 1–21.
Kinghorn, K. 2010. "Authoritarian Tennis Parents: Are Their Children Any Worse Off?" In *Tennis and Philosophy*, edited by D. Baggett, 90–106. Lexington: University Press of Kentucky.
O'Sullivan, P. 2015. *Breaking Away: A Harrowing True Story of Resilience, Courage, and Triumph*. Toronto: Harper Collins Canada.
Slote, M. 1983. *Goods and Virtues*. New York: Oxford University Press.
Tomlin, P. 2018. "Saplings or Caterpillars? Trying to Understand Children's Wellbeing." *Journal of Applied* 35: 2946. https://doi.org/10.1111/japp.12204
Turner, S. 2002. *Something to Cry About: An Argument Against Corporal Punishment of Children in Canada*. Waterloo: Wilfrid Laurier University Press.

11

Labor Exploitation

A Left-Libertarian Analysis

Roderick T. Long

Critics of libertarianism often charge that the fully free market society favored by libertarians would be pervaded by exploitation, including exploitation in the workplace. For their part, mainstream libertarians often deny or downplay the existence, and/or the wrongness, of forms of exploitation that do not involve the violation of libertarian rights; even the scope of rights-violating forms of exploitation is often interpreted in such a way as to restrict it fairly narrowly to direct state actions such as taxation—precisely the sort of action that libertarianism's critics tend *not* to interpret as exploitative.

Mainstream libertarians also tend to regard most workplaces (including sweatshops) as non-exploitative, or at least not wrongly exploitative, even in existing state-regulated capitalist economies, and to be suspicious of labor unions and other mechanisms for worker empowerment, whereas many of libertarianism's critics tend to regard labor exploitation as a serious problem that can be addressed only by the sorts of state regulations that libertarians oppose.

Drawing on the traditions of classical liberal class theory, individualist anarchism, and contemporary left-libertarianism,[1] I shall defend an account of exploitation that:

(a) differs from the libertarian mainstream in:

This chapter has benefited (I hope) from written comments by Ben Ferguson, Michael J. Green, and Matt Zwolinski, and from discussion with participants at the Alabama Philosophical Society, the Athens Institute for Education and Research, and the University of San Diego Exploitation Workshop.

[1] I here use the term "left-libertarian" as it is generally used within the (free market) libertarian movement: to refer to the left wing of that movement, which arose from the rapprochement between libertarianism and the New Left in the 1960s and 1970s (cf. Carson 2008, 1–2; Chartier 2012). The term "left-libertarianism" in this sense, dating from the 1970s (Childs 1971; Konkin 2012), is not to

(a1) recognizing problematic forms of exploitation that libertarians qua libertarians have reason to condemn even though they do not involve violations of libertarian rights

(a2) identifying a thoroughly pervasive incidence of morally problematic private exploitation, and in particular labor exploitation (including not only sweatshop conditions but more ordinary workplace hierarchies as well), that is indirectly enabled by rights-violating state interventions on behalf of the more affluent

(b) differs from libertarianism's critics in

(b1) identifying most state action, including taxation, as exploitative

(b2) maintaining that the incidence of nominally private exploitation, and in particular of the most egregious forms of labor exploitation, would be much lower in a fully freed market than in virtually any realistically achievable system of state intervention

1. The Contours of Exploitation

Let me begin by saying something about the concept of exploitation. I shall not choose among the multitudinous competing definitions of exploitation in the literature (I regard such definitions as properly downstream, rather than upstream, from investigations like this one),[2] nor shall I settle whether exploitation is (a) not always wrong, (b) wrong by definition, or (c) not wrong by definition but nevertheless in fact always wrong. However, the sort of exploitation I am interested in here is the sort that is at least *presumptively* wrong, and so when I mention exploitation that is the kind I have in mind. Moreover, while not offering a definition, I do agree with the general consensus that exploitation can be broadly characterized as taking unfair advantage of someone. And while I don't plan to give that broad characterization the full specification that it would ultimately require, I do think we can lay down some general parameters.

---

be confused with its more recent use to denote a position, associated with Peter Vallentyne, Hillel Steiner, and Michael Otsuka, that combines self-ownership (the libertarian part) with some sort of common ownership of natural resources (the "left" part).

[2] See Valdman's proposal to start from "paradigm cases of wrongful exploitation" and "base our analysis of exploitation's wrongness on them" (2009, 3) For a defense of this reflective-equilibrium approach to moral epistemology, see Long 2000, 2003.

First, the stock case of the rescuer who demands that a drowning person agree to an exorbitant fee prior to rescue seems to me to establish convincingly that in order for a transaction to be (wrongfully) exploitative, it need not be involuntary on the exploited person's part, nor need it make her worse off—though the case for a relationship's being exploitative is plausibly *strengthened* by the presence of involuntariness or net harm.

Second, I do not think it makes sense to condemn as (wrongful) exploitation every transaction in which one person benefits from the need of another,[3] as this would condemn most forms of trade and cooperation. Given that trade and cooperation are the basis of all human society, an account of exploitation that condemns them in toto deserves to be regarded with skepticism. But the case for describing a transaction as exploitative is strengthened when the exploited person's need is desperate and the price she must pay is exorbitant. Hence Michael Valdman's suggestion that we commit exploitation when we "extract excessive benefits from people who cannot, or cannot reasonably, refuse our offers"[4] is closer to the mark—though I think the degree of cost to the exploited person matters more than the degree of benefit received by the exploiter.[5]

Is an exchange exploitative simply in virtue of one party to an exchange receiving a disproportionate share of the products of their cooperation, even if neither force nor disadvantage in bargaining power is present? That's far from obvious. If a generous billionaire decides to offer me an unusually high price for my service or product (staggeringly high for me, trivial for her), then I've benefited disproportionately from our exchange, but it's hard to see how I've exploited her. Exploitation seems to involve some defect in the *origin* of the disproportionate benefit, and the two most salient candidates—force, for one, and disadvantage in bargaining power, for the other—both seem to have more to do with disrespectful treatment. (To be sure, disproportionate benefit from exchanges is frequently a *sign* of exploitative origins, but hardly an infallible one.)

---

[3] Allen Wood does not quite say this, but his claim that we (wrongfully) exploit others whenever we "treat their vulnerabilities as opportunities to advance our own interests or projects" (Wood 1995, 150–151) comes perilously close. (The view is often attributed to Montaigne, but mistakenly so; see Long 2008a.)

[4] Valdman 2009, 3.

[5] Moreover, I would not want to limit exploitative transactions to *offers*; if Dracula keeps me locked in his dungeon to serve as an ongoing source of blood for his sustenance, he is arguably exploiting me even though there is no offer involved. It also seems to me that exploitation can occur even when the exploiter is not seeking, let alone receiving, a benefit (see Long 2011, 3–4). But I shall not pursue these issues here.

2. Against the Cost Principle

Some left-libertarian thinkers—and in particular, the nineteenth-century individualist anarchists Josiah Warren and Stephen Pearl Andrews—have defended a fairly extreme theory of exploitation, called the cost principle, which holds that A (wrongfully) exploits B whenever A charges B more for some good or service than what that good or service cost A to produce. Unlike some of their successors such as Benjamin Tucker and Francis Tandy, or more recently Kevin Carson,[6] who defend the cost principle as a *prediction* of what will generally happen once governmental impediments to free competition are removed (the idea being that those who persist in selling above cost will thereby motivate competitors to undersell them, thus bidding down the price), Warren and Andrews take the cost principle to be a *moral* imperative. Charging prices above cost thus becomes not merely *evidence* of a background of exploitation but in itself the essence of exploitation.[7]

Mainstream libertarians often reject attempts to make cost the standard of price by pointing out that costs are subjective. But Andrews is well aware that costs are subjective, and incorporates this point into his theory by appealing to degrees of subjective disutility (or "repugnance") of labor, defining cost as "the amount of repugnance overcome."[8] Andrews's version of the cost principle, then, amounts to a requirement that one sell one's good or service for the lowest price at which one would still be willing to make the exchange.

Andrews's case for this requirement proceeds, in part, as follows. He takes what he calls the value principle (namely, that one may legitimately charge whatever price the market will bear) as the only viable alternative to the cost principle, and then constructs an example—broadly like our familiar drowning example, but instead involving a vital medicine—intended to serve as a reductio of the value principle: "Am I, then, entitled to demand of you for the nostrum the whole of your property, more or less? Clearly so, if *it is right to take for a thing what it is worth*, which is theoretically the highest ethics of trade."[9] With the value principle thereby disposed of, only the cost principle remains—or so Andrews supposes.

Why does Andrews take the cost principle and the value principle to be the only viable options? The answer seems to be that there is no scientifically

---

[6] Tucker 1893; Tandy 1893; Carson 2007.
[7] Andrews 1970, 104 (§ 157).
[8] Andrews 1970, 75, §§ 78–79.
[9] Andrews 1970, 99, § 144.

precise standard for determining equity anywhere between those two extremes. Andrews notes that the popularity of an intermediate solution, whereby it is permissible to charge what the market will bear *except* when doing so poses an undue burden, is motivated by a recognition of the illegitimacy of an unrestricted application of the value principle. But he thinks there are no principled grounds for picking any particular point between charging the least one is willing to charge and charging the most one can get, and so if one extreme is indefensible, the other extreme must be unavoidable.[10]

But Andrews's assumption that the requirements of moral virtue must be susceptible to unambiguous scientific exactness is unwarranted; in Aristotle's terms, he is demanding more precision than the subject matter allows.[11] After all, we can identify clear cases of blue and of green even if we cannot say precisely where in the spectrum one ends and the other begins.

There are also difficulties with the cost principle itself, and not just with Andrews's defense of it. First, by forbidding arbitrage, the principle obstructs the equilibrating effect of the price system. This is perhaps not a decisive objection, since social benefits and harms are plausibly not the sole criterion of morality; but they, again plausibly, form *part* of the criterion of morality, so the tension between the cost principle and economic equilibration presents at the very least a serious challenge to that principle's legitimacy.[12]

Second, the cost principle requires that we first figure out what a transaction costs and on that basis determine its moral status. But for a morally decent person, the recognition that a choice is immoral raises that choice's subjective cost; hence one cannot determine the cost of a transaction *independently* of moral considerations.

Third, the cost principle, at least as Andrews glosses it, makes the wrongness of exploitation turn more on the benefit to the exploiter than on the cost

---

[10] Andrews 1970, 100, §146. According to Cicero's report, the Stoic philosopher Diogenes of Babylon took a view of the options that was much like Andrews's but drew the opposite moral: if price gouging during a famine were to be deemed wrong, then we would have no basis for avoiding the condemnation of all trade for gain, and so no basis for avoiding the condemnation of private property itself; but such a condemnation is unacceptable, and so price gouging during a famine must be regarded as morally permissible (*De Officiis* III.12.52-53; Cicero 1913, 321-323). Cicero himself follows a rival Stoic, Antipater of Tarsus, in taking an intermediate position like the one I defend here.

[11] Aristotle, *Nicomachean Ethics* I.3, 1094b12-26. Likewise, Adam Smith writes that while the "rules of justice" are "precise and accurate," those of "the other virtues" are "loose, vague, and indeterminate," so that "the first may be compared to the rules of grammar," while the second are like "those which critics lay down for the attainment of what is sublime and elegant in composition," which provide only a "general idea of the perfection we ought to aim at" rather than a rigorous algorithm (Smith 1774, 412, VI.4).

[12] For defense of an ethical approach that gives social consequences *some* weight but not *sole* weight, see Long 2012b, 2013, 2020.

to the person exploited—though he recognizes that there need be no correlation in magnitude between the two,[13] so it's not as though whatever the exploiter gains must be lost by the person exploited. Yet surely, again, what is primarily wrong with exploitation is the burden borne by the exploited person, not the benefit reaped by the exploiter.

Fourth, it's not clear that the cost principle can even be coherently applied. Suppose I grow bananas and you grow coconuts, and our respective subjective preferences are such that I would be willing to trade two bananas for one coconut, and you would be willing to trade two coconuts for one banana. It seems that there is an attractive opportunity for mutually beneficial trade here; but if the cost principle is right, how can any exchange between us be equitable? If I give you anything less than two bananas per coconut, I am exploiting you; if you give me anything less than two coconuts per banana, you are exploiting me. Hence there is no possible rate of exchange that will avoid having at least one of us exploited (and at most rates of exchange we are *both* exploited), and so we are morally obligated to refrain from trading. Inasmuch as the aim of the cost principle was to make exchange equitable, not to abolish it, this seems an awkward consequence.

I conclude that, Andrews's mockery notwithstanding, "Don't gouge *too* deep" (as he sarcastically words it)[14] is indeed a more defensible principle than its more absolutist rivals, "Gouge all you want" and "Don't gouge at all." Or, in more accurate terminology, "Don't take *excessive* advantage of *extreme* need" is a more defensible principle than either "Never take advantage of anyone's need" or "Take as much advantage as you like of anyone's need no matter how extreme." If the more defensible principle is also more difficult to apply than its rivals, this is simply another reminder that developing practical wisdom involves more than memorizing a bunch of rules.

3. The State as Exploiter

Just as mainstream libertarians are often reluctant to recognize exploitation outside of state action, so non-libertarians are often reluctant to recognize the state itself as an exploiter. As Matt Zwolinski notes, although the "modern

---

[13] "The burden or cost may be very great and the benefit or value very little, or *vice versa*" (Andrews 1970, 93, § 131).
[14] Andrews 1970, 100, § 146.

centralized state bears significant responsibility in structuring almost every transaction that persons enter into, commercial, professional, legal, social, and otherwise," contemporary exploitation theory nevertheless deals almost exclusively with "exploitation that occurs *within* that structure." The state is generally invoked only as "a kind of *deu[s] ex machina* the powers of which can be brought to bear to correct exploitation in the market, the family, and elsewhere," and the possibility that "the state itself can be a significant source and tool of exploitation" is "almost never mentioned."[15]

Nevertheless, most state action seems paradigmatically exploitative. Consider two of the state's most fundamental attributes: its power of taxation and its territorial monopoly. In the case of taxation, the state makes its citizens an offer: surrender an amount of the state's choosing, or face various penalties. This seems even more clearly exploitative than the rescuer's offer to save a drowning person for an exorbitant fee, for the rescuer is offering to save the victim from a threat not of the rescuer's making, whereas the state is itself the source of the threat it offers to remove. Likewise, in banning competing service providers within the same territory, the state deprives its citizens of the option of seeking better service at a lower price. Moreover, if taking advantage of people's weaknesses or vulnerabilities is problematically exploitative, a state vastly more powerful than the individual it coerces is surely making suspect use of an enormous strength differential.

What defeaters might there be to the claim that taxation and territorial monopoly constitute exploitation? It may be claimed that citizens benefit from these programs, or have consented to them. But these claims are open to challenge, given that monopoly provision tends to be more expensive and inefficient than competitive provision.[16]

There may be some citizens who are net beneficiaries of state redistribution. Both mainstream libertarians and their non-libertarian critics tend to identify that class with the poorest citizens, while left-libertarians tend to identify that class with the richest citizens. But if libertarian analyses—either left or right—of the effects of government intervention on economic growth are correct, it is also possible that in the long run there are no net beneficiaries of state redistribution.

---

[15] Zwolinski 2012, 175.

[16] For discussion of the advantages of non-state provision of such services as legal adjudication and rights protection, including the citation of successful historical examples, see Anderson and Hill 2004; Bell 1992; Benson 2011; Casey 2012; Chartier 2011, 2013; Friedman 1989; Leeson 2014; Long and Machan 2008; Stringham 2005, 2007, 2015; Tucker and de Bellis 2016.

As for consent, the social-contract arguments intended to show that citizens have tacitly consented to the state's authority by remaining within the territory it claims or accepting the services it offers are notoriously weak.[17] In any case, as Crispin Sartwell points out, if I "consent to abide by the law when that law is enforced by a huge body of men with guns and clubs," then "it is never clear . . . whether my consent is genuine or not," and thus the "mere existence of an overwhelming force by which the laws will be enforced compromises conceptually the possibility of voluntarily acceding to them."[18]

So, the first problem with an appeal to citizen benefit or citizen consent as a defeater to the claim that taxation and monopoly status are exploitative is that the claim that citizens benefit from or consent to these programs seems unfounded. But the second problem with such an appeal is that even if citizens did benefit from or consent to these programs, benefit and (highly pressured) consent are not per se defeaters to a charge of exploitation (as the rescue-from-drowning example shows). Suppose, for example, that continuing to reside within the territory claimed by a state *did* constitute consent to that state's authority.[19] It would still remain true that, given the burdensome costs of withholding such consent (viz., by having to relocate to another country), most citizens will have no reasonable alternative to consenting to the state, and so will resemble the drowning person who has no reasonable alternative to promising their life savings to the rescuer.

A different potential defeater to the charge that taxation in particular is exploitative is the claim that the citizen owes taxes as a just repayment for the benefits of participation in social cooperation. Here the argument is not that taxes are a payment *to the state* for services that *it* proposes to provide (a transaction that looks uncomfortably like a protection racket) but rather that taxes are owed *to society* (on whose *behalf* the state proposes to collect) as a payment for benefits one has all along been receiving. But even if it were true that receiving benefits generates enforceable obligations of repayment,[20] it's unclear why the state would be the appropriate agency to collect it (given that

---

[17] For an especially effective recent critique of such arguments, see Huemer 2012.
[18] Sartwell 2008, 50–51; cf. Johnson 2009.
[19] Of course I don't think it does. To begin with, in order for continued residence within the territory claimed by a state to constitute consent to that state's authority, the state's claim to that territory must be legitimate. (Otherwise I could obligate you to accept my authority simply by declaring myself the legitimate ruler of the territory in which you reside.) But it will then be circular to appeal to consent-via-continued-residence as a justification for the state's claim to authority over a given territory, if that claim's being justified is in turn a *precondition* for continued residence to count as consent in the first place.
[20] For reasons to doubt this, see Robert Nozick's public-address example: Nozick 1974, 92–94.

the relations of social cooperation in which any particular citizen participates need not correspond at all closely to state boundaries) or why the state's unilateral edict on the amount to be paid should be respected (for even if A genuinely owes a debt to B, empowering a third party, C, not only to collect that debt but to decide unilaterally how much it should be—and, once collected, how it should be spent—seems like a recipe for abuse).

In addition to taxation and territorial monopoly, most of the other things the state does have the appearance of exploitation. The state issues edicts—millions of them—that threaten citizens with penalties if they do not behave in certain ways. Many of these cases are regulatory arcana where disobedience to the edict is only a *malum prohibitum* rather than a *malum in se*; that, is it requires or forbids what no one would take to be inherently required or forbidden were it not for the edict. Moreover, the number of such edicts is so great, and their wording so opaque, that no citizen can reasonably be expected to know the totality of what she is required or forbidden to do. Furthermore, even when what is prohibited is a *malum in se*, the penalty for committing the prohibited act is typically morally disproportionate to the offense (e.g., incarceration as a penalty for theft),[21] and the means of enforcement is frequently not only excessively violent but also heedless of the likely guilt or innocence of those targeted (think of widespread cases of police abuse and brutality, particularly against minorities). To top it off, the cost of hiring a lawyer to defend oneself against the state's charges is frequently prohibitive, and the free counsel provided to indigent defendants is often of poor quality.[22] When a massively powerful institution such as a state takes advantage of its citizens' powerlessness and ignorance to direct their behavior as it prefers and to impose punitive treatment they have little capacity to challenge, it's hard to see how this can be described as anything other than exploitation.

4. Labor Exploitation and State Intervention

Our chief concern at present, however, is not exploitation in general, but *labor* exploitation. In what ways does the state exploit labor? In some instances it literally compels labor, as in the case of military conscription,

---

[21] For a general critique of the institution of punishment, see Long 1999.
[22] See Roach 2014.

compulsory jury service, prison labor, filling out tax forms, and—in some countries—compulsory voting. Taxation is also, as Robert Nozick points out, an indirect form or analogue of compulsory labor, since "taking the earnings of n hours labor" is tantamount to "forcing the person to work n hours for another's purpose."[23] There is also a vast amount of labor exploitation that is still more indirect than this, but for which the state nevertheless continues to bear responsibility.

In the classical liberal version of class theory, the ruling or exploiting class is taken to owe its position not (as in Marxist theory) to its control of the means of production, but rather to its access to political power.[24] For the nineteenth-century French liberal Adolphe-Jérôme Blanqui, for example, society is divided into two great parties: "those who wish to live by their own labour, and those who wish to live off the labour of others."[25] He cites as examples taxes, monopolies, and customs duties. Likewise in England, liberal reformer James Mill (father of John Stuart Mill) divided society into "the ruling Few," or "Ceux qui pillent" (those who pillage), and "the subject Many," or "Ceux qui sont pillés" (those who are pillaged), such pillaging being carried on primarily through the agency of the state.[26]

The nineteenth-century individualist anarchists[27] took over the classical liberal theory of class and radicalized it. Unlike the classical liberals, and like the Marxists, they stressed the importance of control over the means of production in maintaining the power of the ruling class. But unlike the Marxists,[28] they saw the ruling class's control of the means of production as mainly a byproduct of state privilege and political power, and so rather than seeking to suppress private property and market exchange, as the Marxists advised, they sought—like, but to a still greater extent than, the classical liberals—to expand private property and market exchange by suppressing the power of the state.

---

[23] Nozick 1974, 169.
[24] See, e.g., Hart 1994; Long 2012a.
[25] Blanqui 1860, 4–5; translation mine.
[26] Mill 1835.
[27] See Hodgskin 1825, 1832; Warren 1852; Andrews 1970; Spooner 1846; Heywood 1985; Tucker 1893; Tandy 1893; Lum 1887, 1890; de Cleyre 1914.
[28] More precisely, when Marxists are replying to those who defend existing economic inequality on the grounds that it resulted from a free market, Marxists insist, to the contrary, on the historical role of state violence, rather than anything like a free market, in establishing and perpetuating such inequality; in those moments the Marxists sound like the individualist anarchists. But when Marxists are replying to defenses of the free market itself, they tend to act as though they've forgotten the role of state violence, and now charge free markets with creating existing economic inequalities. On this dynamic, see Carson 2007, 89–164.

The individualist anarchist position has since been revived by the contemporary left-libertarian movement. Left-libertarians regard competition as a leveling force; when legal impediments to the imitation of success are removed, imitators are generally able to bid down the prices charged by the successful, thus limiting the extent to which market actors can reap exorbitant and long-lasting profits from their successes. Hence whenever economic inequalities are large, systematic, and enduring, left-libertarians identify interference—generally state interference—with free competition as the likeliest explanation. In particular, left-libertarian authors have identified a multitude of ways in which state interventions, even (or especially) those advertised as protecting ordinary people against the powerful, serve in practice to monopolize control of the means of production in the hands of the capitalist class, largely forcing the rest of the population into the position of wage laborers.[29] Nor is this an accidental feature of state intervention, one that could be remedied through reformist efforts. On the contrary, given the incentival and informational perversities associated with territorial monopolies, it is virtually inevitable that state interventions will tend on the whole to promote class rule. Hence left-libertarians seek at the very least to minimize state intervention, and ideally (for most left-libertarians) to abolish the state entirely.

While I cannot give a full account here of left-libertarian economic analysis,[30] let me offer a brief sketch. As I've written elsewhere:

> The existence of regulations, fees, licensure requirements, et cetera does not affect all market participants equally; it's much easier for wealthy, well-established companies to jump through these hoops than it is for new firms just starting up. Hence such regulations both decrease the number of employers bidding for employees' services (thus keeping salaries low) and make it harder for the less affluent to start enterprises of their own. Legal restrictions on labor organizing also make it harder for such workers to organize collectively on their own behalf.[31]

---

[29] Chartier and Johnson 2011; Carson 2007, 2008.
[30] For details, I'll simply point the interested reader to the growing body of left-libertarian literature. See in particular Carson 2007, 2008; Chartier and Johnson 2011; and Massimino and Tuttle 2016; cf. Long 2012a, 2019b. For left-libertarian analysis of exploitation in particular, see MacKenzie 2007 and Johnson 2007.
[31] Long 2008b.

Thus on the one hand, government policies tend to reduce the number of firms, thereby reducing the competition that employers face *from other employers*. And on the other hand, through policies that concentrate the means of production in fewer hands, thus making it harder for employees to start their own businesses (whether as workers' cooperatives or as individual proprietorships), the state reduces the competition that employers face *from self-employment*. This is particularly true in the third-world countries to which sweatshops gravitate, where peasants have typically been kicked off their land by local kleptocracies. But it is true as well in first-world countries like the United States, where most land west of the Mississippi is owned by governments or nominally private but government-privileged land companies, where intellectual property laws criminalize competition-by-imitation, and where legal barriers to self-employment are often prohibitive—all means of monopolizing the means of production in the hands of a ruling class. While some state interventions do benefit the least affluent, they generally do so merely by moderating the effects of other, more deeply embedded interventions that run the other way.

The nineteenth-century individualist anarchist Benjamin Tucker, a forerunner of today's left-libertarians, accused mainstream free market advocates of believing "in liberty to compete with the laborer in order to reduce his wages, but not in liberty to compete with the capitalist in order to reduce his usury."[32] The essence of the left-libertarian critique of the prevailing capitalist system is that *labor is prevented from competing with capital*.

Does this mean that in a freed market wage labor would wither away, or only that it would become less exploitative? The answer is: some of each. The left-libertarian argument is that large hierarchical firms are subject to Hayekian knowledge problems, creating diseconomies of scale that would place such firms at a competitive disadvantage in relation to smaller, flatter firms were it not for a multitude of state actions that serve to insulate them from such competition. Hence if the legal barriers to self-employment were removed, many more workers' cooperatives and individual proprietorships would flourish.

We do not assume, however, that all wage labor would cease to exist; there are various reasons that individuals might choose to work for wages. What we oppose is not wage labor but the wage *system*—that is, the system in which the working class has *no viable alternative* to working for wages. It

[32] Tucker 1888, 3.

would be much harder for employers to behave exploitatively or oppressively if their employees had access to attractive alternatives to wage labor; and the result is that those who do choose to work for wages would be able to successfully demand more workplace autonomy, and a status more like independent contractors than like micromanaged employees.

Once again, although neither involuntariness nor net harm is necessary for exploitation, the presence of these conditions strengthens the case for regarding a transaction as exploitative. If left-libertarian social analysis is correct, most workers receive less revenue, and receive it under more oppressive and hierarchical work conditions, then they would were it not for the state's interventions; hence they suffer a net harm. Moreover, this harm arises through laws that are imposed on them by the armed force of the state; hence their participation is involuntary. So, from a left-libertarian perspective, the working class is exploited by the state on behalf of the capitalist class—or (essentially equivalently, given the capitalist class's influence on the state), the working class is exploited by the capitalist class through the mechanism of the state.[33]

5. Labor Exploitation Without State Intervention

Now, there is a possible left-libertarian position (and more than possible; I know some adherents) that makes exploitation, or at least the wrongness of exploitation, consist *exclusively* in the background of rights violations that it involves. But this is not the majority position among left-libertarians, and for good reason: left-libertarians typically want to say that *one of the reasons* (though not generally the only one) that state intervention is bad is that it enables exploitation. This would be a vacuous claim if the exploitativeness and/or badness of exploitation were exhausted by its origins in state intervention (and thus in aggression). Consequently, from a left-libertarian perspective exploitation must be identifiable, and bad, even apart from its basis in aggression.[34] And if this is so, then the door is at least open to there

---

[33] It is not essential to the left-libertarian analysis that the class effects of state intervention be intentional (although left-libertarians suspect they often are). If (for obvious reasons) legislation negatively affecting the powerful tends to be combated more often and more successfully than legislation negatively affecting the powerless, then the overall pattern of legislation will tend to have a class character regardless of whether anyone intended it to do so.

[34] This, incidentally, seems to me to be a weakness of Hillel Steiner's (1984) account of exploitation, which assumes that all genuine exploitation must be unjust, in the sense of being rights-violating or depending on a background of rights violations; there are of course weaker conceptions of justice,

being forms of (wrongful) exploitation that do not involve aggression, even if (given left-libertarian analysis) aggression makes such exploitation much likelier and more difficult to address.[35]

Most (though not all) left-libertarians accept "libertarian thickness"—the idea that there are certain value commitments that, while not logically entailed by libertarian principles, are nevertheless bound up either conceptually or causally with those principles in such a way as to make them part of reasonable libertarian advocacy—perhaps by being part of, or implied by, the most reasonable defense of libertarianism (*grounds* thickness), or being needed in order to choose between alternative ways of applying libertarian principles (*application* thickness), or being needed to render a libertarian social order achievable or sustainable (*strategic* thickness), or being independently recognizable values for whose secure implementation a libertarian social order is needed (*consequence* thickness).[36] Thus libertarians qua libertarians have reason to promote such values together with libertarianism as part of a unified program. (For left-libertarians, these will be left-wing values, but it is not part of the concept of libertarian thickness that the values be left-wing.)[37]

There are multiple reasons for exploitation to be opposed by libertarians qua libertarians, as part of a "thick" bundle, independently of whether it involves the rights violation of aggression. For one thing, as we've seen, inasmuch as a tendency to enable exploitation is part of what makes aggression bad, those who oppose aggression have reason to oppose exploitation. For another, the other features of aggression that make it bad, apart from its tendency to enable exploitation, display significant overlap with the features that also make exploitation bad (e.g., lack of respect for persons, or pushing people around), and so here too those who oppose aggression have

---

on which see Long 2019b. Forcing all exploitation into the straitjacket of rights violations would seem to force us into either unduly contracting the scope of recognized exploitation (the problem I complain of in mainstream libertarianism) or else shifting the scope of rights so as to render non-libertarian claims enforceable (and thereby abandoning libertarianism per se). (For my reasons for saying "shifting" rather than "expanding," see Long 2014.)

[35] Right-libertarian critics sometimes charge that by classifying both rights-violating acts and non-rights-violating acts as instances of "exploitation," left-libertarians are thereby trying to erase the difference between rights-violating acts and non-rights-violating acts. (See, e.g., Rachels 2016.) By that logic, I suppose those who classify both horses and dolphins as "mammals" must be trying to erase the difference between horses and dolphins.

[36] For further exposition of the concept of libertarian thickness, see Johnson 2008, 2010. For an application of libertarian thickness to exploitation in particular, see MacKenzie 2007 and Johnson 2007; I am in substantial agreement with what they say there.

[37] For an extreme right-wing version of thick libertarianism, see Hoppe 2014.

reason to oppose exploitation. For yet another, a libertarian society that was characterized by widespread exploitation would be unlikely to remain libertarian, as the exploiters would tend to make use of the power differential between themselves and the exploited to establish political power. Hence opposing exploitation is strategically important to the defense of a libertarian social order. (The first two reasons are ones of grounds thickness; the last is one of strategic thickness.)

One reason, it seems, that mainstream libertarians are reluctant to accept the existence of non-rights-violating forms of exploitation is the fear that recognizing them would entail endorsing state intervention as a remedy for them. But this is a non sequitur; acknowledging the existence of a problem does not entail endorsing any particular remedy for it.[38] And given that left-libertarians regard state intervention as, on the one hand, far more likely to cause further exploitation than to reduce it, and, on the other hand, wrong for many of the same reasons that exploitation is wrong, the left-libertarian case for recognizing non-rights-violating forms of exploitation can hardly be accused of providing a basis for statist solutions.

It's worth noting that libertarian thickness, in its left-libertarian form, does not merely offer libertarians reason to embrace left-wing concerns such as social justice,[39] but also offers left-wingers reason to embrace libertarian concerns. Grounds thickness, for example, runs in both directions; if the best reasons for embracing libertarian concerns have substantial overlap with the best reasons for embracing left-wing concerns, this is as much a reason for left-wingers to go libertarian as for libertarians to go left. And strategic thickness and consequence thickness are complementary; any strategic-thickness case for libertarians to go left will constitute a consequence-thickness reason for left-wingers to go libertarian, and likewise any consequence-thickness case for libertarians to go left will constitute a strategic-thickness reason for left-wingers to go libertarian.

---

[38] Moreover, such a response risks incoherence; if thick libertarianism is the thesis that there are values not directly entailed by libertarian principle that libertarians qua libertarians nevertheless have reason to accept, there is something self-undermining about claiming that libertarians qua libertarians have reason to reject thick libertarianism. Mainstream libertarian arguments against thick libertarianism frequently amount, paradoxically, to denying that there are additional values thickly bound up with libertarianism *and* in the same breath claiming that that very denial is *itself* an additional value thickly (usually via strategic thickness) bound up with libertarianism.

[39] Long 2019b; cf. Chartier 2012.

6. Labor Exploitation and Employer Responsibility, with Particular Reference to Sweatshops

According to left-libertarian social analysis, workers are exploited by the capitalist class as a whole, through the mechanism of the state. But what is the responsibility of *individual* employers in this context? With regard specifically to the issue of sweatshops, mainstream libertarians often argue in their defense that sweatshop employment is the best available option for many third-world workers. This is a good reply to those critics of sweatshops whose proposed solution is simply to ban them; it's hardly obvious that workers would benefit from such an intervention. (If I'm drowning and you are offering to rescue me in exchange for my life savings, at which point a humanitarian comes along, denounces your offer as exploitative, and so shoots you, while doing nothing to rescue me, I have little cause to be thankful.) But from the fact that banning sweatshops is a poor solution, it does not follow that sweatshop owners are doing nothing wrong.

In response to mainstream libertarian defenses of sweatshops as workers' best option, left-libertarians frequently raise the question of *how it comes to be* that sweatshop employment is the workers' best option—and typically argue that this is because preferable alternatives have been systematically closed off by state intervention. Hence sweatshop owners are beneficiaries of state privilege; the low wages they pay and the harsh working conditions they provide are possible only because predatory states are sheltering them from grassroots competition.

For many left-libertarians, this analysis makes sweatshop owners (and their analogues) count as exploiters. Brad Spangler, for example, writes that when "one robber (the literal apparatus of government) keeps you covered with a pistol while the second (representing State-allied corporations) just holds the bag that you have to drop your wristwatch, wallet and car keys in," then "both gunman and bagman together are the true State."[40]

Matt Zwolinski is skeptical of this sort of critique of sweatshops. While he acknowledges that it may be only against a background of "suppression of unions, seizure of land and natural resources, and protectionism, including the enforcement of so-called intellectual property rights"[41] that sweatshops are possible (and these are precisely the sorts of conditions to

---

[40] Spangler 2012.
[41] Zwolinski 2012, 169–170.

which left-libertarians would indeed point), Zwolinski argues that *so long as sweatshop owners are not themselves responsible for the background conditions of which they take advantage*, they cannot be fairly charged with (wrongful) exploitation.

I agree that merely benefiting from a situation arising from others' injustice is not in itself wrong; inasmuch as we are all overwhelmingly likely to be descendants of rape, we owe our very existence to injustice regardless of what we do. There is, in MacKenzie's (2007) formulation, a difference between "taking advantage (in conditions) of unfairness and taking unfair advantage." But I think this does less to get sweatshop owners off the moral hook than Zwolinski does; for, first of all, once one traces all the lobbying efforts that firms do to obtain favorable trade agreements and so on, I reckon sweatshop owners will often turn out to bear more responsibility for the background conditions than it might at first have appeared. Second, bearing responsibility for the background conditions of aggressive rights violations that make sweatshops possible is not necessary for sweatshops to be exploitative, because—recall the moral of the drowning case—*aggressive rights violations themselves are not a necessary condition for exploitation*. Subjecting one's employees to inhumane and degrading treatment (and here I have in mind the working conditions more than the low salaries) would be wrong (and, given thickness, wrong from a *libertarian* standpoint) even if the vulnerabilities that enable one to do so had come about without any violation of libertarian rights.

Zwolinski asks how it can be "permissible to *neglect* workers in the developing world, but impermissible to *exploit* them," given that workers benefit more from exploitation than from neglect.[42] I would answer as follows. Suppose you are a desperately poor person, and I approach you with an offer of money in exchange for your licking the mud off my boots (and you accept the deal). Even though my making this offer is more beneficial to you than the diddly-squat I would otherwise be doing for you, is it really at all surprising that my conduct might be judged more reprehensible than if I'd done nothing?

Similarly, Valdman offers a variation on the drowning case. "Suppose that Steve is drowning in rough, dangerous waters, and that Bob, a mediocre swimmer, is the only potential rescuer around." Given the significant risk that a rescue attempt would involve for Bob, Valdman reasons that

---

[42] Zwolinski 2012, 167.

"Bob would not be morally obligated to come to Steve's aid." Nevertheless, Valdman assumes we will agree (and I do agree) that if Bob did decide to take the risk, "it would still be wrong for Bob to turn Steve's plight to his advantage ... by offering to help but only for" an exorbitant price.[43] Here again, an exploitative rescue seems morally worse on Bob's part than a failure to rescue, even though the exploitative rescue is more beneficial to Steve than the failure to rescue would be. Thus it is no surprise that neglect can in some circumstances be morally preferable to exploitation even if the latter would be more beneficial.

One might think that what makes a price unreasonably high and thus exploitative is that it is *gratuitous*, since the exploiter would have been willing to accept a much lower price.[44] On such a view, what makes my action exploitative in the bootlicking case is that I would have been willing to offer the same price for a more conventional shoeshine. But if this analysis were correct, then it would seem that I'd be *justified*, and no longer an exploiter, in demanding the bootlicking if I would *not* in fact be satisfied with a more conventional shoeshine. Such an analysis seems to miss the fact that what is wrong with demanding the bootlicking is that it is degrading to the bootlicker, a fact that remains unchanged regardless of whether or not I would be satisfied with less. Indeed, if anything, I'm inclined to think that having a *more inelastic* demand for bootlicking would make me look *worse*, not better; one does not get off the hook by having *stronger* desires to degrade others.

For another argument against the claim that an exchange must be permissible and non-exploitative if it is mutually beneficial, consider the case of slavery contracts. While some libertarian thinkers[45] have endorsed such contracts as legitimate, the dominant view within the libertarian tradition has long been that the self is inalienable.[46] In particular, many libertarian thinkers (myself included) accept a title-transfer theory of contract,[47] according to which contractual obligations are grounded in conditional

---

[43] Valdman 2009, 4. Valdman actually says "only for a price that far exceeds what would reasonably compensate him for the risks involved," but as with Andrews above, I think this puts too much emphasis on the benefit to Bob and not enough on the cost to Steve. Again, what's wrong with exploitation is primarily what it does to the exploited person, not how much it benefits the exploiter.

[44] I owe this objection to Michael J. Green; it also seems to be implied by Andrews's account.

[45] Nozick 1974, 58; Block 2003. As in so many cases, academic philosophers who are familiar with no libertarian thinker other than Nozick have often mistakenly taken his views as representative of the movement as a whole.

[46] See, e.g., Spooner 1846, 60–61; Tucker 1887; Evers 1977; Rothbard 1998, chs. 7 and 19; Barnett 1986. Note that the inalienability of the self is, strictly speaking, a claim about what *cannot be done*, not a claim about what *should not be allowed*; for elaboration, see Long 2019a.

[47] See, again, Evers 1977; Rothbard 1998, chs. 7 and 19; Barnett 1986; Long 2019a.

transfers of alienable goods. Since personal services are not alienable, contracts for personal services may thus be enforced only by money damages or the like, not by specific performance; this rules out not only literal slavery contracts but also any contract requiring the compelled performance of any service.

I agree with the dominant position in holding that slavery contracts are illegitimate (in the sense of not being legitimately enforceable). But suppose they *were* legitimate. It seems plain that it would still be morally wrong, because disrespectful of personhood, to treat any moral agent as one's literal slave. Consider, then, the following example offered by Walter Block on behalf of such contracts:

> My child has now fallen ill with a dread disease. Fortunately, there is a cure. Unfortunately, it will cost one million dollars, and I, a poor man, do not have such funds at my disposal. Fortunately, you are willing to pay me this amount if I sign myself over to you as a slave, which I am very willing to do since my child's life is vastly more important to me than my own liberty, or even my own life.[48]

A consistent defender of the thesis that a voluntary exchange is permissible if it is mutually beneficial, it seems to me, ought to claim that in the case described, it is better to enslave Block than to neglect him. But while this may be a *modus ponens* for Block, I suspect it will be a *modus tollens* even for most defenders of the thesis—in which case they must abandon the thesis.

Still, even if we are convinced *that* conduct can be more reprehensible when it is also more beneficial, it remains to be explained *how* this can be so. It can be tempting to think that if A receives a net benefit from B's intervention, then B's intervening cannot involve harm to A. But this line of thought involves excessive aggregation. It's perfectly possible for an action that is beneficial on net to include a harm. So in the case of my offer to trade money for bootlicking, let X be the harm I prevent by giving you the money, and let Y be the harm I cause by making you lick my boots. If my offer is beneficial on net, then X must be greater than Y. But if X is greater than Y, does it follow that causing Y is more defensible than failing to prevent X?

It *would* follow, if one rejected the moral distinction between doing and allowing—say, between killing and letting die, or more generally between

[48] Block 2003, 40.

causing harm and failing to prevent it. But libertarians, of all people, cannot reject that distinction, since for libertarians those who cause rights violation may legitimately be met with force, whereas those who merely fail to prevent a rights violation may not. It is of course open to a libertarian to maintain that the distinction holds only for harms that involve rights violations, but this seems indefensibly ad hoc. And once one grants that, even in the case of harms that do not involve rights violations, it can be worse to cause a harm than to fail to prevent that harm, the conceptual space is opened for a more interesting possibility: that even when harm X is greater than harm Y (so that it would be in one's interest to submit to harm Y in exchange for the prevention of harm X), *causing* harm Y might nonetheless be morally worse than *failing to prevent* harm X. And that is why it seems plausible to regard my getting you to lick my boots as morally worse than my failing to relieve your desperate financial need, even if you benefit by the transaction. By the same token, then, it can be worse to run a sweatshop than not to run one, even if workers would benefit more from the sweatshop's presence than from its absence.

Mainstream libertarians often ask, "Well, what if sweatshop conditions are the best that a given employer can afford? Is the employer at moral fault for offering them, as opposed to offering nothing?" I would say, as a general rule, no; however, this question seems to envision "sweatshop conditions" as merely a matter of low wages, lack of modern facilities, and the like, and so misses much of the point of the critique of sweatshops. Even leaving aside those practices by sweatshop owners or supervisors that involve literal forcible aggression, or the threat thereof, against employees (whether direct, as in physical abuse and sexual assault, or indirect, as in calling upon the police or army to harass workers attempting to form unions, even off-site, or to begin legal deportation proceedings against those demanding to receive long-withheld paychecks), "sweatshop conditions" typically involve a range of humiliating, abusive, and dangerous forms of treatment such as sexual harassment, confiscation of passports, and the locking of fire doors, for which it's generally hard to imagine a justification as being the best that employers can afford.[49]

To be sure, with regard specifically to the locking of fire doors—a practice that led to mass death in, for example, the Tazreen Fashion factory fire in Dhaka, Bangladesh, in 2012,[50] in an incident reminiscent of the similar

---

[49] Congressional Subcommittee 2010.
[50] Burke and Hammadi 2012.

Triangle Shirtwaist factory fire in New York City a century earlier[51]—such a policy is evidently motivated by the desire to save money by cutting down on break time, making theft more difficult, and the like, and so might indeed be defended by an impecunious employer as the best she can afford. But even assuming that no more cost-effective way of cutting down on revenue loss owing to theft or unauthorized breaks is available (and this seems questionable; it would surely be more reasonable for the employer to make use of local knowledge and incentives by *asking the employees themselves* to try coming up with an alternative policy),[52] this justification strikes me as much more morally problematic than a mere justification of, say, low wages. Even if workers would benefit more from, and so would consent to, working in a factory with locked fire doors, by comparison with the absence of the factory, how are we to imagine the state of mind and character of the employer who orders, or the supervisor who carries out, the actual locking of the doors? They are, in effect, consenting to the mass death of their employees in the event of a fire, a moral attitude that is difficult to condone.

From all this, does it follow that third parties would be justified in forcibly shutting down such sweatshops? No, because this would be a violation of the rights of both the sweatshop owners and the sweatshop workers. (In cases where sweatshop owners do bear responsibility for the background of rights violations that gives them privileged access to desperate workers, forcibly shutting down the sweatshops would no longer be a violation of the rights of the sweatshop owners, but it would still be a violation of the rights of the sweatshop workers.) Instead, third parties can legitimately focus on forcibly shutting down the background rights violations, while in the meantime pressuring employers to improve conditions. Both strategies might well involve helping the sweatshop workers to empower themselves.[53] Mainstream libertarians tend to be hostile to labor unions, but here if anywhere they seem like the optimal solution. (Someone friendlier to state intervention might hold that a governmental regulatory or prohibitory solution is justified in those cases where sweatshop employers *would* be willing and able to offer the same number of jobs at better terms or wages, but not justified in cases where employers are either unwilling or unable.[54] But given the knowledge

---

[51] Von Drehle 2004.
[52] Perhaps, e.g., via a profit-sharing scheme that would give employees an incentive to police one another.
[53] For a left-libertarian approach to strategies for labor empowerment, see Carson 2010; cf. Prychitko 2019.
[54] I owe this suggestion to Michael J. Green.

problems that beset hierarchical institutions in general and monopoly states in particular, I'm skeptical as to the state's ability to draw the relevant line with anything approaching accuracy.)

I've focused on the case of sweatshops, but a similar analysis applies to the petty tyrannies of ordinary workplaces as well. Expressing enthusiasm for Elizabeth Anderson's (2017) discussion of the "power-ridden and authoritarian nature of many of today's firms," libertarian David Prytchitko asks why we should settle for a vision of libertarianism that "grants people the freedom to spend money as they see fit—but retains, in principle, hierarchy . . . and regimentation throughout the working day."[55] If left-libertarian economic analysis is correct, the imbalances of power that sustain such conditions are primarily the product of governmental intervention. But even if they were not, or for any instances that are not, systematically pushing people around in these ways is to be condemned as objectionably exploitative for reasons that substantially overlap with the reasons that violations of libertarian rights are to be condemned.

In conclusion, then, libertarianism's critics are right: existing labor markets are systematically exploitative, and not all cases of exploitation need involve violations of libertarian rights. But libertarianism's critics are also wrong: state intervention, far from being a cure for labor exploitation, is the chief (albeit not sole) enabler of such exploitation, so most labor exploitation would wither away without the state's assistance, and what did not wither away would be small enough to be combated by left-libertarian grassroots social activism.[56] Left-libertarian analysis thus opens a space for a position on labor exploitation that is both libertarian and leftist: libertarian without economic elitism, and leftist without political elitism.

References

Anderson, E. 2017. *Private Government: How Employers Rule Our Lives (and Why We Don't Talk About It)*. Princeton, NJ: Princeton University Press.
Anderson, T. L., and P. J. Hill. 2004. *The Not So Wild, Wild West: Property Rights on the Frontier*. Stanford, CA: Stanford University Press.

---

[55] Prychitko 2019, 180–181.
[56] For discussion of left-libertarian grassroots social activism, see Richman 2011; Johnson 2011, 2013; Long and Johnson 2005; and, again, Carson 2010.

Andrews, S. P. 1970. *The Science of Society*. Weston, MA: M & S Press.
Barnett, R. E. 1986. "Contract Remedies and Inalienable Rights." *Social Philosophy and Policy* 4, no. 1: 179–202.
Barnett, R. E. 2014. *The Structure of Liberty: Justice and the Rule of Law*, 2nd edition. Oxford: Oxford University Press.
Bell, T. W. 1992. "Polycentric Law." *Humane Studies Review* 7, no. 1: 1–92. https://www.the ihs.org/w91issues/.
Benson, B. L. 2011. *The Enterprise of Law: Justice Without the State*. Oakland, CA: Independent Institute.
Blanqui, A.-J. 1860. *Histoire de l'économie politique en Europe*. Paris: Gauillaumin.
Block, W. 2003. "Toward a Libertarian Theory of Inalienability: A Critique of Rothbard, Barnett, Smith, Kinsella, Gordon, and Epstein." *Journal of Libertarian Studies* 17, no. 2: 39–85. https://cdn.mises.org/17_2_3.pdf.
Burke, J., and S. Hammadi. 2012. "Bangladesh Textile Factory Fire Leaves More than 100 Dead." *The Guardian*, November 25, 2012. www.theguardian.com/world/2012/nov/25/bangladesh-textile-factory-fire.
Carson, K. A. 2007. *Studies in Mutualist Political Economy*. Charleston, SC: BookSurge. www.mutualist.org/sitebuildercontent/sitebuilderfiles/MPE.pdf.
Carson, K. A. 2008. *Organization Theory: A Libertarian Perspective*. Charleston, SC: BookSurge. www.mutualist.org/sitebuildercontent/sitebuilderfiles/otkc11.pdf.
Carson, K. A. 2010. "Labor Struggle: A Free Market Model." Center for a Stateless Society, Research Paper No. 10. https://c4ss.org/wp-content/uploads/2010/09/C4SS-Labor.pdf.
Casey, G. 2012. *Libertarian Anarchy: Against the State*. London: Bloomsbury.
Chartier, G. 2011. *The Conscience of an Anarchist: Why It's Time to Say Good-bye to the State and Build a Free Society*. Apple Valley, CA: Cobden Press.
Chartier, G. 2012. "The Distinctiveness of Left-Libertarianism." Bleeding Heart Libertarians, November 5, 2012. bleedingheartlibertarians.com/2012/11/the-distinctiveness-of-left-libertarianism/
Chartier, G. 2013. *Anarchy and Legal Order: Law and Politics for a Stateless Society*. Cambridge, UK: Cambridge University Press.
Chartier, G., and C. W. Johnson, eds. 2011. *Markets Not Capitalism: Individualist Anarchism Against Bosses, Inequality, Corporate Power, and Structural Poverty*. London: Minor Compositions.
Childs, R. A., Jr. 1971. "How Bad Is the U.S. Government?" *The Abolitionist*, May, 2–3. www.unz.org/Pub/Abolitionist-1971may-00002.
Cicero. *De Officiis*. Translated by W. Miller. London: Heinemann.
Congressional Subcommittee on Interstate Commerce, Trade, and Tourism. 2010. *Overseas Sweatshop Abuses, Their Impact on U.S. Workers, and the Need for Anti-Sweatshop Legislation*. Washington, DC: U.S. Government Printing Office. www.govinfo.gov/content/pkg/CHRG-110shrg35685/html/CHRG-110shrg35685.htm.
De Cleyre, V. 1914. *Selected Works*. Edited by A. Berkman. New York: Mother Earth.
Evers, W. 1977. "Toward a Reformulation of the Law of Contracts." *Journal of Libertarian Studies* 1, no. 1: 3–13. https://cdn.mises.org/1_1_2_0.pdf.
Friedman, D. D. 1989. *The Machinery of Freedom: Guide to a Radical Capitalism*, 2nd edition. La Salle, IL: Open Court.
Hart, D. 1994. "Class Analysis, Slavery and the Industrialist Theory of History in French Liberal Thought, 1814–1830: The Radical Liberalism of Charles Comte and Charles

Dunoyer." Ph.D. diss., King's Colege, University of Cambridge. http://davidmhart.com/liberty/Papers/ComteDunoyer/CCCD-PhD/CCCD-Book-2010.pdf.

Heywood, E. H. 1985. *Collected Works*. Edited by Martin Blatt. Weston, MA: M & S Press.

Hodgskin, T. 1825. *Labour Defended Against the Claims of Capital, or, The Unproductiveness of Capital Proved with Reference to the Present Combinations of Journeymen*. London: Knight and Lacey.

Hodgskin, T. 1832. *The Natural and Artificial Right of Property Contrasted*. London: B. Steil.

Hoppe, H.-H. 2014. "A Realistic Libertarianism." LewRockwell.com, September 30, 2014. www.lewrockwell.com/2014/09/hans-hermann-hoppe/smack-down.

Huemer, M. 2012. *The Problem of Political Authority: An Examination of the Right to Coerce and the Duty to Obey*. Basingstoke, UK: Palgrave Macmillan.

Johnson, C. W. 2007. "Remarks on Matt MacKenzie's 'Exploitation: A Dialectical Anarchist Perspective.'" *Rad Geek People's Daily* (blog), January 12, 2007. radgeek.com/gt/2007/01/12/remarks_on.

Johnson, C. W. 2008. "Libertarianism Through Thick and Thin." *Rad Geek People's Daily (blog)*, October 3, 2008. radgeek.com/gt/2008/10/03/libertarianism_through/.

Johnson, C. W. 2009. "Can Anybody Ever Consent to the State?" *Rad Geek People's Daily (blog)*, January 8, 2009. radgeek.com/gt/2009/01/08/can_anybody.

Johnson, C. W. 2010. "Liberty, Equality, Solidarity: Toward a Dialectical Anarchism." *Rad Geek People's Daily* (blog), March 2, 2010, radgeek.com/gt/2010/03/02/liberty-equality-solidarity-toward-a-dialectical-anarchism.

Johnson, C. W. 2011. "We Are Market Forces." In *Markets Not Capitalism: Individualist Anarchism Against Bosses, Inequality, Corporate Power, and Structural Poverty*, edited by G. Chartier and C. W. Johnson, 391–394. London: Minor Compositions.

Johnson, C. W. 2013. "Women and the Invisible Fist: How Violence Against Women Enforces the Unwritten Law of Patriarchy." charleswjohnson.name/essays/women-and-the-invisible-fist/women-and-the-invisible-fist-2013-0503-max.pdf.

Konkin, S. E., III. 2012. "SEK3's History of the Libertarian Movement." Center for a Stateless Society, December 7, 2012. c4ss.org/content/13240.

Leeson, P. T. 2014. *Anarchy Unbound: Why Self-Governance Works Better than You Think*. Cambridge, UK: Cambridge University Press.

Long, R. T. 1999. "The Irrelevance of Responsibility." *Social Philosophy and Policy* 16, no. 2: 118–145. praxeology.net/RTL-irrelevance.pdf.

Long, R. T. 2000. *Reason and Value: Aristotle Versus Rand*. Poughkeepsie, NY: Objectivist Center. atlassociety.org/sites/default/files/Reason_Value.pdf.

Long, R. T. 2003. Review of *Ethics as Social Science: The Moral Philosophy of Social Cooperation* by Leland B. Yeager. *Quarterly Journal of Austrian Economics* 6, no. 1: 89–98. mises.org/library/review-ethics-social-science-moral-philosophy-social-cooperation-leland-b-yeager.

Long, R. T. 2008a. "Montaigne on Profit and Loss." *Austro-Athenian Empire (blog)*, May 5, 2008. web.archive.org/web/20210418053518/https://aaeblog.com/2008/05/05/montaigne-on-profit-and-loss/.

Long, R. T. 2008b. "Corporations Versus the Market; or, Whip Conflation Now." Cato Unbound, November 10, 2008. www.cato-unbound.org/2008/11/10/roderick-t-long/corporations-versus-market-or-whip-conflation-now.

Long, R. T. 2011. "Comment on Ruth Sample's 'Is the State Exploitative?' and Matt Zwolinski's 'Toward a Theory of State Exploitation.'" Remarks at the Pacific Division of the American Philosophical Society, April 20, 2011. praxeology.net/pacific-apa-state-exploitation.pdf.

Long, R. T. 2012a. "Left-Libertarianism, Market Anarchism, Class Conflict and Historical Theories of Distributive Justice." *Griffith Law Review* 21, no. 2: 413–431.

Long, R. T. 2012b. "Eudaimonist Libertarianism." *Bleeding Heart Libertarians (blog)*, February 4, 2012. https://bleedingheartlibertarians.com/2012/02/eudaimonist-libertarianism.

Long, R. T. 2013. "Eudaimonism and Non-Aggression." *Bleeding Heart Libertarians (blog)*, April 30, 2013. https://bleedingheartlibertarians.com/2013/04/eudaimonism-and-non-aggression.

Long, R. T. 2014. "Why Libertarians Believe There Is Only One Right." Center for a Stateless Society. c4ss.org/content/25648.

Long, R. T. 2019a. "Getting Self-Ownership in View." Working paper. praxeology.net/RTL-self-ownership-PPE2019.pdf.

Long, R. T. 2019b. "Why Libertarians Should Be Social Justice Warriors." In *The Dialectics of Liberty: Exploring the Context of Human Freedom*, edited by R. E. Bissell C. M. Sciabarra, and E. W. Younkins, 235–253. Lanham, MD: Lexington Books.

Long, R. T. 2020. "Virtue's Unity and the Liberal Quest for Principled Moderation." Working paper. http://praxeology.net/PPE2020-unity-virtue-full.pdf.

Long, R. T., and C. W. Johnson. 2005. "Libertarian Feminism: Can This Marriage Be Saved?" charleswjohnson.name/essays/libertarian-feminism/.

Long, R. T., and T. R. Machan, eds. 2008. *Anarchism/Minarchism: Is a Government Part of a Free Country?* Aldershot, UK: Ashgate.

Lum, D. D. 1887. "On Anarchy." In Albert R. Parsons, *Anarchism: Its Philosophy and Scientific Basis*, ch. 6. Milwaukee, WI: A. R. Parsons.

Lum, D. D. 1890. *The Economics of Anarchy: A Study of the Industrial Type*. New York: Twentieth Century.

MacKenzie, M. D. 2007. "Exploitation: A Dialectical Anarchist Perspective." *Upaya: Skillful Means to Liberation (blog)*, March 20, 2007. praxeology.net/Exploitation-DRAFT.pdf.

Massimino, C., and J. Tuttle, eds. 2016. *Free Markets and Capitalism? Do Free Markets Always Produce a Corporate Economy?* Auburn, AL: Center for a Stateless Society.

Mill, J. 1835. "State of the Nation." *London Review* 1, no. 1: 1–24. oll.libertyfund.org/titles/2520#Mill_1624_2954.

Nozick, R. 1974. *Anarchy, State, and Utopia*. New York: Basic Books.

Prychitko, D. L. 2019. "Context Matters: Finding a Home for Labor-Managed Enterprise." In *The Dialectics of Liberty: Exploring the Context of Human Freedom*, edited by R. E. Bissell, C. M. Sciabarra, and E. W. Younkins, 175–183. Lanham, MD: Lexington Books.

Rachels, C. C. 2016. "The Sophistry of Left-'Libertarianism.'" Facebook, February 29, 2016. www.facebook.com/christopher.rachels/posts/10205445720933382.

Richman, S. 2011. "Context-Keeping and Community Organizing." In *Markets Not Capitalism: Individualist Anarchism Against Bosses, Inequality, Corporate Power, and Structural Poverty*, edited by G. Chartier and C. W. Johnson, 421–424. London: Minor Compositions.

Roach, M. 2014. "Indigent Defense Counsel, Attorney Quality, and Defendant Outcomes." *American Law and Economics Review* 16, no. 2: 577–619.

Rothbard, M. N. 1998. *The Ethics of Liberty*. New York: New York University Press. cdn.mises.org/The%20Ethics%20of%20Liberty%2020191108.pdf.

Sartwell, C. 2008. *Against the State: An Introduction to Anarchist Political Theory*. Albany, NY: SUNY Press.

Smith, A. 1774. *The Theory of Moral Sentiments; Or, An Essay Towards an Analysis of the Principles by Which Men Naturally Judge Concerning the Conduct and Character, First of Their Neighbors, and Afterwards of Themselves*, 4th edition. London: W. Strahan.

Spangler, B. 2012. "Recognizing Faux Private Interests that Are Actually Part of the State." *Spangler Pensieve* (blog), December 15, 2012. spanglerpensieve.wordpress.com/2012/12/15/recognizing-faux-private-interests-that-are-actually-part-of-the-state.

Spooner, L. 1846. *Poverty: Its Illegal Causes and Legal Cure, Part First*. Boston: Bela Marsh.

Steiner, H. 1984. "A Liberal Theory of Exploitation." *Ethics* 94, no. 2: 225–241.

Stringham, E. P. 2005. *Anarchy, State and Public Choice*. Cheltenham, UK: Edward Elgar.

Stringham, E. P. 2007. *Anarchy and the Law: The Political Economy of Choice*. New Brunswick, NJ: Transaction.

Stringham, E. P. 2015. *Private Governance: Creating Order in Economic and Social Life*. Oxford: Oxford University Press.

Tandy, F. D. 1893. *Voluntary Socialism: A Sketch*. Denver: Tandy.

Tucker, A., and G. P. de Bellis, eds. 2016. *Panarchy: Political Theories of Non-Territorial States*. New York: Routledge.

Tucker, B. R. 1887. "A Puppet for a God." *Liberty* 4, no. 19 (April 9): 4–5.

Tucker, B. R. 1888. "State Socialism and Anarchism: How Far They Agree, and Wherein They Differ." *Liberty* 5, no. 16 (March 10): 2–3, 6.

Tucker, B. R. 1893. *Instead of a Book, by a Man Too Busy to Write One: A Fragmentary Exposition of Philosophical Anarchism*. New York: B. R. Tucker.

Valdman, M. 2009. "A Theory of Wrongful Exploitation." *Philosophers' Imprint* 9, no. 6: 1–14.

Von Drehle, D. 2004. *Triangle: The Fire That Changed America*. New York: Grove Press.

Warren, J. 1852. *Equitable Commerce: A New Development of Principles, as Substitutes for Laws and Governments, for the Harmonious Adjustment and Regulation of the Pecuniary, Intellectual, and Moral Intercourse of Mankind, Proposed as Elements of New Society*. New York: Fowlers and Wells.

Wood, A. 1995. "Exploitation." *Social Philosophy and Policy* 12, no. 2: 136–158.

Zwolinski, M. 2012. "Structural Exploitation." *Social Philosophy and Policy* 29, no. 1: 154–179.

12
Decommodification as Exploitation

Vida Panitch

1. Introduction

Anti-commodification theorists argue that to preserve the inherent or socially dominant values of many important goods, they must be exchanged in accordance with the altruistic norms proper to personal or civic relationships, and never in accordance with the supposedly self-interested norms of the marketplace. These theorists argue that "putting a price on the good things in life can corrupt them ... because markets ... express and promote certain attitudes toward the good being exchanged."[1] Markets are said to degrade the value of important goods along with the social relations that depend on their altruistic exchange, because the "worth of goods depends on the motives that people have in providing them."[2] The norm of self-interest that is thought to dominate market transactions, it is argued, supplants the reciprocity and beneficence necessary to the proper enjoyment of the goods and to relationships essential to human flourishing.[3] The anti-commodification argument is often applied to bodily goods and indeed has roots in Titmuss's study of paid blood donation, from which he concluded that introducing payment into a sphere as intimate as the body "represses the expression of altruism and erodes the sense of community."[4]

Many anti-commodification theorists appeal to the concept of exploitation to strengthen their case against payment for body parts and intimate services. On their view, commodifying the body is wrongful because it exploits the vulnerable. They appeal to two different, and at times competing, accounts of exploitation to make this case: exploitation as *wrongful advantage-taking*, and exploitation as *wrongful use*. On both accounts, a vulnerable

---
[1] Sandel 2012, 9.
[2] Anderson 1990, 186.
[3] Anderson 1990b. See also Radin 1996.
[4] Titmuss 1997, 314.

party is deprived of something she is rightly due. According to exploitation as wrongful advantage-taking, what a vulnerable party is due is a fair share of a cooperative surplus to which she has contributed.[5] According to exploitation as wrongful use, what a vulnerable party is due is the respect owed to all bearers of humanity.[6] Anti-commodification theorists who appeal to the former account of exploitation endeavor to show that payment for bodily goods and intimate services is unfair, while those who appeal to the latter account endeavor to show that payment for such items is degrading.

Making an exploitation claim inevitably adds something of rhetorical force to an anti-commodification argument, but it is not altogether clear that it adds anything of normative value, and indeed I will try to show that it does not. What I will argue is that rather than payment for bodily goods and intimate services being either unfair or disrespectful, it is the lack of payment that meets both of these criteria. Anti-commodification theorists who seek to condemn financial transactions involving the body by appealing to claims about the exploitation of providers have got things the wrong way around and their arguments do more to legitimate exploitative transactions than to curtail them. Exploitation occurs in the realm of body sales not when providers are paid, I will show, but when payment is withheld from them by those who profit from bodily commodification while simultaneously claiming that the body should never be commodified. The failure to remunerate suppliers of bodily goods and intimate services is both unfair and disrespectful and warrants the making of an exploitation claim understood as either, or both, wrongful advantage-taking and wrongful use.

I will begin in section 1 with the account of exploitation as wrongful advantage-taking and argue that too much attention has been devoted by anti-commodification theorists who appeal to this account to a worry about coercion, and too little to the issue of fairness. When adequate attention is devoted to the criterion of fairness central to this account, it becomes evident that instead of payment for bodily goods and intimate services constituting an unfair distribution of the cooperative surplus of an exchange, it is a rather a lack of payment to providers that is exploitatively unfair. In section 2, I will turn to the account of exploitation as wrongful use. I will reject the connection between personhood and body parts on which this account relies and

---

[5] Wertheimer 1996.
[6] Sample 2003.

argue that where a refusal to pay suppliers of bodily goods and intimate services is grounded in the social expectation of gendered altruism, it is a lack of payment that threatens both respect for persons and the social bases of women's self-respect.

By this point I will have shown that a failure to pay providers of body parts and intimate services is both unfair and disrespectful. This alone will suffice to generate a claim that withholding payment from providers is exploitative both in terms of wrongful advantage-taking and in terms of wrongful use. And I will have thereby already arrived at my conclusion that it is not the commodification of the body that is regularly exploitative but its decommodification. What I will do in section 3 is go on to argue that a form of deception occurs in many exploitative bodily transactions that typically accompanies, if not contributes to, the relevant unfairness and disrespect. Such deception occurs when one party initiates a market transaction for the purposes of profit, while misinforming the other party that it is wrong to commodify the body, and on this fraudulent basis withholds payment.

Arguably, deception undermines the consent of the vulnerable party. But I will not make that case here. Nor will I argue that an impairment of consent is a necessary component of an exploitative transaction, as mutually advantageous exchanges can be voluntary and still exploitative. What I will argue in section 3 is that deception is an unambiguously worse-making feature of already exploitative transactions, and that a particular type of deception frequently occurs in unpaid bodily exchanges. The denial of payments to providers of bodily goods and intimate services is exploitative; for this exploitation to be justified by appeal to the false claim that the body shouldn't be commodified while profits, wages, and other financial benefits accrue to the very parties who make such a claim, renders it that much more dissolute.

2. Exploitation as Wrongful Advantage-Taking

Exploitation as wrongful advantage-taking is a rich and complex view. Most contemporary exploitation theorists regard themselves as offering a view of this kind. While myriad debates persist among them, there is consensus that exploitation consists in a violation of fairness in either the transactional process or the transactional outcome of an exchange (or both). Broadly speaking, the central idea is that fairness can be impaired procedurally by coercive measures and/or consequentially by an unjust distribution of the cooperatively produced surplus of a transaction.[7] How best to understand the nature of the relevant coercion, and how much injustice should be tolerated before an interaction ought to be interfered with, has been the source of much debate among exploitation theorists. I will touch briefly on this later, but for the most part I will avoid getting into these debates, as my intent is rather to demonstrate how exploitation as wrongful advantage-taking has been appealed to in the service of anti-commodification arguments, and unsuccessfully so.

Much of the opposition to payments for body parts or intimate services comes from those who worry that payment is coercive. The argument goes like this: "The fewer alternatives a person has to obtain the financial means . . . the higher the coercive influence or pressure exerted through the offer of payment . . . [O]ffering someone in extreme material need and without alternative opportunities for income, money for [body parts] instead of other, more meaningful options . . . [is] an unacceptable way of compromising this person's autonomy."[8] The trouble with payment in the realm of the body is, on this line of thought, that an agent's desperate need for money is being taken unfair advantage of by those who offer it. The fact of their need obscures their ability to rationally consider whether the offer is in their best interest, to such a degree that it renders their acceptance of the offer invalid, supposedly generating a claim of exploitation as wrongful advantage-taking. Or so the argument goes.[9]

But this argument is problematic for two main reasons. First, it is empirically unsound. The argument that offering payment for bodily goods and services is coercive across the board is simply false. Not everyone who sells eggs, sperm, plasma, or gestational services is in a position where they cannot decline to do so for material reasons. As the argument above shows, the offer must be made to someone who is in dire material need and who is without alternative options for us to even consider the claim that it might be coercive. But many egg donors and surrogates, for example, have plenty of alternative options. The average American egg donor or surrogate has a college education and a host of professional opportunities available to her.[10] The same certainly cannot be said of the global egg provider or surrogate.[11] But what

---

[7] Wertheimer 1996.
[8] Buyx 2009, 330.
[9] As applied to organs, see Rippon 2014; Greasley 2014; Hughes 1998, 2009. As applied to surrogacy, see Kirby 2014; Baylis 2014. As applied to sex work, see Overall 1992; Shrage 1989.
[10] Busby and Vun 2010; Krawiec 2010; Steiner 2013; Epstein and Whitehouse 2020.
[11] Twine 2011.

this suggests is that a claim of coercion in all instances of payment cannot be sustained. Exploitation as wrongful advantage-taking asks us to examine coercion and distributional fairness in discrete transactions. This creates a problem for anti-commodification theorists trying to use this account to ground indiscriminate bans on (or even to generate wholesale moral condemnation of) payment for bodily goods. It is obviously true that in some cases the provider of a body part or intimate service has no other alternatives and accepts a paid offer because of this. But it is not true in all cases, so this argument cannot condemn the practice of paying for bodily goods.

Second, the argument that offering money for bodily goods is coercive is normatively unconvincing. Offering someone money for their plasma, sperm, eggs, gestational capacities, or kidney is not like putting a gun to their head. The gunpoint ultimatum "your money or your life" works by removing the victim's other options until his best course of action is the one the gunman prefers. This is coercive because the gunman restricts the victim's options until his own preference becomes the victim's most attractive one. By contrast, offering payment adds to a person's range of options, and the offer succeeds only if it is preferred by the recipient to the other options he had before. A coercive offer restricts your options; by contrast, an incentivizing offer adds to them. It is thus coercive to offer a desperate person money if you rendered them desperate in the first place with the intent of pressing them for advantage.[12] It is equally coercive to make the fulfillment of a duty you have to them contingent on their compliance with terms that serve your interests.[13] Threatening to make someone worse off if they refuse to accept your offer is coercive. Refusing to rescue someone to whom you owe a duty of rescue unless they pay you is coercive. Making someone an offer they find more attractive than their alternatives is not.

If a claim of coercion isn't empirically or normatively sustainable, we should look more closely at what might be operating in the background of such claims. The worry might be that, while the vulnerable party may be able to refuse an offer, they may not be able to negotiate its terms, lest the offer be made to someone else eager to take their place. If the poor can't bargain, enlisting them in certain financial enterprises could certainly expose them to unfair advantage-taking.[14] The worry might also be that we all have an

---

[12] Wertheimer 1996, 247–277.
[13] Ferguson, 2020.
[14] Panitch 2013.

obligation to meet the needs of the vulnerable that is actualized or heightened when we transact with them.[15] Or the worry might be that the introduction of payment for bodily goods or services would change the option set of the desperate in a problematic way, because while some individuals might opt to partake in bodily sales, others may prefer that such transactions not be permissible at all lest they find themselves unable to secure other sources of financial support once this one becomes available.[16] These are all legitimate worries. But these are worries about *justice*, not coercion.

Coercion carries such a great deal of rhetorical force that the case for exploitation is often rested there. But if the real worry is that the person who offers payment gets away with something she shouldn't because the recipient of the offer is desperate, then I propose that what we are dealing with is the simple egalitarian dictum that "no citizen shall ever be wealthy enough to buy another, and none poor enough to be forced to sell himself."[17] The rich shouldn't be able to get whatever they want from the poor just by dangling money in front of them. Obviously, there are many ways of addressing this problem via redistributive channels, and thus without banning payment to providers of body parts and intimate services. This suggests that what often passes for a coercion worry is more likely a distributive justice worry. Which, in turn, suggests that we need to investigate more closely the transactional-outcome (or distributive-unfairness) component of an exploitation-as-wrongful-advantage-taking claim.

There are myriad ways to unpack the unfair-outcome criterion of exploitation as wrongful advantage-taking. But it is straightforward to participants in this debate that if A benefits from the transaction while B is made worse off by it relative to where she began, A has taken unfair advantage of B.[18] In an exploitative exchange, A is made better off as a result of her interaction with B, walking away with the cooperative surplus produced through their interaction, while B is made worse off as a result of her interaction with A, having expended more (time, energy, labor) to produce the surplus than she received back. But there are many cases of mutually advantageous exploitation in which B also benefits from the exchange, albeit less so than A. These are tricky cases for exploitation theorists, who must determine how much mutual benefit is enough to render an exchange not wrongful while still

---

[15] Snyder 2013.
[16] Rippon 2014.
[17] Rousseau ([1762] 2018), book II, ch. XI.
[18] Wertheimer 1996, 18–32.

unfair.[19] Luckily, this need not be settled here. There is agreement among those who understand exploitation as wrongful advantage-taking that if A benefits from an exchange and B does not, there is no mutual advantage, and if A benefits while B loses, B has been the victim of wrongfully unfair advantage-taking by A.

It should indeed offend our egalitarian intuitions that the rich can get what they want from the poor just by dangling money in front of them, including their body parts and intimate services, and perhaps these things above all else.[20] But when we look closely at the distributive-unfairness criterion of exploitation as wrongful advantage-taking, it appears decidedly worse that the rich should get whatever they want from the poor *while the poor get nothing in return*. Payment at least produces mutual advantage. An exchange in which the recipient of a bodily good or service gets what she wants without having to compensate the provider is one in which the recipient gains while the provider loses and is therefore one in which the provider has been the victim of wrongfully unfair advantage-taking. Consider the absurdity of refusing to pay your handyman to clean your eaves because you know he only took the job for the money. The fact of his need should be even more reason to pay him, and to pay him well, rather than to withhold payment because it offends our egalitarian sensibilities that handymen must sell their physical labor to homeowners to survive. Refusing to pay him would not be to mitigate this inequality but to take wrongfully unfair advantage of it.

Two objections may be raised at this point. The first is that one way to solve the problem of the rich getting whatever they want by dangling money in front of the poor is to deny them the option of paying for bodily goods. No exchange, no exploitation. But if one party to a transaction enjoys gains while the other party walks away having lost something without gaining anything in return, the outcome is wrongfully unfair regardless of the respective pre-transaction baselines from which each of the parties began. One party to an exchange gaining a kidney and the other party losing a kidney and gaining nothing is unfair regardless of how well-off each was to begin with. Moreover, removing the option from a person in desperate circumstances to better his circumstances by selling his kidney would seem to leave him in a worse position than one in which he is paid for his kidney, or even underpaid for it. We

---

[19] Wertheimer 1996, 207–246; Zwolinski 2007; Ferguson 2016.
[20] Panitch 2019.

may commit a greater injustice against the poor by removing the option of receiving payment for bodily goods than by allowing it.[21]

But this brings us to the second possible objection, which is that my argument may seem to imply that all persons who choose to engage in non-commercial sex or non-compensated pregnancy are being taken unfair advantage of. Some certainly are, but this is not a point I will press here. I am strongly tempted by the view according to which exploitation is a concept best reserved for the sphere of the marketplace.[22] But this is also not a point I intend to defend here. Suffice it to say that intimate sexual relations and family building through pregnancy are perhaps best thought of as acts undertaken by parties who want the same things and who anticipate the same gains. Nothing is lost exclusively by one party or gained exclusively by the other. Both parties (ideally) gain back from the other in proportion to what they give, and both gain what they hoped to achieve.

What I have tried to show in this section is that when we probe the coercion claim offered by anti-commodification theorists who seek to condemn payment for body parts and intimate services as exploitative, it reveals itself to be empirically and normatively problematic. I suggested that the coercion concern is at base a distributive-justice concern, and that with respect to distributive justice, a party who receives nothing from a transaction to which she has contributed is taken unfair advantage of. A failure to pay providers of body parts and intimate services thus satisfies the unfair-outcome criterion of exploitation as wrongful advantage-taking. It is a failure to pay providers that is exploitative, not the reverse, as anti-commodification theorists would have it. I will now turn to the account of exploitation as wrongful use to examine the argument according to which the commodification of the body is exploitative not for reasons of unfairness but for reasons of disrespect.

3. Exploitation as Wrongful Use

On this account, there is no price at which it would be permissible to pay someone for their body parts or intimate services, because the very assignment of a price value to these goods violates the respect individuals are owed as persons. This view tracks the Kantian contrast between dignity and

---

[21] Radcliffe-Richards 1996.
[22] Hussain 2017.

price: "What has a price is such that something else can be put in its place as its equivalent; by contrast, that which is elevated above all price, and admits of no equivalent, has a dignity."[23] Here, the wrong of exploitation consists in interacting with another human being in a way that fails to demonstrate appropriate respect for that being's inherent value.[24] Accordingly, although exploiters may cause injustice, the harm they commit lies rather in the disrespect they show another by denying the inherent value the other possesses as a member of humanity.[25]

For anti-commodification theorists moved by this account, the exploitation of providers of bodily goods and intimate services can't be avoided by fair payment, because exploitation arises from the indignity of a price being attached to the body in the first place.[26] Exploitation occurs not when A denies B a fair share of their cooperative surplus, but rather when A denies B the respect B is owed as a bearer of humanity and thus the dignity she needs to flourish. And A denies B this kind of respect when she puts a price on B's body parts or intimate capacities.[27] The idea that fair payment could render such a transaction non-exploitative "perpetuates the myth that parts of the self can be sold without this impacting the self in general."[28] The exchange of bodily goods and capacities is only consistent with dignity and flourishing, it is argued, when this is undertaken from altruism or reciprocity, because we fail to properly value agents when we regard them instead as suppliers of spare parts and their bodies as mere instruments of use.[29]

On Ruth Sample's account of exploitation as wrongful use, which she calls exploitation as degradation, exploitation involves interacting with another human being in a way that fails to respect the inherent value in that being. Human beings possess a value that exerts a claim on us, and in exploiting them we fail to honor this value for the purposes of advantaging ourselves at their expense. For Sample, we can

> first, fail to respect a person by neglecting what is necessary for that person's well-being or flourishing. Second, we can fail to respect a person by taking advantage of injustice done to him. Third, we can fail to respect a person by

[23] Kant 1996, 84–85.
[24] Sample 2003, 57.
[25] Wood 1995; Snyder 2008; Vrousalis 2013; Gilabert 2019.
[26] Sample 2003, 61.
[27] Sample 2003; Anderson 1990b; Phillips 2011; Radin 1987; Marway, Johnson, and Widdows 2014.
[28] Marway, Johnson, and Widdows 2014, 592; Rippon 2017.
[29] Anderson 1990b, 182.

commodifying or treating as a fungible object of market exchanges, an aspect of that person's being that ought not be commodified.[30]

We fail to demonstrate respect by commodifying a person's body parts or intimate capacities because no one could in principle consent to having such essential aspects of their personhood treated as objects of mere use value.[31]

For Anne Phillips, the commodification of the body is disrespectful in that it leads us to view other agents as beings of lesser moral value. We all have bodies, Phillips argues, and none of us would choose to sell them except under conditions of dire need. This means that body markets can be explained or justified not by appeal to individual preference but only by appeal to social and material inequality.[32] And it means that when we make financial offers to persons for their body parts or intimate services—offers we would never deign to accept ourselves—we regard those who do accept them as beings with less moral worth than we take ourselves to possess. For Phillips, "exploitation is . . . about inequality, and not just inequality . . . in outcomes, but *the inequality that is at stake when one party to an arrangement treats the other as a being of lesser significance* . . . It is not the level of payment that makes it exploitation . . . but what it asserts about our status as [moral] equals."[33] It asserts that people who sell body parts and intimate services are beings of lesser moral worth, and thus deserving of lesser social status.

These views are compelling, but they fail to establish that payment for bodily goods and intimate services indeed constitutes exploitation as wrongful use. This is because the conflation of body parts with selfhood is tenuous at best, the conflation of altruism with respect is tenuous at best, and a genuine worry about respect seems to point toward payment, not away from it. First, the idea that the body should be exempt from sale because it is too intimately tied to personhood runs counter to the philosophical account of personhood on which it rests. We are beings possessed of dignity and deserving of respect, on the Kantian account, in virtue of our rational autonomy, not our organs, gametes, plasma, or intimate capacities. If our body parts and intimate capacities were truly essential to our personhood, we should not be able to alienate ourselves from them for money or for free.

---

[30] Sample 2003, 57. It should be noted that although here these sound like independently sufficient conditions for exploitation, elsewhere Sample suggests they are mutually sufficient (83).
[31] Sample 2003, 69.
[32] Phillips 2011, 744.
[33] Phillips 2017, 110.

And for an account that prioritizes cognitive capacities over physical ones, it is surely more dignity-preserving to respect the rights of individuals to do as they please with their bodies than to limit their choices in this realm.

Second, it is problematic to conceive of payment for body parts and intimate capacities as disrespectful to the extent that it impedes flourishing. Elizabeth Anderson argues that the body must be exchanged altruistically lest we disrespect those whom we deprive of a flourishing life. If sex is exchanged for money, the value of sexual intimacy is supposedly undermined not only for parties to the exchange but also for all those for whom a flourishing life requires that sex be valued for its reciprocal nature.[34] And if gestation is assigned a price, the value of motherhood as the ultimate act of beneficence is undermined for all those according to whom altruistic family relations are central to the good life.[35] But these claims depend on conceptions of the value of sex and gestation, and of their relation to flourishing, espoused by some but not all. And how is it respectful to use a single account of their value to ground coercive interference in the choices of citizens who hold different yet equally reasonable conceptions thereof?

Third, and most importantly for our present discussion, consider that short of payment signifying disrespect in our society, payment is very much how we demonstrate respect for the efforts of others. Recall the handyman who cleans the eaves of wealthy homeowners. They pay him because he expends time and physical effort, and this is recognized and shown appropriate appreciation through compensation. Failing to pay him would signal a serious moral disregard for his time and effort. Or consider tipping as standard practice in the service industry in North America, where a failure to tip your waiter or bartender is an explicit expression of disrespect for their service. There is a tension in claiming that payment for body parts and intimate capacities is disrespectful when compensation is otherwise used to demonstrate respect in our societies. Denying payment for certain activities suggests these activities are not worthy of the recognition payment bestows, and that the people who perform them are not worthy of the respect of those for whom they perform them. Following Brennan and Jaworski, if we worry about the signals that payment sends, we must worry equally about the signals that a lack of payment sends.[36]

---

[34] Anderson 1990b, 187–188.
[35] Anderson 1990a, 75–82.
[36] Brennan and Jaworski 2015.

Consider, further, that much work in our society remains unpaid, and that most of that unpaid work is done by women. The failure to accord material value to women's domestic, care, gestational, and emotional labor is defended by some on the grounds of its supposed non-productiveness, and by others on the grounds of women's essentialist inclination for nurturing. But it is just as often defended by appeal to the value of altruism in the familial and domestic sphere. Payment can never capture the true value of what's given to others through these kinds of labors, it is claimed, so payment would degrade both the work itself and the women who do it. But this view, like the others, reinforces what I call the patriarchal expectation of gendered altruism, which underlies the attitude that women's work isn't work at all. This attitude is clearly degrading to women.

Most body sales involve women. Where the denial of payment is grounded by appeal to the importance of altruism, we must worry about the gendered nature of this burden being assigned primarily to women, and of the attendant disrespect for the value of their bodily work. This consideration may supply a reason to think about the kind of exploitation I am worried about here through a structuralist lens rather than a transactional one, although my reservations about both the normative and practical limitations of structural accounts of exploitation give me pause.[37] This is therefore a consideration I will bracket for the purposes of this chapter.

I have shown so far that exploitation-as-wrongful-use arguments fail to establish that payment for bodily goods and intimate services is indeed exploitative—first, because body parts can't be conflated with selfhood; second, because it is disrespectful to impose one conception of the relationship of bodily goods to flourishing on those who hold other reasonable conceptions thereof; and third, because it is disrespectful to demand an inordinate amount of socially altruistic behavior from women. We might try to address these concerns by thinking about the relationship between body parts, payment, and respect more broadly in terms of the state's obligation to guarantee the social bases of self-respect. As Rawls argued, positive self-appraisal depends on positive social appraisal.[38] We need to find our person and projects appreciated and confirmed by others who are similarly esteemed, because otherwise we may come to believe that what we want to do with our lives is not worthy of pursuit, or that we are not worthy of its pursuit.

---

[37] For an account of the structural approach and my reservations regarding it, see Panitch 2022.
[38] Rawls 1999, 67.

If a particular group of citizens is subjected to denigrating social attitudes about the worth of their projects or their own ability to achieve them, they may come to feel as though they are not worthy of equal participation in society. Social practices that confirm such attitudes are unjust.[39] And many feminist theorists have argued that body sales promulgate such beliefs and attitudes about the inferiority of women and should thereby be banned on grounds of justice.[40]

This version of the respect-based argument against body sales does not depend on a tenuous premise according to which body parts and intimate capacities are too intimately linked to personhood to be assigned a price, nor on appeals to flourishing, which are ultimately doomed as far as grounding legislation in a liberal democracy goes. Unfortunately, however, it can't avoid the third worry that plagued the previous arguments, which is that short of payment signifying disrespect in our society, payment is very much how we demonstrate respect for the supply of goods and the provision of services we deem to be valuable. Failing to pay someone for the work she does not only signals a serious moral disregard for her time and effort but also threatens the social bases of her self-respect by signaling a disregard for the projects she has adopted and her own capacity for carrying them out.

While not all body sales involve women, the vast majority do, including not only surrogacy, sex work, and egg donation but organ and blood donation as well.[41] And where anti-commodification claims are offered to defend non-payment to providers of body parts and intimate services, it is likely the patriarchal expectation of gendered altruism that's at work, just as it is with regard to other undervalued gendered labor. A failure of remuneration may therefore do even more damage to the social bases of women's self-respect than the assignment of price values to their bodies. Claiming that certain kinds of physical undertakings are too valuable vis-à-vis flourishing to be paid may be a loftier way of defending non-compensation than insisting on their lack of productive value, but the resulting disrespect is the same. A lack of payment for body parts and intimate services can therefore reasonably be thought to threaten the social bases of providers' self-respect, as well as their individual dignity as bearers of humanity. It is the withholding rather than

---

[39] Doppelt 2009.
[40] Satz 2010; Pateman 1982; Overall 1992; Shrage 1989; Baylis 2014.
[41] Liberto 2013; Duffner 2015.

the provision of payment to providers of body parts and intimate services that thereby warrants the making of an exploitation-as-wrongful-use claim.

But let me be clear before proceeding that I am not claiming that we show disrespect, and thus exploit, in all instances of non-remuneration. Suppose the handyman who cleans my eaves is also my brother and that while this is his profession, he is also happy to help me out from time to time. In this case, I would insult him by offering him payment. The same point can be raised about non-payment in the realm of intimate relations. Intimate partner sex shouldn't involve payment precisely because introducing cash in this context can be degrading. And a sister offering to be a gestational surrogate for her brother and his partner might similarly feel disrespected by their offer of money. My response here will echo and build on the one I gave to the similar worry about non-payment and unfair advantage-taking considered at the conclusion of the previous section.

In family and intimate relations both parties aim (hopefully) at the same good and approach the interaction with the same set of norms in mind. Intimate sexual relations and family building through pregnancy are best thought of as acts undertaken by parties who want the same things and who anticipate the same gains. Both parties (again, ideally) gain back from the other in proportion to what they give, and both gain what they hope to achieve. But more importantly, in such contexts, the parties do not come to their interaction with a different sense of the relevant norms: no one is trying to profit off another's altruism, nor trying to inculcate a sense of altruism in the other precisely so as to profit from it. If in fact one of the parties were to do so, this would mark the relevant point at which non-payment turns from an act of respect among relations or intimates to one of disrespect, and thereby exploitation, among transactors. It is when a refusal to pay suppliers of bodily goods and intimate services is justified by appeal to the social expectation of gendered altruism, while those who make such an appeal profit from it, that a lack of payment threatens both respect for persons and the social bases of women's self-respect.

4. Decommodification as Deception

I have shown that a lack of payment to providers of body parts and intimate services is exploitative, understood as wrongful advantage-taking, as wrongful use, or both. In evaluating the exploitation-as wrongful-advantage-taking account, I argued that short of payments for body parts and intimate services being coercive or unfair, it is a lack of payment that is unfair where a party contributes to a collective surplus of which she is denied a share. And in evaluating the exploitation-as-wrongful-use account, I challenged the view that payment is degrading, showing instead that a lack of payment threatens the self-respect of providers, as well as the social bases thereof, by reaffirming the patriarchal expectation of gendered altruism and degrading the value of women's bodily work.

What I would like to show now is that there is an additional wrong-making feature of transactions in which providers of body parts and intimate services are unpaid, and that while this additional wrong-making feature is not a necessary component of an exploitative transaction, it is very likely to produce one. This additional wrong-making feature is deception. A lie is damaging to a party's ability to give meaningful consent, by depriving her of important facts, or by misleading her about the nature of the transaction she is entering. I will not delve deeper into the relationship between deception and consent, however. Nor do I intend to make the case that impaired consent is a necessary feature of exploitation, because a transaction can be unfairly or disrespectfully exploitative even if consensual. The point I want to make in this section is that unpaid bodily exchanges are often characterized by the additional wrong of deception, which is wrong in and of itself, and insofar as it contributes to the production of exploitative outcomes.

What kind of deception occurs where payments to providers of body parts and intimate services are withheld? Revisiting Anderson's argument helps shed some light here. She argues that commercial surrogacy is exploitative because the parties involved have different conceptions of the norms appropriate to the exchange. The surrogate "sees in the arrangement some basis for establishing the personal ties she needs to sustain her emotionally."[42] Accordingly, "the surrogate mother operates according to the norms of gift relationships. The surrogate agency, on the other hand, follows market norms. Its job is to get the best deal for its clients and itself, while leaving the surrogate mother to look after her own interests as best as she can."[43] For Anderson, this normative discrepancy gives the prospective parents and their agency an edge, which they can use to take advantage of the surrogate's emotional attachment.

---

[42] Anderson 1990a, 86.
[43] Anderson 1990a, 84–85.

This discrepancy puts the agencies in a position to manipulate surrogates, and they do this by intentionally screening surrogates for altruistic motives (that is, screening out those who identify need or financial incentives as their motive) and by emphasizing the importance of the motives of generosity and love throughout the exchange. Indeed, "when applicants question some of the terms of the contract, the broker sometimes intimidates them by questioning their character and morality: if they were really generous and loving they would not be so solicitous about their own interests."[44] If women were already coming to surrogacy arrangements with only emotional needs and beneficent norms in mind, as Anderson seems to suggest at first, the agencies would not need to screen for and repeatedly emphasize the importance of altruism. That they do this, she later acknowledges, reveals an intentional attempt to mislead surrogates about the nature of the exchange they are entering, presenting as a gift exchange what is in fact a market exchange, so that they can gain more from surrogates than they intend to offer in return.

For Anderson, this supplies a reason to ban paid surrogacy. But what I think it supplies is a reason to be very wary of altruistic surrogacy, or what should rightly be called unpaid surrogacy. To promote the view that an exchange is an altruistic one, when altruism is in fact demanded only of one party and not of the other, is to deceive the first party about the nature of the exchange. Where a deception is used as grounds to withhold payment for the purposes of increasing the profit share of the deceiver, it becomes fraudulent. While this kind of fraud is not constitutive of the surrogate's exploitation (*pace* Anderson), if its byproduct is a lack of payment to the surrogate that is both unfair and disrespectful, it can certainly produce the features that are constitutive thereof.[45]

Amrita Pande raises similar concerns based on her ethnographic research of Indian surrogacy arrangements. Pande demonstrates that Indian surrogates are frequently told that what they are giving is a gift and that it is rude to bargain in a gift exchange. The clients, meanwhile, are encouraged to view the transaction as a financial one from which they should expect the best possible returns. As a surrogate counselor working for a fertility clinic in Gujarat reported: "My task is to make sure the clients don't get fooled—they get the best deal possible. After all they are investing all this money in my surrogates. I teach my surrogates: don't treat it like a business. . . . Don't be

---

[44] Anderson 1990a, 85.
[45] Anderson 1990a, 84.

greedy."[46] Multiple surrogates in Pande's study reported feeling that it would have been rude to ask for more from the clients, having been encouraged to see them as family members for whom they were doing a favor.[47] The problem is not simply that one party sees their arrangement as a gift exchange and the other a financial exchange, but that one party purposely misleads the other to see it as a gift exchange when it is clearly not one.

Consider the case of egg sales in the United States. Payments to American egg donors were until recently capped at $5,000 (or $10,000 in some exceptional circumstances). The American Society for Reproductive Medicine (ASRM) argued price capping would ensure that ova were not bargained over like mere commodities, which would fail to honor the true worth of women's bodies and their genetic materials.[48] Yet the very fertility doctors who self-regulate through the ASRM continued to charge clients market rates for the ova provided as part of their fertility treatments. A civil suit brought by egg donors against the ASRM recently put an end to this. The plaintiffs argued that the fertility specialists were engaged in price-fixing, and that capping payments to donors enabled them to capture rents on ova in violation of American antitrust law.[49] The very doctors who insisted that eggs should not be accorded market values were nonetheless selling them at market rate for profit. The fees they charged their clients contradicted the anti-commodification arguments they gave to their egg providers to justify depressing their wages. Altruistic rhetoric served as a tool of deception used by ASRM members to increase their profit margin at the expense of the women upon whose contributions their industry depends.

When the reasons given for not compensating providers of bodily goods and intimate services is that the body is not the kind of thing that should be commodified, while the very people who make these anti-commodification claims are profiting from its commercial exchange, we have a deception that can produce the unfairness and disrespect necessary for exploitation. A market clearly already exists for assisted reproduction, from which doctors, agencies, lawyers, brokers, and multiple other service providers and manufacturers profit. The U.S. fertility industry is worth upward of $8 billion annually. When any one of the agents who profit from this industry tell a provider of gametes or gestational services that what she is engaged in is a

---

[46] Pande 2010, 979.
[47] Pande 2009, 160–166.
[48] Krawiec 2010.
[49] Krawiec 2014.

non-market exchange that should be governed by altruistic norms, and that what she gives is a gift too valuable to be accorded a price value, she is being deceived. This puts her at a serious disadvantage from the point of view of obtaining a fair outcome. It can also lead to her subjection to the patriarchal expectation of gendered altruism and to her being denied the esteem demonstrated through the payment of a proper wage for work of considerable financial value.

Granted, the cases I have looked at so far are ones of underpayment, not a lack of payment. But the problem I'm identifying doesn't go away with a lack of payment; it gets worse, because it means the deception has been more effective. In Canada, commercial surrogacy is illegal. While surrogates can be reimbursed for their expenses, they cannot be paid for their gestational services. Canada's Assisted Human Reproduction Act (AHRA) states that "trade in the reproductive capabilities of women and men and the exploitation of children, women and men for commercial ends raise ... ethical concerns that justify their prohibition."[50] These concerns are not clearly spelled out in the law, but defenders argue that payment would erode the value of a benevolent act, which should be protected from the norm of self-interest that inevitably accompanies a market exchange. The AHRA not only prohibits payment to surrogates but also prohibits the brokering of paid gestational services. Yet Canadian surrogacy agencies abound, flouting the law with respect to their own continued operation, while denying payments to surrogates, citing the AHRA. This allows them to attract less legal ire, but also more clients through lower fees. Profits are undeniably made from surrogacy in Canada even as anti-commodification arguments are cited to ensure that surrogates see none of them.

Consider another case of non-payment in the Canadian context, this time outside the realm of assisted reproduction. Canadian Blood Services (CBS) is a non-profit agency mandated to collect blood and plasma in Canada. CBS does not compensate its donors, on the grounds that blood and plasma should not be valued for their price but should be "given altruistically by persons in Canada for the benefit of other persons in this country."[51] Canada's blood collection system, legislators contend, "must remain one that is driven

---

[50] Assisted Human Reproduction Act (2004), Principle 2(f), https://laws-lois.justice.gc.ca/eng/acts/a-13.4/FullText.html.
[51] Krever 1997, 1047.

by the human instinct to help one another, not by personal gain."[52] But just because CBS is a non-profit agency, that doesn't mean plasma is not valued according to its price in Canada, nor that personal gain doesn't enter the picture.[53] Canada purchases 80 percent of its plasma from the United States, where donors can be paid if they choose, because CBS does not collect enough in Canada through unpaid donation. And the plasma that is donated in Canada must be collected, screened, and shipped to fractionation facilities that manufacture plasma-derived medicinal products, which are then sold back to Canadian hospitals for use as treatment. Plasma has a price and makes money for the professionals who carry out these various processes. When Canadian donors are told that they can't be compensated because plasma is too valuable to have a price and that personal gain shouldn't enter the blood system, they are being lied to, and when this deception leads to a lack of payment for a product very much in market demand, it paves the way for their exploitation.[54]

This kind of deception is neither a necessary nor sufficient condition for exploitation. But its occurrence can certainly make exploitation more likely, and more wrongful. When a party initiates an exchange for personal gain yet encourages the other party to view it as a gift exchange, a deception takes place. When an intentional deception produces a gain for the deceitful party, the deception is fraudulent, and when it leads to an outcome for the deceived party that is unfair and disrespectful, it yields exploitation. Unfairness obtains in the exchange of body parts and intimate services when profits are denied to suppliers upon whose contribution profits are made. Disrespect obtains when profits are made from the body parts and intimate services of women through the entrenchment of the patriarchal expectation of gendered altruism and the degradation of the value of their work. The harm of exploitation consists in this unfairness or disrespect but is intensified by deception grounded in anti-commodification rhetoric. Short of identifying transactions involving payment to suppliers of body parts and intimate services as exploitative, anti-commodification theorists have provided the very arguments that increase the likelihood and the wrongfulness of their exploitation.

---

[52] Wallin 2018.
[53] Duffner 2015.
[54] Panitch and Horne 2019.

5. Conclusion

I have argued that when compensation is withheld from suppliers of body parts and intimate services by those who profit from their commodification, this constitutes exploitation as wrongful advantage-taking. I have argued further that when suppliers are denied payment on the basis of the patriarchal expectation of gendered altruism, they are victims of exploitation as wrongful use. When either or both forms of exploitation are justified by appeal to the claim that the body is the wrong type of good to commodify, while profits are made by those who make such claims, the exploitation of suppliers of bodily goods and services is compounded by the additional moral wrong of their deception. When we proclaim ourselves the protectors rather than the exploiters of those to whom we deny payments for their body parts and intimate services, we have got things the wrong way around.

It's true that exploitation wouldn't occur in the realm of bodies at all if no one were able to profit from them. So, we might think we should ban entire practices in which anyone profits from the supply of body parts or intimate services. But this approach can't justify current laws in which only suppliers are deemed unworthy of payment, while markets in plasma, gametes, and assisted reproduction flourish. A ban on all bodily and intimate service-related profits would have to include the wages and fees of doctors, lawyers, and agents. It would therefore have the negative consequence of depressing the number of kidney transplants performed, of plasma-derived medicinal products manufactured and administered, of fertility treatments offered, and so on. These are crucial and in some cases lifesaving practices. Banning them except in instances where no money is made might solve the exploitation problem, but since we could also solve it simply by paying providers, the latter seems the clear choice.

None of what I have argued should be taken to imply that payment for body parts and intimate services can never be morally problematic. Unregulated body markets are worrying for several reasons. One is that they generate inequalities of access, whereby the rich can purchase needed medical goods that the poor cannot, which seems particularly troubling when it comes to lifesaving bodily goods. A possible solution is to centralize payments through state institutions, giving the government a monopsony on acquisition of needed bodily goods, such as kidneys, to ensure fairness in the distribution thereof. While this potential solution requires more investigation than I can offer here, my point is simply to acknowledge that while we may have to regulate payments with respect to medically necessary goods on grounds of equality, this does not provide an argument for banning payments to suppliers altogether, since a centralized scheme could address this concern.[55] Nor does it undermine the central argument of this chapter, which is that withholding payment is exploitative.

Another worry is that unregulated commercial body contracts could involve violations of bodily integrity. If body parts come to be seen as tradeable commodities, they could presumably also be treated as material assets that could, for example, be posted as collateral for a loan.[56] Were a debtor under such conditions to default on his loan, this would seem to give his creditors the right to remove his kidney against his protestations. But this worry is overblown and does not justify withholding payment from suppliers of body parts and intimate services. Creditors would never be justified in removing a debtor's kidney against his will, regardless of what he agreed to initially, because while he may have the right to sell his kidney, he cannot sign away his right to refuse medical intervention at any given time, as this is grounded in his inalienable right to bodily integrity.

The same applies to surrogacy contracts that include fetal reduction or caesarian delivery clauses. If such procedures are carried out against a surrogate's protestations, they constitute violations of her bodily integrity regardless of what she might have agreed to at the outset, because her right to bodily integrity is not something she can contract away for a nine-month period. As with sex work, whatever is agreed to at the outset of the contract nonetheless constitutes assault if consent is withdrawn at any point during the exchange. When it comes to bodily integrity, consent must be ongoing. Permitting financial exchanges involving the body does not commit us to looking the other way in the face of clauses that involve gross violations of bodily integrity. We need not honor contractual clauses according to which suppliers license an invasion of their body at some future time because this is not something they can license except at the time. Sex work, surrogacy, and kidney sale contracts are not unconscionable if money changes hands, but they are unconscionable if they contain clauses that override the signatory's right to later refuse invasions of her body.[57]

---

[55] Satz 2010, 204–207.
[56] Satz 2010, 200.
[57] Panitch 2019, 74–75.

While the worry about inequality of access and the worry about the violation of bodily integrity may offer grounds for regulating body sales, neither undermines the claim that withholding payments from providers of body parts and intimate services is exploitative, nor the claim that withholding payment on anti-commodification grounds is fraudulent. When anti-commodification theorists appeal to claims about exploitation to strengthen their case against paying providers of bodily goods and intimate services, they fail to see the ways in which those very arguments speak against their intended conclusion. Short of the theories of exploitation as wrongful advantage-taking and as wrongful use offering serviceable arguments for the anti-commodification cause, they speak against decommodifying body parts and intimate services, or at least against denying payments to suppliers thereof.

References

Anderson, A. 1990a. "Is Women's Labor a Commodity?" *Philosophy and Public Affairs* 19: 75–82.

Anderson, E. 1990b. "*Ethical Limitations of the Market.*" *Economics and Philosophy* 6, no. 2: 179–205.

Baylis, F. 2014. "Transnational Commercial Contract Pregnancy in India." In Family Making: Contemporary Ethical Challenges, edited by F. Baylis and C. McLeod, 265–286. Oxford: Oxford University Press.

Brennan, J., and P. Jaworski. 2015. "Markets Without Symbolic Limits." *Ethics* 125, no. 4: 1053–1077.

Busby, K., and D. Vun. 2010. "Revisiting 'The Handmaid's Tale': Feminist Theory Meets Empirical Research on Surrogate Mothers." *Canadian Journal of Family Law* 26, no. 1: 13–93.

Buyx, A. M. 2009. "Blood Donation, Payment, and Non-Cash Incentives: Classical Questions Drawing Renewed Interest." *Transfusion Medicine and Hemotherapy* 36, no. 5: 329–339.

Doppelt, G. 2009. "The Place of Self-Respect in a Theory of Justice." *Inquiry* 52, no. 2: 127–154.

Duffner, A. 2015. "Blood Products and the Commodification Debate: The Blurry Concept of Altruism and the 'Implicit Price' of Readily Available Body Parts." *HEC Forum* 27, no. 4: 347–359.

Epstein, S., and P. Whitehouse. 2020. "Inheriting the Ivy League: The Market for Educated Egg and Sperm Donors." *The Crimson,* April 30, 2020. https://www.thecrimson.com/article/2020/4/30/inheriting-the-ivy-league/.

Ferguson, B. 2020. "Are We All Exploiters?" *Philosophy and Phenomenological Research* 103, no. 3: 535–546.

Ferguson, B. 2016. "The Paradox of Exploitation." *Erkenntnis* 81, no. 5: 951–972.

Gilabert, P. 2019. "Exploitation, Solidarity and Dignity." *Journal of Social Philosophy* 50, no. 4: 465–494.
Greasley, K. 2014. "A Legal Market in Organs: The Problem of Exploitation." *Journal of Medical Ethics* 40, no. 1: 51–56.
Hughes, P. M. 1998. "Exploitation, Autonomy, and the Case for Organ Sales." *International Journal of Applied Philosophy* 12, no. 1: 89–95.
Hughes, P. M. 2009. "Constraint, Consent, and Well Being in Human Kidney Sales." *Journal of Medicine and Philosophy* 34, no. 6: 606–631.
Hussain, W. 2017. "False Parallels: Exploitation in Markets, and 'Exploitation' in Social Relationships." In *Exploitation: from Practice to Theory*, edited by M. Deveaux and V. Panitch, 59–74. London: Rowman & Littlefield.
Kant, I. 1996. *Groundwork of the Metaphysics of Morals*. In I. Kant, *Practical Philosophy*. Edited and translated by M. J. Gregor, 84–85. Cambridge: Cambridge University Press.
Kirby, J. 2014. "Transnational Gestational Surrogacy: Does It Have to Be Exploitative?" *American Journal of Bioethics* 14, no. 5: 24–32.
Krawiec, K. D. 2010. "A Woman's Worth." *North Carolina Law Review* 88: 1739–1770.
Krawiec, K. D. 2014. "Egg Donor Price-Fixing and *Kamakahi v. American Society for Reproductive Medicine*." *AMA Journal of Ethics* 16, no. 1: 57–62.
Krever, H. 1997. *Commission of Inquiry on the Blood System in Canada, Final Report*. Ottawa: Government of Canada.
Liberto, H. 2013. "Noxious Markets Versus Noxious Gift Relationships." *Social Theory and Practice* 39, no. 2: 265–287.
Marway, H., S.-L. Johnson, and H. Widdows. 2014. "Commodification of Human Tissue." In *Handbook of Global Bioethics*, edited by B. Gordijn, 581–598. Dordrecht: Springer.
Overall, C. 1992. "What's Wrong with Prostitution? Evaluating Sex Work." *Signs* 17, no. 4: 705–724.
Pande, A. 2009. "Not an Angel, Not a Whore: Surrogates as 'Dirty' Workers in India." *Indian Journal of Gender Studies* 16, no. 2: 969–992.
Pande, A. 2010. "Commercial Surrogacy in India: Manufacturing the Perfect Mother-Worker." *Signs* 35, no. 4: 969–992.
Panitch, V. 2013. "Global Surrogacy: Exploitation to Empowerment." *Journal of Global Ethics* 9, no. 3: 329–343.
Panitch, V. 2019. "Liberalism, Commodification, and Justice." *Politics, Philosophy, and Economics* 19, no. 1: 62–82.
Panitch, V. 2022. "Exploitation." In *The Routledge Handbook of Politics, Philosophy, and Economics*, edited by C. Melenovsky, 217–226. London: Routledge.
Panitch, V., and L. C. Horne. 2019. "Paying for Plasma: Commodification, Exploitation, and Canada's Plasma Shortage." *Canadian Journal of Bioethics* 2, no. 2: 1–10.
Pateman, C. 1982. "Defending Prostitution." *Ethics* 93, no. 3: 561–565.
Phillips, A. 2011. "It's My Body and I'll Do What I Like With It: Bodies as Objects and Property." *Political Theory* 39, no. 6: 724–748.
Phillips, A. 2017. "Exploitation, Commodification, and Inequality." In *Exploitation from Practice to Theory*, edited by M. Deveaux and V. Panitch, 99–119. Lanham, MD: Rowman & Littlefield
Radin, M. J. 1987. "Market Inalienability." *Harvard Law Review* 100, no. 8: 1849–1937.
Radin, M. J. 1996. *Contested Commodities*. Cambridge, MA: Harvard University Press.
Rawls, J. 1999. *A Theory of Justice*, revised edition. Cambridge, MA: Harvard University Press.

Richards, J. R. 1996. "Nephrarious Goings On: Kidney Sales and Moral Arguments." *Journal of Medical Philosophy* 21, no. 4: 375–416.

Rippon, S. 2014. "Imposing Options on People in Poverty: The Harm of a Live Donor Organ Market." *Journal of Medical Ethics* 40, no. 3: 145–150.

Rippon, S. 2017. "Organ Markets and Disrespectful Demands." *International Journal of Applied Philosophy* 31, no. 2: 119–136.

Rousseau, J.-J. ([1762]2018). *On The Social Contract. The Social Contract and Other Later Political Writings*, 2nd edition, edited and translated by V. Gourevitch, 39–156. Cambridge.

Sample, R. 2003. *Exploitation: What It Is and Why It's Wrong*. Lanham, MD: Rowman & Littlefield.s

Sandel, M. 2012. *What Money Can't Buy: The Moral Limits of Markets*. New York: Farrar, Straus & Giroux.

Satz, D. 2010. *Why Some Things Should Not Be for Sale: The Moral Limits of Markets*. New York: Oxford University Press.

Shrage, L. 1989. "Should Feminists Oppose Prostitution?" *Ethics* 99, no. 2: 347–361.

Snyder, J. 2008. "Needs Exploitation." *Ethical Theory and Moral Practice* 11, no. 4: 389–405.

Snyder, J. 2013. "Exploitation and Demeaning Choices." *Politics, Philosophy and Economics* 12, no. 4: 345–360.

Steiner, L. M. 2013. "Who Becomes a Surrogate Mother." *The Atlantic*, November 25, 2013. https://www.theatlantic.com/health/archive/2013/11/who-becomes-a-surrogate/281596/.

Titmuss, R. 1997. *The Gift Relationship: From Human Blood to Social Policy*. Edited by A. Oakley and J. Ashton. New York: New Press.

Twine, F. W. 2011. *Outsourcing the Womb: Race, Class, and Gestational Surrogacy in a Global Market*, New York: Routledge.

Vrousalis, N. 2013. "Exploitation, Vulnerability, and Social Domination." *Philosophy and Public Affairs* 41, no. 2: 131–157.

Wallin, P. 2018. "Time to End For Profit Plasma Donation." *Regina Leader Post*, June 11, 2018.

Wertheimer, A. 1996. *Exploitation*. Princeton, NJ: Princeton University Press.

Wood, A. 1995. "Exploitation." *Social Philosophy and Policy* 12, no. 2: 136–158.

Zwolinski, M. 2007. "Sweatshops, Choice, and Exploitation." *Business Ethics Quarterly* 17, no. 4: 689–727.

13
Exploitation Does Not Justify Prohibiting Canadian Paid Plasma

Mark Wells and Peter Jaworski

People seeking the prohibition, or prohibitive regulation, of paid plasma donation often claim that this practice is wrongfully exploitative of donors. Further, they reason that such wrongful exploitation justifies prohibition or prohibitive regulation.[1] In what follows, we focus on the case of Canada, where this issue has seen the most public discussion and has raised the most political controversy, but the conclusions will apply in other countries as well, including those in the European Union where this issue is also highly contentious.

In 2018, British Columbia joined Alberta (2017), Ontario (2014), and Quebec (1998) in prohibiting the remuneration of plasma donors by private entities.[2] Since the public organizations that collect plasma in Canada do not remunerate, this then amounted to a total ban on paid plasma donation in these jurisdictions. Efforts to extend such prohibition to the remaining provinces and territories continued.[3] Most recently, however, Canadian Blood Services formed a partnership with the Spanish company Grifols, which will allow them to pay for plasma donations in Ontario and British Columbia as

---

[1] Nevertheless, every country that prohibits payment for plasma donations imports from those that permit payment. Excluding China, nearly nine-tenths of the source plasma collected to manufacture plasma protein therapies comes from the five countries that permit commercial companies that use payment, with the United States alone supplying approximately 70 percent of that plasma.

[2] Outside of Quebec, each province passed similar legislation called the Voluntary Blood Donations Act, which prohibits remuneration of blood and plasma donors by commercial entities. In each case, Canadian Blood Services was exempted from the prohibition. In December 2020, the province of Alberta repealed the ban through the Voluntary Blood Donations Repeal Act.

[3] The most recent such effort was an attempt by Independent Senator Pamela Wallin to introduce Bill S-252, the Voluntary Blood Donations Act, before the Senate in 2018. That effort was stalled before the Senate Committee on Science, Technology and Social Affairs, with a unanimous vote by the committee members that the bill should not go forward.

"agents" of Canadian Blood Services, despite the ban.[4] In justifying efforts to ban paid plasma, prohibitionists often claim that such remuneration would constitute or lead to exploitation.

Is it true that paying plasma donors in Canada is, or would be, generally wrongfully exploitative? And, if so, would that justify prohibition? In this chapter, we make the case that paying plasma donors in Canada is not, and would not be, generally wrongfully exploitative. Moreover, even if we are wrong about that, such exploitation does not justify prohibition. As we will argue, current practices in Canadian jurisdictions where prohibition is in effect are more exploitative than elsewhere.

Our main arguments are:

1. Paid plasma donors are wrongfully exploited in being paid for their plasma only if a vulnerability of theirs is generally and wrongfully taken advantage of by those buying their plasma.
2. Plasma buyers in Canada do not generally take wrongful advantage of the donor's vulnerability.
3. So, paid plasma donors in Canada are not generally wrongfully exploited.

If our argument for (3) is unsound and, further, paid plasma donors in Canada are wrongfully exploited, then we argue that:

4. If paid plasma donors in Canada are generally wrongfully exploited, then paid plasma donors are generally wrongfully exploited in the United States.
5. If paid plasma donors are generally wrongfully exploited in the United States, then Canadian Blood Services (CBS) is complicit in the wrongful exploitation of U.S. paid plasma donors.
6. So, CBS is complicit in the wrongful exploitation of U.S. paid plasma donors.

Finally, we consider whether either of our two conclusions (3 and 6) justifies prohibition. We outline three constraints on when exploitation justifies prohibition and argue:

---

[4] See Canadian Blood Services, "Blueprint for greater security of immunoglobulins for patients in Canada," September 7, 2022. Available at https://www.blood.ca/en/about-us/media/newsroom/blueprint-greater-security-immunoglobulins-patients-canada. Accessed September 18, 2023.

7. In either case, wrongful exploitation does not justify prohibition of paid plasma donation.
8. So, wrongful exploitation does not justify prohibition of paid plasma donation.

The rest of the chapter proceeds as follows. In section 1, we detail the paid plasma donation process and the Canadian social context in which it occurs. In section 2, we support our first premise by surveying the most plausible theories of wrongful exploitation. In section 3, we support our second premise by applying our ecumenical standard to the Canadian context. Many concerns about exploitation in Canada with respect to paid plasma rely on an implicit analogy to American paid plasma. As we will show, a better analogy would be to European paid plasma, such as in Germany or Austria. Since U.S. social services provide significantly less than Canadian social services, prohibitionists should accept our fourth premise. Accordingly, in section 4, we support our fifth premise by applying plausible principles of exploitation to the contemporary state of the Canadian-U.S. plasma trade. In section 5, we introduce general constraints on when exploitation justifies prohibition to support our seventh premise. And we conclude in section 6 with a plea for moving this debate away from its narrow fixation on management at commercial paid plasma centers, unpaid blood clinics, and public sector unions. Instead, we should recenter those who are most vulnerable and stand to gain or lose the most depending on the outcomes of this debate: namely, patients who are reliant on human-sourced plasma therapies, and the donors, paid or unpaid, who provide that plasma.

1. The Details: History and Benefits of Plasma

The process of giving plasma takes approximately one and a half hours for the first visit, with each subsequent visit taking approximately an hour. The plasmapheresis process itself lasts from thirty to forty minutes. The rest of the time is spent on paperwork or completing physical examinations and tests to determine that one is healthy enough to give safely.

The paperwork includes a check for a permanent home address. This address must be within the catchment area of the plasma center, which differs depending on factors including how densely populated the city is. These catchment areas are intended to exclude sellers who are less likely to come back for a second donation, but also to make it more likely that transient homes are discovered (homeless donors are not permitted). Donors are also required to present a social security number in the United States or a social insurance number in Canada.

The physical examination checks the donor's health, including blood pressure, iron, and hemoglobin levels, and so on, to ensure that every donor is healthy enough to give plasma, and to check for new tattoos or signs of illicit drug use. Donors are encouraged to eat a healthy meal prior to giving plasma and to consume large quantities of water.

By our best estimates, donors received anywhere from $20 to $50 per donation prior to the pandemic, and now receive an average of around $60 to $80 per donation.[5] In some cases, compensation partly depends on the volume of plasma that can be extracted, which itself depends on the weight of the donor. In all cases, what you are paid depends on a fee structure that encourages repeat donations. Canadian Plasma Resources (CPR) runs two of the three paid plasma centers in Canada and has the following structure: $30 for the first donation in a week, and $60 for a second in that same week. If a seller gives twice per week for two consecutive weeks, they move from the "Orange" tier to the "Silver" tier, thereby increasing the payment for their second donation of the week to $55 to $65, depending on volume. If a seller in the "Silver" tier donates twice a week for three consecutive weeks, they move to the "Gold" tier. The payment for a second donation in a week is then $60 to $70, again depending on volume. There are also additional draws and bonuses, including, for example, a vacation prize.[6] The weighted average payment per sale of plasma works out to roughly $60 now, or $40 then.

Human blood plasma is used to make medicinal products including immunoglobulin, albumin, and clotting factors. Demand for these products has increased significantly in recent years, with increases ranging from 6 to 10 percent per year. Currently, the United States supplies approximately 70 percent of the world's plasma therapies, including over 80 percent of Canada's demand.[7] These therapies are purchased by CBS, the publicly

---

[5] The COVID-19 pandemic resulted in a 20 percent decrease in plasma collections in the United States, which explains the more-than-doubling of the average donor fee. The higher present levels of compensation should strengthen our argument.

[6] "Compensation," Canadian Plasma Resources, https://giveplasma.ca/become-a-donor/compensation/, accessed October 31, 2020.

[7] See Health Canada Expert Panel 2018, vi–vii.

funded collector and blood product distributor in all of Canada outside Quebec (where Hema-Quebec fulfills the same function).

The United States collects such significant quantities of plasma for three primary reasons. First, as in Canada, U.S. centers are permitted to collect from any particular donor twice per week, with at least forty-eight hours between collections, and a maximum of 104 times per year.[8] In most of Europe, for example and by contrast, collections from a particular donor are permitted at most once per week, and are capped at 33 times per year (Germany and Austria are exceptions, allowing 60 and 65 such donations respectively). Second, financial incentives are legally permitted. Only Germany, Austria, Hungary, the Czech Republic, and the United States have had this as a longstanding practice. Parts of Canada, Egypt, Ukraine, and Iran have only recently permitted or seen this practice expand. Third, there are more plasma centers in the United States than anywhere else in the world, both absolutely and proportionately. Counting only commercial plasma centers, there were more than 1,000 plasma centers in the United States in 2020 (there were 299 such centers in 2006, and 601 in 2016).

2. What Wrongful Exploitation Requires

Those theorizing on exploitation broadly agree that the following suffices for exploitation: someone (the exploiter) benefits by taking advantage of a person's (the exploited's) vulnerability.[9] Sometimes exploitation is not wrongful. In poker, for example, one player may take advantage of another player's vulnerability and so win at the expense of the other player. This is exploitation, but it is not wrongful exploitation. Wrongful exploitation requires the violation of some further moral standard.

Which standard? Exploitation theorists disagree. We do not aim to settle the debate here, as our purpose is to put these theories to work rather than to develop an account of wrongful exploitation. However, many contemporary exploitation theorists agree that one or a few of the following criteria capture the relevant standard:

---

[8] In Canada, collections were permitted at a rate of once per six days until July 4, 2019, when Health Canada approved a change in its policies permitting twice-weekly donations, matching the United States.

[9] See Zwolinski and Wertheimer 2017; Vrousalis 2018.

(Division of) Benefits: Wrongful exploitation occurs when a person takes advantage of another's vulnerability where the vulnerable person receives an unfair portion of the benefits.[10]

(Failure to) Aid: Wrongful exploitation occurs when a person takes advantage of another's vulnerability for which they had a prior moral duty to aid or not make worse off.[11]

(Limited) Agency: Wrongful exploitation occurs when a person takes advantage of another's vulnerability when the vulnerable person cannot exercise their full agency.

(Bad) Meaning: Wrongful exploitation occurs when a person takes advantage of another's vulnerability in a way that expresses or embodies disrespect to the dignity of the vulnerable person (e.g., commodification).[12]

(Bad) Attitudes: Wrongful exploitation occurs when a person takes advantage of another's vulnerability when acting with an attitude of disrespect to the dignity of the vulnerable person.[13]

In keeping with our ecumenical approach, we will take each to suffice for wrongful exploitation. Though contemporary exploitation theorists may disagree with some, we expect wide agreement that at least one criterion suffices and that, jointly, these cover, we hope, the plausible positions. Given such broad support from theorists with otherwise significant theoretical differences, we take our approach to be concessive. In what follows, we will consider each criterion in the context of Canadian paid plasma.

3.1. Division of Benefits

Opponents of paid plasma, whether commercial or not, sometimes argue that these donors do not receive enough compared with what the commercial entities receive. It is, however, not obvious to us that the current practices of commercial paid plasma collections in Canada are unfair in this way.

---

[10] See Cohen 1995; Valdman 2009; Arneson 2016. Though he does not endorse this criterion, Vrousalis distinguishes between two kinds of failure here. On the first, one party, A, receives "something from B without giving an equivalent in return" (2018, 4). On the second, A benefits "by offering B an unfair, excessively low price" (2018, 8). In minimizing our substantive commitments to such substantive frameworks, we follow Koplin (2018) in characterizing both as concerning improper benefit.

[11] See Roemer 1994; van Donselaar 2009.

[12] See Goodin 1987; Sample 2003; Vrousalis 2013.

[13] See Koplin 2018; Ferguson 2020.

While it is generally difficult to get the financial data from commercial plasma centers, CPR publicized its offer of the plasma they collect to CBS after CBS rejected their offer, which included many of the financial details.[14] As mentioned, Canadian paid plasma donors received, on average, $40 per donation at CPR, which results in an average of 800 mL of plasma. The standard commercial unit of plasma is 1 liter. So, roughly $50 was the average cost of compensation for CPR per liter. CPR offered to sell their plasma to CBS for $166 per unit in 2017, which represented an approximate 20 percent discount compared with the then-current global price of plasma of roughly $200 (today, despite much higher donor fees, the cost is around $230 per liter). Had the offer been accepted, Canadian plasma donors would have received roughly 30 percent of the total revenue per liter. Since the offer was rejected, CPR probably sold at the global price, and so the donor's share was roughly 25 percent. The donor fee at CPR, much like plasma centers in the United States, makes up the highest proportion of total revenue. Salaries for employees constitute the next-highest proportion. It would not surprise us if profit at CPR was less than zero in 2017, given the high costs of starting plasma collection centers and the typical three-year timeframe for such centers to "mature." But the profit could be as much as 5 to 10 percent per unit. Additional costs include infrastructure, electricity, testing of plasma, shipping, and so on.

Judgments about these numbers will vary, but they do not seem unfair to us. More than that, we think it is a good deal for donors. Nonetheless, those who disagree or are ambivalent can consult their favored principle of fair distribution for individual transactions. Even if these numbers represent an unfair distribution—for example, if all profit is exploitation—a challenge remains: to demonstrate that paid plasma donors, rather than the employees involved in the process, receive an unfair distribution of the benefits.[15]

---

[14] "Open Letter to Provincial and Territorial Ministers of Health," Canadian Plasma Resources, March 6, 2017, https://giveplasma.ca/wp-content/uploads/Open-letter-to-ministers-of-health.pdf. CPR had a standing offer to contract with CBS should CBS change its mind about purchasing from CPR. They are now likely to be bought out by Grifols by 2025.

[15] Readers familiar with the industry may note that many companies that run plasma centers are vertically integrated and derive revenue from the finished plasma therapies as well. How does that revenue figure into our analysis? First, only Prometic Plasma Resources, which runs a single center, manufactures some plasma therapies. So, this is not generally relevant to the Canadian context. Second, fractionation differs and warrants a different analysis. The cost structure of fractionators includes significant risk and overhead (e.g., fractionation plants that cost half a billion to a billion dollars, and the 12-month timeframe for fractionating immunoglobulin). Third, this concern requires that the division of benefits between the fractionators and the non-vertically-integrated source plasma suppliers be unfair, which is unlikely.

The above responds to exploitation objections at the level of individual transactions. But we could reformulate the objection, drawing on the work of Roemer and Koplin, by making the relevant unit of analysis categories or groups of people.[16] The objection might then be that the poor, as a group, receive payment for their plasma, while the wealthy, as a group, receive the much more valuable plasma therapy, and so the latter exploit the former.

This reformulated objection will not succeed. Rich and poor alike use plasma therapies. In addition, further reformulations must account for Canada's provision of these therapies at no cost to patients. The complaint that, for example, American plasma donors cannot afford the therapies made with their own plasma does not apply in the Canadian context.[17]

3.2. Failure to Aid

Even if the division of the benefits is fair, an exchange can still be wrongfully exploitative if there is a defect in the process that leads to the exchange. This is so when, for example, someone owes a vulnerable person aid but instead secures personal advantage. To illustrate, a person in need of emergency medical assistance on the side of the road is plausibly owed that assistance, but a passerby who happens to be a physician could see this as an opportunity to sell their aid. Even if the physician only charges her typical rate, and so does not gain unfair benefit, we might think that the outcome is exploitative. Why? There was a background duty to help (e.g., a duty to rescue).[18]

Applying this to the case of paid plasma: Plasma collectors may owe desperate people a hand, not an intravenous line. Even if the benefits from the exchange, holding all else constant, are fairly divided, that still leaves open the question of whether or not they fail to discharge one or another duty to help, and so exploit paid plasma donors by failing to give them the hand potential donors may be entitled to. Meanwhile, locating clinics in poorer

---

[16] See Roemer 1982; Koplin 2018.

[17] It is also unlikely to succeed in the U.S. since these therapies are covered by insurance, and since recipients are overwhelmingly also covered by Medicare or Medicaid.

[18] It is possible that this analysis reduces to a fair-benefits analysis in the following way: When we owe aid, we have a standing debt to the person who is entitled to our help. A "fair benefit" would have to recognize this debt in accounting for what would be fair. If I owe you $20, and we agree to an exchange of a pair of shoes in your possession for $40, then the exchange would not be fair if I delivered $40. I would have to give you $60. But we can parse out the question of whether $40 for a pair of shoes is fair from the further question of what is fair all things considered, and so for that reason we can treat the failure-to-aid criterion as separate from the fair-benefits criterion.

neighborhoods where desperation from poverty is higher makes it likelier that collectors will have donors who are owed this duty, and, if so, we may conclude that this is exploitative.

Concerns about the location of plasma centers were brought up repeatedly in the Canadian paid plasma debate. The chair of Canadian Doctors for Medicare, for example, wrote: "Choosing these locations brings up many ethical and public health concerns, including targeting people who may be living in poverty."[19] The prohibitionist group Bloodwatch accused CPR of "setting up collection centres next to methadone clinics, homeless shelters and payday loan businesses."[20] The National Union of Public and General Employees issued a press release on behalf of the Canadian Health Professionals Secretariat (CHPS) on April 12, 2016, that stated, "Paying donors for blood products also preys on the poor and vulnerable in our society. . . . For-profit blood and plasma collection clinics are often established near homeless shelters and addiction treatment facilities."[21]

In deriving principles from these cases, we should avoid absurd implications. People need food, but, provided they charge a fair price, grocery stores do no wrong when they choose a location where there are no other nearby grocery stores or restaurants.[22] In fact, in standard cases, we think it is good for grocery stores to locate in food deserts. Similarly, people need medical assistance and medical care, but medical providers do no wrong in locating nearer to places with higher incidences of medical emergencies provided they charge a fair price.[23] Indeed, we have reason to prefer that medical providers prioritize these locations when choosing where to locate a hospital precisely because they will thereby do more good.

So, similarly, and again in standard cases, we should think that paid plasma centers do not exploit anyone in locating near populations for whom paid

---

[19] Monika Dutt, "For-Profit Plasma Clinics Are Risky Business," Healthy Debate, July 22, 2013. (Available at, https://healthydebate.ca/opinions/for-profit-plasma-clinics-are-risky-business, accessed Oct. 31, 2020.)

[20] James Hopkin, "Blood Safety Groups Want Saskatoon Plasma Clinic's Licence Pulled," CBC News, April 12, 2016, https://www.cbc.ca/news/canada/saskatoon/blood-donations-money-plasma-licence-pulled-1.3532031.

[21] "Health Professionals Call on Governments to Prevent Another Tainted-Blood Scandal," National Union of Public and General Employees, April 12, 2016, https://nupge.ca/content/health-professionals-call-governments-prevent-another-tainted-blood-scandal.

[22] This is about the choice of location. It would be exploitative to charge a very high price for the groceries, but this would make this a question relevant to fair benefits, not about a failure to aid.

[23] This claim is not a claim about universal healthcare, which is a debate over *who* should be charged for medical services. When they charge, medical providers have an obligation to charge a fair price for their services *whomever* they charge. But in standard cases a fair price is not zero. Medical providers are not always obligated to volunteer their services.

plasma donation is an attractive option provided they receive a fair price. Given that donating plasma is very rarely harmful to the seller, it is difficult to see how choosing such locations is anything other than non-exploitatively net-beneficial. We should prefer it.

There may be individual, non-standard cases where a paid plasma donor is owed a duty of rescue, and so plasma centers may be obligated to help. But this is also true of grocery stores and CBS. Unlike a duty of rescue, however, we typically have some leeway (whether in the form of discretion or latitude or both) in how we discharge our duty to aid.[24]

In cases where poverty is both desperate and systemic, we plausibly discharge our duty to aid by participating in institutions whose function it is to help. This happens when, for example, governments provide sufficiently good social safety nets to mitigate standard emergencies through an improvement in the background circumstances. In those cases, plasma centers do what they are obligated to when they pay taxes or provide charitable giving.

3.3. Limited Agency

Many prohibitionists think plasma selling involves a failure to recognize the basic value of people—what Kant calls "dignity." Some prominent prohibitionists in the Canadian debate can be understood this way. Kat Lanteigne said paid plasma centers represent "blood farms on the backs of the poor."[25] Senator Pamela Wallin, meanwhile, claimed, "Canadian donors are not meant to be a revenue stream for private companies looking to make a profit."[26]

Dignity can be violated in different ways. First, a person might violate another's dignity by manipulating them or otherwise preventing them from exercising a substantially autonomous choice. Various formal or legal

---

[24] By "discretion" we mean permission for the agent "to determine whether or not to fulfill the duty in a particular occasion," and by "latitude" we mean that the agent has permission to decide "how the duty is to be fulfilled, when it should be fulfilled, or to whom should it be fulfilled" (Santiago Mejia, "Which Duties of Beneficence Should Agents Fulfill on Behalf of Principals?" unpublished manuscript, 4).

[25] Claire Brownell, "Blood Money: Legislated out of Ontario, Canadian Plasma Resources Courts Controversy with Saskatoon Clinic," *Financial Post*, March 18, 2016, https://financialpost.com/entrepreneur/small-business/blood-money-legislated-out-of-ontario-canadian-plasma-resources-courts-controversy-with-saskatoon-clinic.

[26] "Voluntary Blood Donations Bill. Bill to Amend—Second Reading—Debate Adjourned," Senator Pamela Wallin, Senate of Canada, May 31, 2018, https://sencanada.ca/en/speeches/sen-wallin-bills252-bill-amend-second-reading-debate-adjourned/.

trappings, such as signed papers or rote presentations of information, can give the appearance of autonomy without it having been exercised. Second, someone might violate the dignity of another by treating them in a disrespectful way, regardless of the violator's intentions. For example, a person might neglect the needs of others by narrowly attending to their own. Similarly, a person might merely be inconsiderate or inadvertently disrespectful, as is common when a person enters a new cultural context. Third, someone can give the outward appearance of respect, and even ensure the substantial autonomous choice of others, but inwardly have the wrong intentions toward other people (e.g., objectifying others or thinking of them as mere means to be used). We will consider each in turn.

Even if plasma purchasers satisfy their duty to aid their impoverished neighbors, they might still be taking unfair advantage of their limited agency. While exploitation objections to the location of plasma centers in poorer neighborhoods fail when we attempt to ground them in a failure to aid, we may instead try to ground them by appealing to limited agency. When we say that the offer collectors make is "very attractive" to paid plasma donors, it raises the question of whether the background circumstances of the donor are such that she does not make a fully autonomous choice in donating her plasma. When this is so, the offer would be a coercive offer and autonomy would be compromised, which would be an offense to the dignity of the donor.

Poverty correlates with an array of cognitive and motivational limitations. An offer of quick money, like those made by plasma centers, might be an undue inducement for people with such limitations. As Steve Weimer writes, "One of the main arguments against compensated donation systems is that many donors do or would come from circumstances of poverty that restrict their alternatives in a way that compromises those donor's autonomy."[27] Alena M. Buyx presents the case similarly:

> The fewer alternatives a person has to obtain the financial means offered through blood donation, the higher the coercive influence or pressure exerted through the offer of payment. If no alternatives for income present themselves, refusing the offer of payment for blood would be very unreasonable.... [O]ffering someone in extreme material need and without alternative opportunities for income money for blood instead of other, more

[27] Weimer 2015, 1.

meaningful options could be understood as an unacceptable way of compromising this person's autonomy.[28]

Plausibly, the very same limitations to agency that make an exchange exploitative also license paternalistic intervention. In each case, the person's limited agency changes which moral principles apply. In both cases, that change shares common ground: the vulnerable person's ability to act on reasons has been compromised. That inability to act on reasons is precisely why it is inappropriate to engage in an exchange with them regardless of the exchange's fairness.

But it is a shallow (and disrespectful) paternalism that gets its license from mere poverty. Impoverished people can act on reasons—that is, recognize a potential transaction's gains and autonomously decide to pursue those gains. When this is so we have an obligation to respect their choices and not interfere by, say, prohibition. Our obligation to respect another's decisions can dissolve only when hunger turns to starvation, when a medical emergency becomes critical, or when poverty becomes desperate. And even then, *not always*.

In addition, current policies of commercial paid plasma centers in Canada, when followed, would exclude those whose agency may be sufficiently limited to raise the concern that they are being coerced. The mandatory physical upon first donation, for example, checks for illicit drug use among other health vulnerabilities that may limit agency. The requirement of a permanent home address, coupled with the steps they take to check known transient addresses, means that only those with a permanent home address are permitted to sell their plasma, thereby limiting concerns about coercion. These centers, then, either do not, or at least do not intend to, exchange with those whose autonomy is sufficiently compromised (or who are sufficiently desperate to engage the duty of rescue).

We do not here assume perfect compliance, and we note that there is evidence from the United States that motivated donors can bypass some of the exclusion criteria at these centers.[29] However, there is no particular reason to believe that this is an issue in Canada, nor that it would be for anything other than exceptional cases.

---

[28] Buyx 2009, 330.
[29] See the documentary *Blood Trade: Health vs. Dollars* (2019), dir. Stefanie Dodt, ARD TV (Germany).

We think part of what motivates this specific concern—that paid plasma donors have limited agency when choosing to donate plasma—is the thought that no one would choose to do this unless they were in dire straits. This might be because donating plasma comes with risks that people with more options would not choose, or, alternatively, that it is perceived as "undignified" and so not the sort of thing people with means choose to do. We deal with versions of the latter worry in section 3.4, below, but we note that opponents of paid plasma need to be careful to avoid begging the question. That something is stigmatized is not enough to ground the claim that it is undignified, since we need to establish that the grounds for stigmatization are justified. With respect to the former worry, if plasma donation turn out to be unduly risky, then this would raise the question of whether the choice to donate plasma is a robustly autonomous choice after all.

As we suggested in section 1, the risks are low and there are stringent procedures in place to avoid risky donations. Publicly available evidence on risk includes three published studies on frequent donors and an ongoing study on the safety of long-term intensive plasmapheresis in donors (SIPLA) by the Plasma Protein Therapeutics Association, for which we have preliminary results about "donor-adverse events." The preliminary results from the SIPLA study (N = 7.6 million donations) show that donor-adverse events occur at a rate of 20.93 per 10,000 donations, with hypotensive adverse events at 14.77 per 10,000.[30] These preliminary results reaffirm the long-standing consensus expert opinion that plasmapheresis itself is safe. For a comparison, the rate of bicycle accidents reported to emergency medical services in Boston, Massachusetts, in 2010 was 100.21 per 10,000.[31]

The evidence on long-term, frequent plasmapheresis is not conclusive but does suggest it too is safe. Three separate studies have been conducted, with one indicating that there are "significant differences . . . in plasma protein levels in plasmas collected with different techniques and frequencies."[32] In particular, less frequent plasma donors had higher levels of albumin than more frequent plasma donors. The authors called for more studies but also said, "Whether these significant differences have relevant health implications

---

[30] Mary Gustafson, "PlasmaVigilance: Source Plasma Donor Hemovigilance Activities and Results," presentation at AABB annual meeting, October 8, 2017, http://www.pptaglobal.org/images/presentations/2017/Gustafson_PlasmaVigilance100817.pdf.
[31] "Cyclist Safety Report 2013," City of Boston, https://www.cityofboston.gov/news/uploads/167 76_49_15_27.pdf.
[32] Laub et al. 2010.

for the donors is questionable."³³ Another found that "long-term intensive donors of plasmapheresis under conditions investigated in this study is safe."³⁴ The third concluded that "regular donor plasmapheresis of up to 45 l of plasma per year appears to be as safe as more moderate plasmapheresis programmes, with respect to the parameters analysed in this study."³⁵

In addition to these studies, there are tens of millions of Americans who have donated plasma, with millions who have done so frequently. There is some reason to expect to hear about significant adverse events, and we have not heard about these. This adds some weight to the conclusion that donating plasma, even as frequently as twice per week, is not unsafe. Finally, both the Food and Drug Administration in the United States and Health Canada have approved twice-a-week frequencies (so up to 104 times per year), the latter doing so in 2019. These agencies reflect on the evidence prior to issuing regulatory guidance, and so, to the extent we find either or both trustworthy, we have some additional reason to think it is not unsafe.

While it is true that the desperation of a donor can compromise autonomy, the details regarding the risk of plasma donation appear to us to be robust, as do the procedures in place to ensure that only a certain kind of person gets to donate plasma in the first place. These risks and procedures make the claim of wrongful exploitation for this reason implausible.

Even if we are wrong in thinking that the risks are minimal and the exclusion criteria adequate, Canadian (and European) paid plasma centers operate in a significantly different context of poverty than U.S. centers. Plausibly, Canada has fairer background circumstances than the United States has, because of a more robust social safety net. These practical considerations show that the heart of the problem is the desperation and a lack of options and not that people relieve their desperation through paid plasma donation. Prohibiting paid plasma does not address the underlying causes of desperation; it just forecloses this way of helping to alleviate it. Shuttering a paid plasma center doesn't put $50 in an impoverished person's pocket. As we will elaborate in sections 4 and 5, these concerns about aid and agency suggest the American context is more plausibly exploitative than the Canadian one. And this has implications for whether exploitation justifies prohibition in Canada.

---

[33] Laub et al. 2010.
[34] Schulzki et al. 2006.
[35] Tran-Mi et al. 2004.

3.4. Bad Meaning

Failing to take heed of someone's limited agency is one form of disrespecting dignity. But there are other ways of doing so. Consider the following prohibitionist line of reasoning: Following Kant, certain objects might be such that selling them disrespects the dignity of persons. Blood plasma is one such object.[36] Buyx describes this view as follows: "From a Kantian perspective, some consider the offer and acceptance of payment for blood to constitute an instrumentalisation of a person, in that the paid donor becomes a mere means to the ends of others."[37] So, permitting people to sell their plasma constitutes disrespect for people's dignity, and it is exploitative to purchase such plasma.[38] But this view proves too much. The Red Cross, for example, sells blood and plasma to hospitals. If plasma is not the sort of thing that ought to be bought and sold, then this common practice would need to be condemned.

A more plausible reformulation of this objection is that permitting paid plasma expresses a tacit endorsement of injustice. As we've discussed, the distribution of benefits from social cooperation can be unfairly distributed, and this unfairness can play an expressive function. When people complain that plasma selling is farming the poor, for example, they might be objecting to the message such plasma selling sends—namely, that people living in poverty are a resource to be harvested and distributed for the benefit of others.

This improved objection also fails. The therapies derived from plasma do not go just to the wealthy in Canada. Given Canada's universal healthcare system, these therapies go to those who require them to survive or thrive, rich and poor alike. Those who think that the poor are being harvested for the sake of the rich are mistaken. This mistake is important because the message itself is not as important as its accuracy. Otherwise, prohibitionist claims would be self-fulfilling.

3.5. Bad Attitudes

Finally, let us consider the possibility that those operating plasma collection centers think of paid plasma donors not as persons with dignity but as mere

---

[36] Kerstein 2009.
[37] Buyx 2009, 331.
[38] As Panitch and Horne (2019) point out, objections to commodification sometimes run in tandem with exploitation in the following way: establishing that it is wrong to commodify plasma thereby establishes that a person is exploited if she sells her plasma.

instruments for profit. We should notice that even if this is true, the very same attitude can be evinced by management at unpaid plasma centers as well. Management is paid a salary at CBS, with more than four hundred CBS employees making six figures, and the CEO, Graham Sher, collecting over $800,000.[39] Those salaries are dependent on donors providing blood and plasma without themselves receiving any payment. It is at least possible that management at CBS regards donors as mere instruments for their salaries.

Indeed, some opponents of commercial paid plasma have insisted that current management at CBS has the wrong attitude toward donors. For example, Ron Stockton, a business agent for the Nova Scotia Union of Public Employees, which opposes paid plasma, was quoted as saying:

> With CBS it is never about delivering service, it is always about getting the biggest bang for your buck. . . . CBS is being transformed into a business, as opposed to a public service or a humanitarian organization. These days it's all about automation and squeezing efficiencies out of donors and workers. . . . [T]o CBS you are a piece of meat giving blood, you could be a bag.[40]

Thus, in practice, opponents recognize that the wrong attitude can be evinced by both paid and unpaid plasma collectors. Objecting to bad attitudes does not differentiate paid from unpaid plasma centers or for-profit from not-for-profit or public agencies. Without empirical evidence, we only have the prejudice that employees and managers vary in attitude merely based on the business model within which they do their work.

4. Canadian Complicity in the Exploitation of U.S. Paid Plasma Donors

We have given our reasons for thinking paid plasma in Canada is not exploitative. But we've been open about the limitations regarding evidence. So, let us entertain the possibility that both our reasoning and our conclusions have

---

[39] "2019 Salary List of Canadian Blood Services Employees Earning $100,000 or More," Canadian Blood Services, 2019, https://www.blood.ca/sites/default/files/Salary_Disclosure_Information_2019_Final.pdf.

[40] Robert Devet, "Canadian Blood Services: A Bloody Shame," *Nova Scotia Advocate*, April 26, 2016, https://nsadvocate.org/2016/04/26/canadian-blood-services-a-bloody-shame/.

gone wrong and that paid plasma is, in fact, exploitative. If so, then agents of CBS are currently complicit in exploitation, if not exploiters themselves.

This conclusion follows from the fact that CBS purchases plasma therapies that they know are made with paid plasma. They therefore do not avoid exploiting paid plasma donors; they merely offshore or outsource the exploitation, primarily to the United States. All we do is shift who is exploited, from Canadian paid plasma donors to American paid plasma donors. This is how exploitation functions in paradigmatic cases, like corporations. Owners contract with a host of executives and managers who, in turn, contract with laborers. Yet, if that corporation exploits its laborers, then the owners alongside contracted executives like the CEO are themselves complicit in exploitation.

Perhaps it will be said that CBS does not control what happens in the United States, and so it is permissible for CBS to turn a blind eye to how plasma is collected there. Unlike a contract that directs people to engage in something that is exploitative, purchasing the finished therapies does not engage the kind of control necessary to conclude that CBS is complicit in exploitation, rather than a participant or mere beneficiary of it. This challenge might vindicate small-time stockholders but fails in the case of CBS. It fails because the volume of therapies purchased by CBS through contracts with Grifols, CSL, and Takeda suffice to directly increase the number of people who are offered (and accept) money for their plasma. This volume of sales is controlling some of these companies' behavior. To paraphrase Al Gore, if paid plasma is exploitative, then CBS treats Americans as a source of spare parts for Canadians.[41]

In reply, a prohibitionist might argue that Canadian legislators owe a special obligation to their constituents and that such an obligation makes the particularities of the exploited relevant. That is, it is not exploitation that justifies the ban but exploitation *of these constituents*. We reject this reply, as it presumes that political boundaries serve to limit or negate some of our basic moral obligations, rather than add to them. But special obligations are additive. We cannot avoid our basic obligations to others by incurring special obligations to some.

---

[41] Koplin's (2018) remarks suggest this approach. In his view, political agents who permit kidney markets knowing that people will sell their kidney out of desperation are exploiters too. These agents ought to fix the background circumstances causing such desperation.

We have argued that paid plasma is not exploitative, so we do not believe that CBS is complicit in exploitation. But opponents of paid plasma suggest that such sales are exploitative and so, for them, CBS must be complicit, if not an exploiter itself.

5. Constraints on Exploitation as Justification for Prohibition

The question remains: if paid plasma donors in Canada would generally be exploited, then does that justify a prohibition on paid plasma? To answer this, we consider three constraints on such justification for prohibiting some exploitative process:

- *Special*: The prohibited practice must reasonably differ from permitted exploitative practices.
- *Success*: The prohibition must (be expected to) end the exploitative practice.
- *Cost*: The costs of the exploitative practice must outweigh or undermine both the practices' benefits and the costs of the prohibition itself.

We begin with a plausible, if somewhat controversial, constraint, *Special*. It is worth considering whether the exploitation of paid plasma donors is particularly egregious. On many of the accounts considered, as well as on Marxist accounts, if Canadian paid plasma centers wrongfully exploit donors, then almost every employment contract, or other kind of exchange, will turn out to be wrongfully exploitative. But why then expend our finite time and energy prohibiting paid plasma, especially with the benefits it provides to the ill, rather than something else? Picking strawberries is arduous, backbreaking labor typically done by poor immigrant workers on special farm visas for very low pay. Meanwhile, no one's life is saved by having access to affordable strawberries. On grounds of exploitation, we should prefer to prohibit paid strawberry picking rather than paid plasma, since what is at stake is morally much less urgent. We might worry about fairness here, too. We may have reason to forgo a ban on some behavior, when we cannot apply that ban consistently across all similar behavior.[42] So set *Special* aside.

---

[42] See Feinberg 1974.

We think *Success* is widely shared and needs little support. However, if we are correct in section 4, then a Canadian prohibition on paid plasma fails to clear even this low bar. The provincial governments have merely changed *who* is being exploited, rather than eliminated exploitation. Ontario, for example, prohibited paid plasma in 2014. It did so with no plans in place for securing an alternative, domestic, unpaid source of plasma. So legislators knew that reliance on paid American donors would continue. Not only did it continue, but it increased from meeting roughly 70 percent of Ontarians' needs all the way up to just under 87 percent by 2019. It would be one thing to prohibit paid plasma with a funded plan for an alternative method of procuring plasma, but this is not what any of the Canadian provinces that passed a prohibition did.

We take *Cost* to also be widely shared. While a hardliner might disagree, we take the lives saved and improved by the therapies derived from paid plasma to be relevant, even if gained by exploitative means. Tens of thousands of individuals rely on a regular supply of plasma to survive or thrive, with unpaid donations unable to meet current demand and not increasing, while demand for plasma therapies increases by approximately 6–10 percent per year with no sign of abating.[43] If the choice is between having to forgo supply (and thereby failing to save lives) or permitting some exploitation of the sort we might find in Canadian plasma centers, choosing the former seems morally better.

We discuss these constraints to show how the existence of an exploitative process might not justify a political prohibition. While we think *Success* establishes that Canadian prohibition is unjustified, we think *Cost* and *Special* are worth considering too.

6. Conclusion: Refocus on the Vulnerable

We have argued as follows: Paid plasma in Canada is not generally wrongfully exploitative even on an ecumenical account of wrongful exploitation. Even if it is, CBS wrongfully exploits American paid plasma donors. So, the exploitation argument for prohibiting paid plasma in Canada faces a dilemma: either it is baseless or it cannot succeed without great cost. While

---

[43] See Health Canada Expert Panel 2018.

we have focused on Canada, much of what we have said applies mutatis mutandis to prohibitions on paid plasma within the European Union, Australia, and New Zealand. The United Kingdom is worth a similar, independent treatment, especially since the National Health Service directly operated paid plasma collection centers in the United States from 1999 until at least 2016, when it sold off all but 30 percent of its interests in BPL Plasma to Bain Capital. Only now is the United Kingdom restarting domestic plasma collections for purposes of further manufacture into plasma therapies after ending it in 1998 in the wake of an outbreak of variant Creutzfeld-Jakob disease and the concern that prion diseases may be passed on through plasma therapies. From 1999 to 2021, the United Kingdom was entirely dependent on American paid plasma for U.K. patients' supply of plasma therapies.

We conclude with a plea for a recentering of this debate on the voices and views of the vulnerable. This includes patients with rare diseases whose survival or quality of life depends on human-sourced blood plasma, who too often are spoken about, rather than with. In Canada, the voices of patient groups are nearly univocal: do not ban paid plasma.[44]

These voices also include those of paid plasma donors. Public opinion polls show Canadians support paid plasma, including thinking it "morally appropriate."[45] Presumably, at least some of these people would be the ones who would be selling their plasma but for a law that prevents it. Prohibiting something that a person would choose based on their judgment about what their best options are, even given their often unfair background circumstances, is prima facie disrespectful.

Very significant harms or benefits might sometimes justify paternalism. But genuine paternalism will countenance likely alternatives to avoid removing people from a frying pan only to place them in a fire. Banning paid plasma does not improve the fairness of the background circumstances that,

---

[44] The Network of Rare Blood Disorder Organizations (NRBDO) describes itself as a "pan-Canadian coalition of not-for-profit organizations representing people with rare blood disorders and/or people with chronic conditions who are regular recipients of blood or blood products or their alternatives." They have issued a number of statements and press releases arguing against prohibiting paid plasma donations, and have an official position paper on the topic. With respect to ethics, the position paper says, "We believe that paying Canadians is no more or less ethical than paying Americans, as we do today for most of the plasma-derived medicinal products used across Canada." See "Position Statement: Compensated Collection of Plasma," NRBDO, September 2018, https://www.nrbdo.ca/uploads/8/5/3/9/8539131/nrbdo_-_position_paper_-_paid_plasma.pdf. The only exception to univocality is the British Columbia chapter of the Canadian Hemophilia Society, which issued a position in favor of prohibition.

[45] See "Canadians Think That Pay-for-Plasma Is Morally Appropriate," Donation Ethics, August 14, 2019, https://donationethics.com/plasmapoll2019.

ex hypothesi, leads some to sell their plasma. Whether or not such a ban will lead to greater harms, we note that a failure to investigate what the likely alternative options will be for people constrained by prohibition demonstrates disrespect without the justification of genuine concern.

References

Arneson, R. 2016. "Exploitation, Domination, Competitive Markets, and Unfair Division." *Southern Journal of Philosophy* 54, no. S1: 9–30.
Buyx, A. M. 2009. "Blood Donation, Payment, and Non-Cash Incentives: Classical Questions Drawing Renewed Interest." *Transfusion Medicine and Hemotherapy: Offizielles Organ der Deutschen Gesellschaft fur Transfusionsmedizin und Immunhamatologie* 36, no. 5: 329–339.
Cohen, G. A., ed. 1995. *Self-Ownership, Freedom, and Equality*. Cambridge: Cambridge University Press.
Feinberg, J. 1974. "Noncomparative Justice." *Philosophical Review* 83, no. 3: 297–338.
Ferguson, B. F. 2020. "Are We All Exploiters?" *Philosophy and Phenomenological Research* 103, no. 3: 535–546.
Gerrand, N. 1999. "The Misuse of Kant in the Debate About a Market for Human Body Parts." *Journal of Applied Philosophy* 16, no. 1: 59–67.
Goodin, R. E. 1987. "Protecting the Vulnerable: A Reanalysis of Our Social Responsibilities." *Ethics* 97, no. 3: 659–661.
Health Canada Expert Panel. 2018. "Protecting Access to Immune Globulins for Canadians." Health Canada. https://donationethics.com/static/IGReport.pdf.
Kerstein, S. J. 2009. "Kantian Condemnation of Commerce in Organs." *Kennedy Institute of Ethics Journal* 19, no. 2: 147–169.
Koplin, J. 2018. "Beyond Fair Benefits: Reconsidering Exploitation Arguments Against Organ Markets." *Health Care Analysis* 26, no. 1: 33–47.
Laub, R., S. Baurin, D. Timmerman, T. Branckaert, and P. Strengers. 2010. "Specific Protein Content of Pools of Plasma for Fractionation from Different Sources: Impact of Frequency of Donations." *Vox Sanguinis* 99, no. 3: 220–231.
Panitch, V., and L. C. Horne. 2019. "Paying for Plasma: Commodification, Exploitation, and Canada's Plasma Shortage." *Canadian Journal of Bioethics / Revue canadienne de bioéthique* 2, no. 2: 1–10.
Roemer, J. E. 1982. "Property Relations vs. Surplus Value in Marxian Exploitation." *Philosophy and Public Affairs* 11, no. 4: 281–313.
Roemer, J. E. 1994. *Egalitarian Perspectives: Essays in Philosophical Economics*. Cambridge: Cambridge University Press.
Sample, R. J. 2003. *Exploitation: What It Is and Why It's Wrong*. Lanham, MD: Rowman & Littlefield.
Schulzki, T., K. Seidel, H. Storch, H. Karges, S. Kiessig, S. Schneider, U. Taborski, K. Wolter, D. Steppat, E. Behm, and M. Zeisner. 2006. "A Prospective Multicentre Study on the Safety of Long-Term Intensive Plasmapheresis in Donors (SIPLA)." *Vox sanguinis* 91, no. 2: 162–173.
Taylor, J. S. 2006. "Stakes and Kidneys: Why Markets in Human Body Parts Are Morally Imperative." *Philosophical Quarterly* 56, no. 225: 627–629.

Tran-Mi, B., H. Storch, K. Seidel, T. Schulzki, H. Haubelt, C. Anders, D. Nagel, K. E. Siegler, A. Vogt, D. Seiler, and P. Hellstern. 2004. "The Impact of Different Intensities of Regular Donor Plasmapheresis on Humoral and Cellular Immunity, Red Cell and Iron Metabolism, and Cardiovascular Risk Markers." *Vox Sanguinis* 86, no. 3: 189–197.

Valdman, M. 2009. "A Theory of Wrongful Exploitation." *Philosophers' Imprint* 9: 1–14.

Van Donselaar, G. 2009. *The Right to Exploit: Parasitism, Scarcity, and Basic Income.* New York: Oxford University Press.

Vrousalis, N. 2013. "Exploitation, Vulnerability, and Social Domination." *Philosophy and Public Affairs* 41, no. 2: 131–157.

Vrousalis, N. 2018. "Exploitation: A Primer." *Philosophy Compass* 13, no. 2: 1–14.

Weimer, S. 2015. "'I Can't Eat if I Don't Plass': Impoverished Plasma Donors, Alternatives, and Autonomy." *HEC Forum* 27, no. 4: 361–385.

Wertheimer, A. 1996. *Exploitation.* Princeton, NJ: Princeton University Press.

Zwolinski, M., and A. Wertheimer. 2017. "Exploitation." *Stanford Encyclopedia of Philosophy* (Summer 2017 edition), edited by Edward N. Zalta. https://plato.stanford.edu/archives/sum2017/entries/exploitation/.

Index

For the benefit of digital users, indexed terms that span two pages (e.g., 52–53) may, on occasion, appear on only one of those pages.

Tables and figures are indicated by *t* and *f* following the page number

Agassi, Andrew, 194, 195–96
agential accounts of exploitation, 2–4, 18, 23–24, 44–45
anarchism, 212–14
Anderson, Elizabeth, 224, 239, 243–44
Andrews, Stephen Pearl, 206–8
Aristotle
    domains of justice and, 37–39, 42–43, 44, 47
    exactness in science and, 207
    historical accounts of exploitation and, 2
Assisted Human Reproduction Act (AHRA), 246

Bathurst, Bella, 14–16
Berkey, Brian, 6
Bertram, Christopher, 141–42
Bhattacharyya, Gargi, 73
Blanqui, Adolphe-Jérôme, 212
Block, Walter, 221
Bloodwatch, 261
Breaking Away (O'Sullivan), 192–94
Brennan, J., 6–7
Brennan, Samantha, 6–7
Broome, John, 143
Buyx, Alena M., 263–64, 267

Canadian Blood Services (CBS), 246–47, 253–54, 259, 267–70, 271–72
Canadian paid plasma
    argument overview on, 254–55
    bad attitudes argument against, 267–68
    bad meaning argument against, 267
    benefits of plasma and, 255–57
    CBS and, 253–54, 259, 267–70, 271–72
    complicity in exploitation of U.S. donors and, 268–70
    constraints on exploitation as justification and, 254–55, 270–71
    CPR and, 256, 259, 261
    dignity and, 258, 262–63, 267–68
    division of benefits argument against, 258–60
    failure to aid argument against, 260–62
    fairness and, 264, 267, 270, 272–73
    historical context for, 255–57
    limited agency argument against, 262–66
    overview of, 253–55, 271–73
    paternalism and, 264, 272–73
    refocus on the vulnerable and, 271–73
    risks of donation and, 265–66
    United States plasma and, 257, 268–70
    wrongful exploitation requirements and, 257–68
Canadian Plasma Resources (CPR), 256, 259, 261
Capital (Marx), 73, 181
Caraway, Teri, 73
Carson, Kevin, 206
CBS (Canadian Blood Services), 246–47, 253–54, 259, 267–70, 271–72
Chen-Wishart, Mindy, 51–52
children and parental responsibilities
    appreciation of childhood and, 190
    best interests and, 190–91
    children's choices and, 200

children and parental responsibilities (*cont.*)
  criticism of account of, 198–99
  goods of childhood and, 187–90, 192, 196
  language of exploitation and, 191
  misuse of childhood as resource and, 190, 192–96
  overview of, 187–90
  parents' choices and, 200
  physical discipline and, 188–89
  threshold account of parental obligations and, 187–88, 197
citizenship exploitation, 165, 176–80
classical liberalism, 203, 212
climate change, public debt, and resource depletion
  creating preconditions and, 152–55
  distributive justice and, 140–41
  efficiency without sacrifice and, 143
  exploiting the future and, 140–44
  extortion view and, 143–44
  fairness and, 149–50, 151–52
  intergenerational exploitation and, 146–52
  mutually beneficial exchange and, 147–50
  overview of, 139–40, 155
  political responsibilities and, 145–46, 150–52, 154–55
  reciprocity account and, 141–42
  structural accounts and, 144–46
Cohen, G. A., 40–41, 72n.40
Coleman, Jules, 118–19
commodification. *See* decommodification as exploitation
Commonwealth of the Northern Marianas Islands (CNMI), 115
contract law, 31–33, 35–39, 43–44, 47–52
corrective justice
  aptness concern and, 44–45
  contract law's relation to, 31–33, 35–39, 43–44, 47–52
  disruption concern and, 47
  distributive justice's relation to, 31–32, 37–44, 46
  domains of justice and, 31–32, 37–39, 42–43, 44, 47
  efficacy concern and, 45–47
  fairness and, 33, 34, 35, 39–41

  ideal theory and, 38–43, 45–46
  identifying an orthodoxy and, 33–37
  monistic and pluralistic conceptions of contract law and, 48–52
  non-ideal theory and, 43–48
  normative legal redundancy of exploitation and, 32–37
  overview of, 31–32, 52–53
  philosophical theories of exploitation and, 33–34
  purposes of contract law and, 48–52
  replication claim and, 32, 48–49
  structural and transactional accounts and, 33–36, 44–45, 49–50
  voluntariness and mutual benefit and, 33–36, 47–48
  wrongness of exploitation and, 33
cost principle, 206–8
CPR (Canadian Plasma Resources), 256, 259, 261

decommodification as exploitation
  blood donation and, 229, 241–42, 246–47
  coercion and, 232–34
  deception as form of, 242–47
  dignity and price distinction and, 236–42
  distributive justice and, 233–34, 236
  egg sales and, 245
  fairness and, 230–33, 235, 236, 245–46, 247, 248–49
  overview of, 229–31, 248–50
  surrogacy and, 241–46, 249
  unfair-outcome criterion and, 234–35
  wrongful advantage-taking and, 229–36, 242–43, 248, 250
  wrongful use and, 236–42
definition of exploitation. *See also* deontic view of exploitation; labor exploitation; moral injury; paradox of exploitation; structural accounts of exploitation; who is wronged
  agential accounts of exploitation, 2–4, 18, 23–24, 44–45
  overview of, 2–5
  taking unfair advantage, 2, 31, 33, 47–48, 64–65, 86, 87–88, 204, 219, 263

transactional accounts, 33–36, 44–45, 49–50, 58–59, 64, 71, 76
unequal exchange, 2, 142, 163, 164, 167, 173–76, 181
wrongful advantage-taking, 229–36, 242–43, 248, 250
wrongful use, 236–42
deontic view of exploitation
agential accounts and, 23–24
collateral damage and, 18–19, 23–24
consequentialism and, 18–19
duty of benevolence and, 16
instrumentalization and, 13, 21–22n.7
libertarianism and, 22–24
market forces and, 24–26
omission based exploitation and, 16–18
Oosterenders and, 13–16, 27–29
overview of, 13–16
sacrifice and reservation price and, 19–21
side constraints and, 22–23
sweatshops and, 22–23
Swonans and, 14, 15–17, 18–19, 20–21, 24–27
treating others as a means and, 13
dignity, 120, 236–42, 258, 262–63, 267–68
distributive justice
basic structure and, 40–41
climate change and, 140–41
coercion and, 234, 236
corrective justice's relation to, 31–32, 37–44, 46
decommodification as exploitation and, 233–34, 236
fairness and, 5, 37–38
fair trade and, 81–82, 86
global distributive justice, 164–65, 179–80, 181
rules of initial acquisition and, 39–40
domains of justice, 31–32, 37–39, 42–43, 44, 47, 118–20
Donselaar, Gijs van, 5
Dworkin, Ronald, 41–43

egg sales, 245
embedded acts, 63–65
employer responsibility, 218–24
Exploitation (Wertheimer), 117

exploitation overview. *See also* definition of exploitation
agents or structures, 2–4
definition of exploitation, 2–5
distribution or more, 4–5
three questions, 1, 7–8
what should be done about exploitation, 6–7
wrongness of exploitation, 5–6

failure to aid argument, 260–62
fairness
Canadian paid plasma and, 264, 267, 270, 272–73
climate change and, 149–50, 151–52
contract law and, 35, 42–43, 51
corrective justice and, 33, 34, 35, 39–40
decommodification as exploitation and, 230–33, 235, 236, 245–46, 247, 248–49
disagreements about, 33
distributive justice and, 5, 37–38
domains of justice and, 37–38, 39–41, 42–43
international justice and, 177–78, 181–82
labor exploitation and, 219
moral injury and, 6
non-worsenessclaim and, 117–18
procedural and substantive forms of, 34–35
Rawlsian theory of justice and, 39–41
wrongness of exploitation and, 6
fair trade, bargaining, and respect for persons
concern and respect, relation between, 81
demands of justice and, 83–86
disrespect supervenes upon injustice and, 88
distributive justice and, 81–82, 86
motivating shoppers and, 81–82
non-worseness claim and, 93–94, 97, 98, 105, 106, 107
normative features and, 80–81
opportunity and, 81–83
overview of, 79, 90
reiterative equalization system and, 85–86
taking unfair advantage and, 86
will theory of rights and, 84–85

Fairtrade Foundation, 80–81
Faraci, David, 104–5n.16
Feinberg, Joel, 120–21, 122, 126, 134n.6, 188–89
Ferguson, Ben, 86n.9, 117n.2, 191
forced transfers, 61, 63, 69

game theoretical account of exploitation, 165–66, 176–77
Gardiner, Stephen, 143, 146–47
global distributive justice, 164–65, 179–80, 181
Goodin, Robert, 190–91
goods of childhood, 187–90, 192, 196
Grapes of Wrath, The (Steinbeck), 59–60, 76

Hampton, Jean, 113–14, 118–28, 129–31, 136–37
harm and wrongdoing, 118–20
Hartley, L. P., 139
Haslanger, Sally, 65–67, 70–71, 73
Hayek, Friedrich, 22–23, 214
Holmes, Oliver Wendell, 121–22, 126–27
Horne, L. C., 267n.38
Hugo, Victor, 161

ideal theory, 38–43, 45–46, 163, 164, 165
intergenerational exploitation. *See* climate change, public debt, and resource depletion
international justice
    bargaining power and, 182–83
    citizenship exploitation and, 165, 176–80
    cosmopolitan justice and, 161–65, 173–80
    definitions for model and, 169, 173–74, 177–79
    fairness and, 177–78, 181–82
    game theoretical account of exploitation and, 165–66, 176–77
    liberal egalitarian framework and, 170–72
    model of international economy and, 166–70
    original position and, 161–63, 166–67, 168, 172, 176, 182

overview of, 161–66, 181–83
proofs of propositions of model and, 184–85
reproducible solution and, 169–70
theorems of model and, 173–76, 179–80
unequal exchange and, 163, 164, 167, 173–76, 181

Jamaica Inn (du Maurier), 14–15, 18
Jaworski, Peter, 6–7, 239
joint advantage-taking, 70–71, 72–74
Jones, Bill T., 130–31
justice. *See* corrective justice; distributive justice; fairness; international justice

Kaneko, S., 166
Kant, Immanuel
    agential accounts and, 23–24
    demands of justice and, 83–84
    dignity and, 236–37, 262, 267
    duties of love and, 16
    instrumentalization and, 13, 21–22n.7
    respect for persons and, 88
    treating others as a means and, 13
    value of persons and, 120–21
Kinghorn, Kevin, 194
Koplin, J., 269n.41
Krugman, Paul, 117–18

labor exploitation
    anarchism and, 212–14
    citizen benefit and, 209–10
    classical liberalism and, 203, 212
    contours of exploitation and, 204–5
    against the cost principle and, 206–8
    employer responsibility and, 218–24
    fairness and, 219
    left-libertarianism and, 203–4, 213–14, 215–19, 224
    Marxism and, 212
    overview of, 203–4
    personhood and, 221
    state as exploiter and, 208–11
    state intervention and, 211–15
    sweatshops and, 218–24
    taxation and, 203, 204, 209, 210–12
    territorial monopoly and, 209, 211
    without state intervention, 215–17

Lake Erie Transportation Co., Vincent v. (1910), 119–20
Lancaster, Kelvin, 80n.2
left-libertarianism, 213–14, 215–19, 224
legal redundancy of exploitation, 32–37
liberal egalitarian framework, 170–72
libertarianism, 22–24, 203–4, 213–14, 215–19, 224
Liberto, Hallie, 140–41
Locke, John, 148
Long, Roderick, 3–4

MacKenzie, M., 219
Madison, James, 147–48
Malmqvist, Erik, 97, 108–10
market forces, 24–26
Marx, Karl. *See also* labor exploitation
  anonymous and impersonal nature of capitalism and, 60–61
  definition of exploitation and, 2, 5
  fair distribution and, 5
  need for those without capital to sell labor and, 67–68
  reproduction of exploitation and, 73
  structural relations and, 58
  transformation analysis and, 181
Mayer, Robert, 27, 28–29, 58n.6, 61n.14
McKeown, Maeve, 61, 63, 65, 74–75
Meyers, Chris, 20
Mill, James, 195, 212
Mill, John Stuart, 134–36, 195–96
Miller, David, 44–45
Mills, Christopher, 5
moral injury
  benefit and, 130–32
  consent and, 132–37
  definition of, 120–22
  as exploitation, 129–30
  expressive content and, 124–29
  fairness and, 6
  possibility of, 122–24
  regard and, 124–29
Mulkeen, Nicola, 6
Müller, Mirjam, 3
mutual benefit and voluntariness, 33–36, 47–48, 114–17

Nagel, Thomas, 161–62

Network of Rare Blood Disorder Organizations (NRBDO), 272n.44
Nicomachean Ethics (Aristotle), 37–38
non-ideal theory, 43–48
non-worseness claim, 93–94, 97, 98, 105, 106, 107, 117–18, 133
normative legal redundancy of exploitation, 32–37
North American Free Trade Agreement (NAFTA), 114–15
Nozick, Robert
  distributive justice and, 39–40
  involuntary receipt of benefits and, 142
  Rawls critiqued by, 39–40
  taxation and, 211–12
  threats and offers distinction of, 148–49

Open (Agassi), 194
original position, 39–40, 161–63, 166–67, 168, 172, 176, 182
O'Sullivan, Patrick, 192–94, 196–98

paid plasma. *See* Canadian paid plasma
Pande, Amrita, 244–45
Panitch, Vida, 6–7, 267n.38
paradox of exploitation
  benefit and, 130–32
  consent and, 132–37
  definition of, 113–14
  domains of justice and, 118–20
  exploitation as moral injury and, 129–30
  expressive content and, 124–29
  harm and wrongdoing and, 118–20
  moral injury and, 113–14, 120–37
  NAFTA and, 114–15
  non-worseness claim and, 117–18, 133
  overview of, 113–14
  possibility of moral injury and, 122–24
  regard and, 128–29
  shadow contracts and, 115–16
  sweatshops and, 114–17
  voluntariness and mutual benefit and, 114–17
  wrongness and what to do about wrongness distinction and, 116–17
parental responsibilities. *See* children and parental responsibilities

Parijs, P. van, 165, 179
personhood, 221, 230–31, 238–39, 241
Phillips, Anne, 238
Plasma Protein Therapeutics
    Association, 265
plasma sales. *See* Canadian paid plasma
Pogge, Thomas, 23n.10, 162–63, 172n.19
Prytchitko, David, 224
public debt. *See* climate change, public
    debt, and resource depletion

Rawls, John
    distributive justice and, 38–43
    ideal theory and, 38–39
    international justice and, 161–63
    justice as fairness and, 39–41
    libertarian objections to,
        responses to, 40
    objections to, 40–42
    original position and, 39–40, 161–63,
        166–67, 168, 172, 176, 182
    positive self-appraisal and, 240–41
    rule-based distinction and, 40–41
Records of a Family of Engineers
    (Stevenson), 15
Red Cross, The, 267
Reiman, Jeffrey, 61
Rendall, Matthew, 140–41
resource depletion. *See* climate change,
    public debt, and resource depletion
respect for persons. *See* dignity; fair trade,
    bargaining, and respect for persons
Risse, Mathias, 145–46
Roemer, John, 4, 162n.1, 164–65, 166–67,
    173, 175, 176–77, 179–80
Royal Philips, 25

Sachs, Jeffrey, 117–18
Sample, Ruth, 6, 237
Sartwell, Crispin, 210
shadow contracts, 115–16
Sher, Graham, 267–68
Sil de Strandjutter (Bruijn), 13
Slote, Michael, 187–88
Stayman, Allan, 116
Steinbeck, John, 62
Steiner, Killel, 3, 4–5
Sternberg, Elaine, 27–28

Stockton, Ron, 268
structural accounts of exploitation
    capitalism and, 60–61
    climate change and, 144–46
    constraints and opportunities
        and, 65–67
    cultural schemas and, 65–66
    dividend of servitude and, 63–64
    embedded acts and, 63–65
    forced transfers and, 61, 63, 69
    impersonal and anonymous
        exploitation and, 59–62
    individual relations and, 74–75
    joint advantage-taking and, 70–
        71, 72–74
    overview of, 33–36, 57–59, 75–
        76, 144–46
    passivity and, 63
    reproducing exploitation and, 71–75
    social structures and, 65–68
    taking advantage of vulnerability
        and, 68–70
    vulnerability and social positions
        and, 67–68
surrogacy, 241–46, 249
sweatshops
    deontic view of exploitation
        and, 22–23
    economic defenses of, 117–18
    labor exploitation and, 218–24
    moral injury and, 130–31
    non-worseness claim and, 117–18
    overview of, 3–4
    paradox of exploitation and, 114–17
    structural accounts and, 144–45
    who is wronged and, 106–7
Szigeti, András, 97, 108–10

taking unfair advantage, 2, 31, 33, 47–48,
    64–65, 86, 87–88, 204, 219, 263
Tandy, Francis, 206
taxation, 203, 204, 209, 210–12
Tazreen Fashion factory fire
    (2012), 222–23
Tessman, Lisa, 120–21
Tomlin, Patrick, 189
transactional accounts of exploitation, 33–
    36, 44–45, 49–50, 58–59, 64, 71, 76

Triangle Shirtwaist factory fire (1911), 222–23
Tucker, Benjamin, 206, 214

unequal exchange, 2, 142, 163, 164, 167, 173–76, 181

Valdman, M., 219–20
Van Donselaar, G., 28n.12
Veneziani, Roberto, 4, 6–7, 162n.1, 166, 181–82
Vincent v. Lake Erie Transportation Co. (1910), 119–20
voluntariness and mutual benefit, 33–36, 47–48, 114–17
Vrousalis, Nicholas, 60–62, 63–64, 68–69, 142, 258n.10

Wallin, Pamela, 262
Walmart, 115
Warren, Josiah, 206
Wells, Mark, 6–7
Wertheimer, Alan, 19–20, 93–94, 117–18
who is wronged
   conditional obligations and, 107
   identification of, 97–105
   One Dose of Drug, One Person in Need scenario and, 97–98, 104
   One Dose of Drug, Ten People in Need scenario and, 98, 101–4, 105–7, 110
   overview of, 93–97
   relational harms and, 109
   remedial duties and, 108–11
   Sweatshop Hiring scenario and, 101–3, 106–7
   sweatshops and, 106–7
   Sweatshop Siting and Hiring scenario and, 102–3, 106–7
   wrongful exploitation and, 97–105
   wrong-making features and, 105–8
will theory of rights, 84–85
Wollner, Gabriel, 60–62, 63–65, 145–46
Wood, Allen W., 21–22n.7, 205n.3
wrongful advantage-taking, 229–36, 242–43, 248, 250
wrongful use, 236–42
wrong-making features, 5–7, 32, 33, 35–36, 44–45, 95–97, 105–8, 147, 149–50

Yoshihara, Naoki, 4, 6–7, 166, 181–82
Young, Iris Marion, 67n.32, 145–46, 150

Zheng, Robin, 69n.36
Zwolinski, Matt, 19–20, 22–24, 105n.17, 208–9, 218–19

The manufacturer's authorised representative in the EU for product safety is Oxford University Press España S.A. of El Parque Empresarial San Fernando de Henares, Avenida de Castilla, 2 – 28830 Madrid (www.oup.es/en or product.safety@oup.com). OUP España S.A. also acts as importer into Spain of products made by the manufacturer.

Printed in the USA/Agawam, MA
March 28, 2025

885041.004